W9-ANR-237

FamilyCircle®

# Healthy Home-Style Cooking

Volume 2

Meredith® Consumer Marketing
Des Moines, Iowa

*Family Circle® Healthy Home-Style Cooking*

## *Meredith Corporation Consumer Marketing*
**Senior Vice President, Consumer Marketing:** David Ball
**Consumer Product Marketing Director:** Steven Swanson
**Consumer Product Marketing Manager:** Wendy Merical
**Business Director:** Ron Clingman
**Associate Director, Production:** Douglas M. Johnston

## *Waterbury Publications, Inc.*
**Editorial Director:** Lisa Kingsley
**Associate Editor:** Tricia Laning
**Creative Director:** Ken Carlson
**Associate Design Director:** Doug Samuelson
**Contributing Copy Editors:** Terri Frederickson, Gretchen Kauffman, Peg Smith
**Contributing Indexer:** Elizabeth T. Parson

## *Family Circle® Magazine*
**Editor in Chief:** Linda Fears
**Creative Director:** Karmen Lizzul
**Food Director:** Regina Ragone, M.S., R.D.
**Senior Food Editor:** Julie Miltenberger
**Associate Food Editor:** Michael Tyrrell
**Assistant Food Editor:** Cindy Heller
**Editorial Assistant:** Allison Baker

## *Meredith Publishing Group*
**President:** Jack Griffin
**Executive Vice President:** Andy Sareyan
**Vice President, Production:** Bruce Heston

## *Meredith Corporation*
**President and Chief Executive Officer:** Stephen M. Lacy
**Chairman of the Board:** William T. Kerr

In Memoriam: E.T. Meredith III (1933-2003)


First Edition.
Printed in the United States of America.
ISSN: 1944-6926
ISBN: 978-0-696-24389-9

All of us at Meredith® Consumer Marketing are dedicated to providing you with information and ideas to enhance your home. We welcome your comments and suggestions. Write to us at: Meredith Consumer Marketing, 1716 Locust St., Des Moines, IA 50309-3023.

**Pictured on the front cover:**
Ginger-Berry Shortcake, page 296

# Do you go weak in the knees at the sight of a bubbling casserole of macaroni and cheese?

Or pork chops pan-fried and smothered in onions? Or meatloaf and mashed potatoes? Or creamy rice pudding topped with whipped cream? Of course you do. It's the kind of hearty, satisfying, universally loved fare that Mom or Grandma makes—the kind you crave when you're in need of comfort. It's good-mood food.

Home-style cooking is synonymous with happiness, but not necessarily with healthfulness. Traditional recipes are made with rich and indulgent ingredients that pack in unwanted calories and fat grams. But they don't have to be made that way.

*Healthy Home-Style Cooking* is filled with more than 400 recipes for favorite family classics revamped for the way you want to eat now—lower in calories and fat, but still packed with flavor.

Although these recipes are updated for today, they're made the old-fashioned way. They start with fresh foods that naturally abound with good-for-you-ingredients but simply call for less fat than the traditional version—or they substitute a more healthful fat. They also take advantage of cooking methods and techniques that don't require large amounts of unhealthy fats and sugar.

Whether you're looking for a 30-minute weeknight dinner or want to spend a leisurely Saturday cooking or baking with friends, *Healthy Home-Style Cooking* offers a buffet of choices.

As an added help, suggested menus are scattered throughout the book to make meal planning easier and more fun. You can enjoy your favorite foods and your good health too.

Because meal planning for a busy family can be challenging, look for these helpful icons throughout the book:

Any recipe that can be made from start to finish in 30 minutes or less.

This symbol denotes recipes approved by kids.

# Contents

page 20
page 19

# Smart &

# Snacks Starters

Sweet Party Mix

## Sweet Party Mix ✪

**MAKES:** 12 cups **PREP:** 20 minutes
**BAKE:** 20 minutes **OVEN:** 300°

- **Nonstick cooking spray**
- **4 cups bite-size corn square cereal**
- **3 cups bite-size rice square cereal**
- **2 cups pretzel knots**
- **⅔ cup sliced almonds**
- **½ cup packed brown sugar**
- **¼ cup butter**
- **2 tablespoons light-colored corn syrup**
- **⅛ teaspoon baking soda**
- **¾ cup dried cranberries, blueberries, or cherries**

**1** Preheat oven to 300°. Lightly coat a large piece of foil with cooking spray; set aside. In a large roasting pan toss together corn cereal, rice cereal, pretzels, and almonds; set aside.
**2** In a medium saucepan combine brown sugar, butter, and corn syrup. Cook and stir over medium heat until mixture just begins to bubble. Continue cooking at a moderate, steady rate, without stirring, for 5 minutes more. Remove saucepan from heat; stir in baking soda. Pour over cereal mixture; stir gently to coat.
**3** Bake for 15 minutes; stir cereal mixture and bake 5 minutes more. Remove from oven; stir in dried fruit. Spread on prepared foil to cool. Store in an airtight container at room temperature for up to 1 week.

**PER ⅓ CUP MIX:** 31 cal., 0 g total fat, 0 mg chol., 50 mg sodium, 6 g carbo., 1 g fiber, 1 g pro.

## Herbed Mixed Nuts

**MAKES:** 3 cups **PREP:** 10 minutes **BAKE:** 15 minutes **OVEN:** 325°

- **1 tablespoon butter, melted**
- **1 tablespoon Worcestershire sauce**
- **2 teaspoons dried basil and/or oregano, crushed**
- **½ teaspoon garlic salt**
- **3 cups walnuts, soy nuts, and/or almonds**
- **2 tablespoons grated Parmesan cheese**

**1** Preheat oven to 325°. In a bowl combine melted butter, Worcestershire sauce, basil, and garlic salt. Add nuts, stirring to coat.
**2** Line a 15×10×1-inch baking pan with foil; spread nuts in pan. Sprinkle with Parmesan cheese; stir to coat. Bake for 15 minutes, stirring twice. Cool in pan on wire rack. Store in an airtight container at room temperature for up to 1 week.

**PER ¼ CUP NUTS:** 221 cal., 19 g total fat (2 g sat. fat), 3 mg chol., 77 mg sodium, 7 g carbo., 4 g fiber, 8 g pro.

## Curried Cashews

**MAKES:** 3 cups **PREP:** 10 minutes **BAKE:** 15 minutes **OVEN:** 325°

- **3 cups whole cashews and/or macadamia nuts**
- **2 tablespoons frozen apple juice concentrate, thawed**
- **½ teaspoon bottled hot pepper sauce**
- **2 teaspoons curry powder**
- **½ teaspoon garlic salt**
- **¼ teaspoon ground ginger**
- **⅛ teaspoon ground allspice or nutmeg**

**1** Preheat oven to 325°. Line a 15×10×1-inch baking pan with foil; grease the foil. In a medium bowl combine nuts, apple juice concentrate, and hot pepper sauce; stir to coat nuts evenly. In a small bowl combine curry powder, garlic salt, ginger, and allspice. Sprinkle over nuts; toss to coat evenly.
**2** Spread nuts in prepared baking pan. Bake about 15 minutes or until toasted, stirring twice. Cool in pan on wire rack. Store in an airtight container at room temperature for up to 2 weeks.

**PER ¼ CUP NUTS:** 203 cal., 16 g total fat (3 g sat. fat), 0 mg chol., 48 mg sodium, 13 g carbo., 1 g fiber, 5 g pro.

Add some crunch and munch to your next party. Buttery cashews are seasoned with curry and roasted until crisp.

Curried Cashews

Arugula-Cannellini Dip

## Arugula-Cannellini Bean Dip 30

**MAKES:** about 1½ cups **START TO FINISH:** 10 minutes

- 3 cups lightly packed arugula leaves
- ¼ cup olive oil
- 2 tablespoons lemon juice
- 2 cloves garlic, halved
- ½ teaspoon salt
- 1 15-ounce can cannellini beans (white kidney beans), rinsed and drained
- ½ cup chopped, seeded tomato (1 medium)
- Assorted crackers, toasted baguette slices, or cut-up vegetables

**1** In a food processor bowl or blender container combine arugula, oil, lemon juice, garlic, and salt. Cover and process or blend until nearly smooth. Add beans. Cover and process or blend just until coarsely chopped and mixture is combined (mixture should be slightly chunky).

**2** Transfer bean mixture to a serving bowl. Gently stir in tomato. Serve immediately or cover and chill up to 24 hours. Serve with crackers, baguette slices, or vegetables.

**PER 2 TABLESPOONS DIP:** 64 cal., 5 g total fat (1 g sat. fat), 0 mg chol., 154 mg sodium, 6 g carbo., 2 g fiber, 2 g pro.

## Asian Shrimp Dip

**MAKES:** 2 cups dip **PREP:** 15 minutes **CHILL:** 2 to 24 hours

- 1 8-ounce carton sour cream
- 1 4- to 4.25-ounce can tiny shrimp, drained
- ½ of an 8-ounce can (½ cup) water chestnuts, drained and finely chopped
- ¼ cup finely chopped green onions (2)
- 2 tablespoons milk
- 1 tablespoon soy sauce
- ½ teaspoon ground ginger
- ¼ teaspoon garlic powder
- Sliced green onion or sweet pepper strips
- Vegetable dippers (such as sugar snap peas, celery sticks, and/or sweet pepper strips)

**1** In a medium bowl combine sour cream, shrimp, water chestnuts, the chopped green onions, milk, soy sauce, ginger, and garlic powder; mix well. Cover and chill for 2 to 24 hours.

**2** Before serving, stir dip and transfer to serving bowl. Garnish with sliced green onion. Serve with vegetable dippers.

**PER 2 TABLESPOONS DIP:** 50 cal., 4 g total fat (2 g sat. fat), 18 mg chol., 80 mg sodium, 2 g carbo., 0 g fiber, 2 g pro.

## Summer Fruits with Ricotta Dip  

**MAKES:** 12 servings **START TO FINISH:** 15 minutes

- ½ cup low-fat ricotta cheese
- 4 ounces cream cheese, softened
- 3 tablespoons orange juice
- 2 tablespoons powdered sugar
- 1 6-ounce container vanilla low-fat yogurt
- 6 cups assorted fresh fruit (such as sliced plums, cubed cantaloupe, cubed honeydew melon, pitted dark sweet cherries, and/or sliced strawberries)

**1** For dip, in a blender or food processor combine ricotta cheese, cream cheese, orange juice, and sugar. Cover and blend or process until smooth.

**2** In a medium bowl stir together cheese mixture and yogurt. Serve immediately or cover and chill for up to 24 hours. Serve with fruit.

**PER SERVING:** 94 cal., 4 g total fat (3 g sat. fat), 14 mg chol., 72 mg sodium, 12 g carbo., 1 g fiber, 3 g pro.

## Herbed Feta Cheese Spread

**MAKES:** 15 to 20 servings **START TO FINISH:** 10 minutes

- 1 8-ounce package reduced-fat cream cheese (Neufchâtel)
- 1 4-ounce package crumbled feta cheese with garlic and herb
- 1 tablespoon milk
- Several dashes ground black pepper
- Sweet pepper wedges, other vegetable dippers, or crackers

**1** In a small bowl stir together cream cheese, feta cheese, milk, and black pepper. Beat with an electric mixer on medium speed until mixture is well combined and of spreading consistency. Serve with pepper wedges, vegetable dippers, or crackers.

**PER SERVING:** 119 cal., 8 g total fat (8 g sat. fat), 18 mg chol., 245 mg sodium, 8 g carbo., 0 g fiber, 3 g pro.

## Creamy Dill Dip

**MAKES:** 2¼ cups **PREP:** 10 minutes **CHILL:** 1 hour

- 1 8-ounce package light cream cheese, softened
- 1 8-ounce carton light sour cream
- 2 tablespoons finely chopped green onion (1)
- 2 to 3 tablespoons snipped fresh dill or 2 to 3 teaspoons dried dill
- ½ teaspoon seasoned salt or salt
- Milk (optional)
- Fresh dill sprig (optional)
- Assorted spring vegetable dippers (such as potato chips, baby carrots, radishes, pea pods, blanched asparagus spears, and/or jicama strips)

**1** In a medium bowl beat cream cheese, sour cream, green onion, the snipped dill, and salt with an electric mixer on low speed until fluffy. Cover and chill for at least 1 hour.

**2** If dip is too thick after chilling, stir in 1 to 2 tablespoons milk until dipping consistency. If desired, garnish with a dill sprig. Serve with vegetable dippers.

**Note:** To make ahead, prepare dip as directed in Step 1. Cover and chill for up to 24 hours. Cut up vegetable dippers and place in resealable plastic bags; chill for up to 24 hours.

**PER 2 TABLESPOONS DIP:** 100 cal., 8 g total fat (6 g sat. fat), 28 mg chol., 204 mg sodium, 2 g carbo., 0 g fiber, 4 g pro.

Creamy Dill Dip

## Low-Fat Blue Cheese Spread

**MAKES:** ¾ cup **START TO FINISH:** 10 minutes

- ¼ cup light mayonnaise or salad dressing
- 3 tablespoons fat-free sour cream
- 1 tablespoon buttermilk
- 1 teaspoon Dijon-style mustard
- ¼ teaspoon Worcestershire sauce
- ½ cup crumbled blue cheese (2 ounces)
- Salt
- Ground black pepper
- Celery sticks, apple slices, and/or pear slices

**1** In a small bowl stir together mayonnaise, sour cream, buttermilk, mustard, and Worcestershire sauce. Stir in blue cheese until mixture is almost smooth. Season to taste with salt and pepper. Serve immediately or cover and chill for up to 3 days.
**2** Serve with celery sticks, apple slices, and/or pear slices.

**PER 2 TABLESPOONS SPREAD:** 76 cal., 6 g total fat (2 g sat. fat), 11 mg chol., 245 mg sodium, 3 g carbo., 0 g fiber, 3 g pro.

## Basil Guacamole

**MAKES:** about 2 cups **START TO FINISH:** 25 minutes

- 2 ripe medium avocados, halved, seeded, and peeled
- ¾ cup snipped fresh basil
- ½ cup chopped seeded tomato
- 2 tablespoons chopped green onion (1)
- 1 tablespoon lime juice
- ¼ to ½ teaspoon salt
- ¼ teaspoon crushed red pepper or few drops bottled hot pepper sauce
- Tortilla chips

**1** In a large mortar mash avocados with a pestle. (Or in a medium bowl mash avocado with a fork.) Stir in basil, tomato, green onion, lime juice, salt, and crushed red pepper. Serve immediately with tortilla chips.

**PER 2 TABLESPOONS DIP:** 40 cal., 4 g total fat (1 g sat. fat), 0 mg chol., 40 mg sodium, 2 g carbo., 1 g fiber, 1 g pro.

Carrot Hummus

## Carrot Hummus

**MAKES:** 2 cups **PREP:** 15 minutes **CHILL:** 1 hour to 3 days

- 1 cup chopped carrots (2 medium)
- 1 15-ounce can garbanzo beans, rinsed and drained
- ¼ cup tahini (sesame seed paste)
- 2 tablespoons lemon juice
- 2 cloves garlic, quartered
- ½ teaspoon ground cumin
- ¼ teaspoon salt
- 2 tablespoons snipped fresh parsley
- Water (optional)
- Assorted dippers (such as toasted whole wheat pita bread triangles, vegetable sticks, and/or whole grain crackers)

**1** In a small covered saucepan cook carrots in a small amount of boiling water for 6 to 8 minutes or until tender; drain. In a food processor bowl combine cooked carrots, beans, tahini, lemon juice, garlic, cumin, and salt. Cover and process until mixture is smooth. Transfer to a small serving bowl. Stir in parsley.
**2** Cover and chill for 1 hour to 3 days. If necessary, stir in enough water, 1 tablespoon at a time, to make of dipping consistency. Serve with assorted dippers.

**PER 2 TABLESPOONS DIP:** 60 cal., 2 g total fat (0 g sat. fat), 0 mg chol., 124 mg sodium, 8 g carbo., 2 g fiber, 2 g pro.

# Fabulous color, fresh flavor.

Salsa Fresca

## Salsa Fresca

**MAKES:** about 3 cups **PREP:** 20 minutes **CHILL:** 1 hour to 3 days

- **1½ cups finely chopped, seeded tomatoes (2 medium)**
- **1 fresh Anaheim pepper, seeded and finely chopped (see note, page 182) or one 4-ounce can diced green chile peppers, drained**
- **¼ cup chopped green sweet pepper**
- **¼ cup sliced green onions (2)**
- **3 to 4 tablespoons snipped fresh cilantro or parsley**
- **2 tablespoons lime juice or lemon juice**
- **1 to 2 fresh jalapeño chile peppers, seeded and finely chopped (see note, page 182)**
- **1 clove garlic, minced**
- **⅛ teaspoon salt**
- **⅛ teaspoon ground black pepper**
- **Tortilla chips**

**1** In a medium bowl stir together tomatoes, Anaheim pepper, sweet pepper, green onions, cilantro, lime juice, jalapeño pepper, garlic, salt, and black pepper.
**2** Cover and chill at least 1 hour or up to 3 days before serving. Serve with tortilla chips.
**Note:** For a slightly smoother salsa, place 1 cup of the salsa in a food processor or blender. Cover and process or blend just until smooth. Stir into remaining salsa.

**PER ¼ CUP SALSA:** 8 cal., 0 g total fat, 0 mg chol., 24 mg sodium, 4 g carbo., 0 g fiber, 0 g pro.

Avocado-Feta Salsa

One bite of a perfectly ripe avocado, and you can taste why this tropical fruit is sometimes called a butter pear. When buying avocados, look for the Hass variety. They have dark, bumpy skin, a creamy texture, and a wonderfully nutty flavor. When ripe, an avocado will yield to gentle pressure. If an avocado is hard, let it sit on your counter for a few days to ripen before using.

## Avocado-Feta Cheese Salsa

**MAKES:** 3 cups **PREP:** 20 minutes **CHILL:** 2 to 6 hours

- ⅔ cup chopped roma tomatoes (2 medium)
- 1 avocado, halved, seeded, peeled, and chopped
- ¼ cup finely chopped red onion
- 1 tablespoon snipped fresh parsley
- 1 tablespoon snipped fresh oregano
- 1 tablespoon olive oil
- 1 tablespoon red or white wine vinegar
- 1 clove garlic, minced
- 4 ounces feta cheese, coarsely crumbled
- Pita chips or tortilla chips

**1** In a medium bowl combine tomatoes, avocado, red onion, parsley, oregano, oil, vinegar, and garlic. Stir gently to mix. Gently stir in feta cheese. Cover and chill for 2 to 6 hours. Serve with pita chips or tortilla chips.

**PER ¼ CUP SALSA:** 63 cal., 5 g total fat (2 g sat. fat), 8 mg chol., 106 mg sodium, 3 g carbo., 1 g fiber, 2 g pro.

## Fruit Salsa

**MAKES:** 2¼ cups **PREP:** 30 minutes **CHILL:** 8 to 24 hours

- 1 cup chopped papaya or mango
- 1 cup finely chopped fresh pineapple
- ¼ cup finely slivered red onion
- ¼ cup slivered yellow, orange, and/or green sweet pepper
- 3 tablespoons snipped fresh cilantro
- 1 teaspoon finely shredded lime or lemon peel
- 2 tablespoons lime or lemon juice
- 2 to 4 teaspoons finely chopped fresh jalapeño chile pepper (see note, page 182)
- 1 teaspoon grated fresh ginger
- Baked tortilla chips

**1** In a medium bowl stir together papaya, pineapple, red onion, sweet pepper, cilantro, lime peel, lime juice, jalapeño pepper, and ginger. Cover and chill for 8 to 24 hours. Serve with tortilla chips.

**PER 2 TABLESPOONS SALSA:** 11 cal., 0 g total fat, 0 mg chol., 1 mg sodium, 3 g carbo., 0 g fiber, 8 g pro.

Fruit Salsa

Shrimp-Avocado Nachos

## Shrimp-Avocado Nachos

**MAKES:** 4 servings **PREP:** 20 minutes **CHILL:** 10 to 60 minutes

- 16 fresh or frozen peeled cooked medium shrimp
- 1 medium avocado, halved, seeded, peeled, and chopped
- 1 small roma tomato, seeded and chopped
- 2 tablespoons bottled green salsa or salsa
- 1½ teaspoons snipped fresh oregano
- 1 clove garlic, minced
- 16 baked tortilla chips

**1** Thaw shrimp, if frozen. Rinse shrimp; pat dry with paper towels. In a medium bowl combine shrimp, avocado, tomato, salsa, oregano, and garlic. Cover and chill for 10 minutes to 1 hour.
**2** Arrange chips on a serving platter. Remove shrimp from salsa mixture. Place 1 shrimp onto each chip. Spoon some of the salsa mixture onto each chip. Serve immediately.

**PER SERVING:** 140 cal., 8 g total fat (1 g sat. fat), 43 mg chol., 134 mg sodium, 11 g carbo., 4 g fiber, 7 g pro.

## Pizza Tortilla Rolls ✪ 

**MAKES:** 24 rolls **PREP:** 20 minutes **BAKE:** 8 minutes **OVEN:** 400°

- 1 tablespoon butter or margarine
- ¾ cup chopped onion
- ½ cup chopped green sweet pepper (1 small)
- ½ teaspoon dried Italian seasoning, crushed
- ¼ teaspoon crushed red pepper
- 6 7-inch flour tortillas
- 1 8-ounce can pizza sauce
- 1 8-ounce package shredded pizza cheese (2 cups)
- 1 tablespoon vegetable oil
- 2 tablespoons grated Parmesan cheese

**1** Preheat oven to 400°. Line a baking sheet with foil. In a skillet melt butter over medium heat. Add onion and sweet pepper; cook and stir in hot butter until vegetables are tender. Stir in Italian seasoning and crushed red pepper.
**2** Spread each tortilla with about 1 tablespoon of the pizza sauce, leaving a ½-inch border around edge, reserving remaining sauce. Spoon some of the onion mixture onto each tortilla. Sprinkle with pizza cheese, leaving a ½-inch border around edge.
**3** Roll up tortillas. Place, seam sides down, on prepared baking sheet. Brush with oil and sprinkle with Parmesan cheese. Bake about 8 minutes or until pizza cheese is melted.
**4** Meanwhile, in a small saucepan heat the remaining pizza sauce. To serve, cut each tortilla roll into four pieces. Serve warm with heated pizza sauce.

**PER ROLL:** 67 cal., 3 g total fat (1 g sat. fat), 7 mg chol., 122 mg sodium, 6 g carbo., 1 g fiber, 3 g pro.

## Vegetable Nachos

**MAKES:** 8 servings **PREP:** 40 minutes
**BAKE:** 5 minutes **OVEN:** 350°

- 8 7- to 8-inch flour tortillas
- 1 6-ounce carton plain low-fat yogurt
- 1 tablespoon finely snipped fresh cilantro
- 1 tablespoon vegetable oil
- 1 small zucchini, quartered lengthwise and thinly sliced (about 1 cup)
- ½ cup chopped red or yellow onion (1 medium)
- ½ cup shredded carrot (1 medium)
- 1½ teaspoons ground cumin
- 1 15-ounce can pinto beans, rinsed and drained
- 1 4-ounce can diced green chile peppers, drained
- ½ cup chopped, seeded tomato (1 medium)
- ¾ cup shredded cheddar cheese (3 ounces)
- Fresh cilantro leaves (optional)
- Salsa (optional)

**1** Preheat oven to 350°. Cut each flour tortilla into six wedges. Arrange wedges in single layers on baking sheets. Bake for 10 to 15 minutes or until dry and crisp. Set aside to cool.
**2** In a small bowl stir together the yogurt and finely snipped cilantro; cover and chill.
**3** In a large skillet heat oil over medium heat. Add zucchini, red onion, carrot, and cumin; cook and stir in hot oil for 3 to 4 minutes or until vegetables are crisp-tender. Stir in beans. Heat through.
**4** Arrange tortilla chips on an 11- or 12-inch ovenproof platter or 12-inch pizza pan. Spoon the bean mixture onto the chips. Sprinkle with chile peppers and tomato; top with cheese. Bake for 5 to 7 minutes or until cheese is melted.
**5** If desired, garnish with cilantro leaves. Serve with yogurt mixture and, if desired, salsa.
**Note:** To make tortilla chips ahead, prepare as directed in Step 1. Cool and store in an airtight container at room temperature for up to 4 days or in the freezer up to 3 weeks.

**PER SERVING:** 231 cal., 9 g total fat (4 g sat. fat), 14 mg chol., 414 mg sodium, 28 g carbo., 4 g fiber, 10 g pro.

# Top toast with something savory.

Hummus-and-Cucumber Bruschetta

## Hummus-and-Cucumber Bruschetta

**MAKES:** 24 bruschetta **PREP:** 25 minutes
**BAKE:** 10 minutes **OVEN:** 400°

- **24** **¼-inch slices baguette-style French bread**
- **Nonstick olive oil cooking spray**
- **1** **tablespoon Italian seasoning, crushed**
- **½** **teaspoon garlic powder**
- **⅔** **cup finely chopped English cucumber**
- **¼** **cup plain low-fat yogurt**
- **1** **tablespoon lemon juice**
- **1** **tablespoon snipped fresh oregano or 1 teaspoon dried oregano, crushed**
- **¾** **cup purchased hummus**
- **Snipped fresh oregano (optional)**

**1** Preheat oven to 400°. Arrange baguette slices in a single layer on a large baking sheet. Lightly coat baguette slices with cooking spray. In a small bowl combine Italian seasoning and garlic powder; sprinkle over baguette slices. Bake about 10 minutes or until slices are crisp and lightly brown. Cool in pan on wire rack.

**2** Meanwhile, in a small bowl combine cucumber, yogurt, lemon juice, and the 1 tablespoon snipped oregano. Spread hummus on top of toasted baguette slices; top with cucumber mixture. If desired, sprinkle with additional snipped oregano.

**PER BRUSCHETTA:** 98 cal., 3 g total fat (0 g sat. fat), 0 mg chol., 170 mg sodium, 15 g carbo., 2 g fiber, 3 g pro.

**Fruit Bruschetta:** Preheat oven to 400°. Arrange twenty-four ¼-inch slices baguette-style French bread in a single layer on a large baking sheet. Lightly coat slices with nonstick cooking spray. Bake and cool as above. In a small bowl combine ⅔ cup finely chopped mango, blood oranges, and/or oranges; ¼ cup low-fat yogurt; and 1 tablespoon snipped fresh mint. Spread tops of toasted baguette slices with ¼ cup light cream cheese spread with strawberries; top with fruit mixture. If desired, sprinkle with additional snipped fresh mint. Makes 24 bruschetta.

**PER BRUSCHETTA:** 51 cal., 1 g total fat (0 g sat. fat), 1 mg chol., 104 sodium, 9 g carb., 0 g dietary fiber, 2 g pro.

Tomato, Basil, and Mozzarella Crostini

## Tomato, Basil, and Mozzarella Crostini 30

**MAKES:** 16 crostini **START TO FINISH:** 20 minutes **OVEN:** 425°

- 1 8-ounce loaf baguette-style French bread, cut into ½-inch slices
- 2 to 3 tablespoons olive oil
- ⅛ teaspoon ground black pepper
- 4 ounces fresh mozzarella cheese, thinly sliced
- 12 red or yellow cherry tomatoes, halved
- 12 yellow or red pear-shape tomatoes, halved
- 1 tablespoon snipped or shredded fresh basil
- 2 tablespoons olive oil
- ¼ teaspoon salt

**1** Preheat oven to 425°. For crostini, lightly brush both sides of bread slices with some of the 2 to 3 tablespoons oil; sprinkle with pepper. Place on a large baking sheet. Bake for 5 to 7 minutes or until crisp and light brown, turning once halfway through baking.
**2** Top crostini with mozzarella cheese, tomatoes, and basil. Drizzle with the 2 tablespoons oil; sprinkle with salt.

**PER CROSTINI:** 95 cal., 5 g total fat (1 g sat. fat), 6 mg chol., 169 mg sodium, 9 g carbo., 1 g fiber, 3 g pro.

## Shrimp Crostini 30

**MAKES:** 16 crostini **START TO FINISH:** 20 minutes

- 16 large fresh or frozen peeled and deveined cooked shrimp (about 8 ounces total)
- ⅓ cup shredded fresh basil
- 1 tablespoon olive oil
- 2 teaspoons white wine vinegar
- ¼ teaspoon salt
- ¼ teaspoon ground black pepper
- 16 ¼-inch slices baguette-style French bread
- 2 large cloves garlic, halved
- 4 teaspoons olive oil

**1** Thaw shrimp, if frozen. Rinse shrimp; pat dry with paper towels. Preheat broiler. In a medium bowl combine shrimp, basil, the 1 tablespoon oil, vinegar, salt, and pepper; set aside.
**2** Arrange bread slices on baking sheet. Broil 3 to 4 inches from heat about 2 minutes or until lightly toasted, turning once halfway through broiling. Rub one side of toasts with cut sides of garlic cloves; brush with the 4 teaspoons oil. Arrange toasts, brushed sides up, on serving platter.
**3** Using a slotted spoon, spoon a shrimp onto each toast. Serve immediately.

**PER CROSTINI:** 52 cal., 2 g total fat (0 g sat. fat), 28 mg chol., 112 mg sodium, 4 g carbo., 0 g fiber, 4 g pro.

## Vegetable Spring Rolls

**MAKES:** 12 servings **PREP:** 30 minutes **CHILL:** 1 hour + 2 hours

- **½ cup shredded daikon or radishes**
- **¼ cup thinly sliced green onions (2)**
- **2 tablespoons rice vinegar**
- **1 small fresh jalapeño or serrano pepper, seeded and finely chopped (see note, page 182)**
- **1 teaspoon sugar**
- **½ teaspoon toasted sesame oil**
- **½ cup shredded carrot (1 medium)**
- **½ cup thin bite-size strips seeded cucumber**
- **2 tablespoons snipped fresh cilantro**
- **1 tablespoon reduced-sodium soy sauce**
- **1 cup warm water**
- **6 8½-inch-square rice papers**
- **1½ cups shredded Boston or curly leaf lettuce**

**1** In a small bowl combine daikon, green onions, vinegar, jalapeño pepper, sugar, and oil. In another small bowl combine carrot, cucumber, cilantro, and the 1 tablespoon soy sauce. Cover both mixtures; chill for 1 hour. Drain both mixtures.

**2** Pour the warm water into a pie plate. Carefully dip rice papers into water, one at a time. Place papers, not touching, on clean, dry kitchen towels. Let soften for a few minutes until pliable.

**3** For filling, place ¼ cup shredded lettuce on each rice paper near one edge. Place about 1 tablespoon of each vegetable mixture on the lettuce. Fold edge over filling; fold in sides and roll up. Place, seam side down, on a serving plate. Cover with plastic wrap. Chill for up to 2 hours.

**4** To serve, cut each roll in half crosswise on a diagonal to make 12 pieces.

**PER SERVING:** 33 cal., 0 g total fat, 0 mg chol., 58 mg sodium, 7 g carbo., 1 g fiber, 1 g pro.

Smoked Salmon Roll-Ups

## Smoked Salmon Roll-Ups

**MAKES:** 28 roll-ups **PREP:** 30 minutes **CHILL:** 1 to 4 hours

- 2 cups cooked short grain rice, cooled
- 2 tablespoons sesame seeds, toasted
- 2 tablespoons rice vinegar
- 2 teaspoons sugar
- 1 teaspoon salt
- ¼ cup mayonnaise or salad dressing
- ⅛ teaspoon cayenne pepper
- 4 10-inch spinach-flavor flour tortillas
- 2 3-ounce packages thinly sliced smoked salmon (lox-style)
- 1 medium avocado, halved, seeded, peeled, and sliced
- ½ of a medium cucumber, halved lengthwise, seeded, and cut into thin bite-size sticks

**1** In a medium bowl combine rice and sesame seeds. In another bowl combine vinegar, sugar, and salt, stirring to dissolve sugar and salt. Pour vinegar mixture over rice mixture; toss to coat. Set aside.

**2** In a small bowl stir together mayonnaise and cayenne pepper. Spread 1 tablespoon of the mayonnaise mixture over one side of each tortilla. Spread ½ cup of the rice mixture onto half of each tortilla. Top tortillas with salmon, avocado, and cucumber. Carefully roll up each tortilla tightly, starting at the filled side. Wrap rolls in plastic wrap. Chill for 1 to 4 hours.

**3** To serve, trim and discard ends from rolls. Cut rolls crosswise into 1-inch slices. If necessary, secure with toothpicks.

**PER ROLL-UP:** 77 cal., 4 g total fat (1 g sat. fat), 5 mg chol., 146 mg sodium, 8 g carbo., 1 g fiber, 2 g pro.

## Spicy Turkey Quesadillas

**MAKES:** 9 (2-wedge) servings **START TO FINISH:** 35 minutes
**OVEN:** 400°

- 1 turkey breast tenderloin, cut into thin strips (about 12 ounces)
- 3 teaspoons chili powder
- ¼ teaspoon ground black pepper
- ⅛ teaspoon salt
- 1 tablespoon olive oil
- ½ of a 15-ounce can (¾ cup) no-salt-added black beans, rinsed and drained
- 2 tablespoons lime juice
- 6 8-inch whole wheat tortillas
- ½ cup bottled salsa
- ½ cup shredded reduced-fat cheddar cheese (2 ounces)
- ½ cup snipped fresh cilantro
- 1 medium fresh serrano chile pepper, finely chopped (see note, page 182)
- ½ teaspoon lime juice
- 1 recipe Lime Sour Cream (optional)

**1** Preheat oven to 400°. In a large bowl toss together turkey strips, 2 teaspoons of the chili powder, the black pepper, and salt. In a large skillet heat oil over medium heat. Add turkey strips; cook and stir in hot oil for 10 to 12 minutes or until turkey is no longer pink. Remove from heat and cool slightly; coarsely chop turkey.

**2** Meanwhile, in a food processor combine the remaining 1 teaspoon chili powder, beans, and the 2 tablespoons lime juice. Cover and process until nearly smooth.

**3** Arrange three of the tortillas on a large baking sheet (do not overlap). Spread some of the black bean mixture evenly over each tortilla. Spoon salsa evenly over bean mixture. Top with chopped turkey; sprinkle with cheese. Place the remaining three tortillas on top. Bake for 12 to 15 minutes or until tortillas are brown and crisp.

**4** Meanwhile, in a small bowl combine cilantro, serrano pepper, and the ½ teaspoon lime juice.

**5** To serve, cut each quesadilla into six wedges; sprinkle with cilantro mixture. If desired, serve with Lime Sour Cream.

**PER SERVING:** 189 cal., 5 g total fat (1 g sat. fat), 24 mg chol., 411 mg sodium, 21 g carbo., 3 g fiber, 15 g pro.

**Lime Sour Cream:** In a small bowl combine ½ cup light sour cream and 1 tablespoon lime juice. Makes ½ cup.

# Try a tasty bite of something

## Artichoke-Feta Tortilla Wraps

**MAKES:** 24 rolls **PREP:** 15 minutes
**BAKE:** 15 minutes **OVEN:** 350°

- Nonstick cooking spray
- 1 14-ounce can artichoke hearts, drained and finely chopped
- ½ of an 8-ounce tub (about ½ cup) reduced-fat cream cheese
- 3 green onions, thinly sliced
- ⅓ cup grated Parmesan or Romano cheese
- ¼ cup crumbled feta cheese (1 ounce)
- 3 tablespoons purchased pesto
- 8 8-inch whole wheat, spinach, tomato, or regular flour tortillas
- 1 7-ounce jar roasted red sweet peppers, drained and cut into strips
- 1 recipe Yogurt-Chive Sauce

**1** Preheat oven to 350°. Coat a 3-quart rectangular baking dish with cooking spray; set aside. For filling, in a large bowl stir together the artichoke hearts, cream cheese, green onions, Parmesan cheese, feta cheese, and pesto.
**2** Place about ¼ cup filling onto each tortilla. Top each tortilla with some of the red pepper strips; roll up. Arrange tortilla rolls in the prepared baking dish. If desired, lightly coat tortilla rolls with additional cooking spray. Bake, uncovered, about 15 minutes or until heated through.
**3** Cut each roll into thirds and arrange on a serving platter. Serve with Yogurt-Chive Sauce.
**Yogurt-Chive Sauce:** In a small bowl stir together 1 cup plain fat-free yogurt and 1 tablespoon snipped fresh chives.

**PER ROLL:** 87 cal., 4 g total fat (2 g sat. fat), 7 mg chol., 234 mg sodium, 8 g carbo., 4 g fiber, 5 g pro.

Artichoke-Feta Tortilla Wraps

## Greek-Style Stuffed Mushrooms

**MAKES:** 20 stuffed mushrooms **START TO FINISH:** 40 minutes
**OVEN:** 425°

- 20 large fresh mushrooms, 1½ to 2 inches in diameter (about 1½ pounds)
- Nonstick cooking spray
- 1 cup finely chopped fresh broccoli
- ½ cup chopped onion (1 medium)
- 2 cloves garlic, minced
- 2 teaspoons snipped fresh oregano or ½ teaspoon dried oregano, crushed
- ⅛ teaspoon salt
- ⅛ teaspoon ground black pepper
- 3 tablespoons crumbled feta cheese
- 2 tablespoons fine dry bread crumbs

**1** Preheat oven to 425°. Clean mushrooms, removing stems. Set stems aside. Lightly coat the rounded sides of mushroom caps with cooking spray. Place mushroom caps, stem sides down, in a 15×10×1-inch baking pan. Bake for 5 minutes. Carefully place mushroom caps, stem sides down, on a double thickness of paper towels to drain.
**2** Meanwhile, for filling, chop enough of the mushroom stems to make 1 cup. Coat a large nonstick skillet with cooking spray. Preheat skillet over medium heat. Add chopped mushroom stems, broccoli, onion, garlic, dried

oregano (if using), salt, and pepper to hot skillet. Cook and stir for 5 to 10 minutes or just until tender and most of the liquid is evaporated. Stir in 2 tablespoons of the feta cheese, the bread crumbs, and fresh oregano (if using).

**3** In the same baking pan arrange mushroom caps, stem sides up. Spoon filling into mushroom caps. Bake for 8 to 10 minutes more or until heated through. Sprinkle with the remaining 1 tablespoon feta cheese.

**PER MUSHROOM:** 19 cal., 1 g total fat (0 g sat. fat), 1 mg chol., 51 mg sodium, 2 g carbo., 0 g fiber, 2 g pro.

Tiny Broccoli Quiches

## Tiny Broccoli Quiches

**MAKES:** 18 (2-quiche) servings **PREP:** 45 minutes
**BAKE:** 25 minutes **COOL:** 5 minutes **OVEN:** 400°

- Nonstick cooking spray
- 1 11-ounce package piecrust mix (for 2-crust pie)
- ½ of a 10-ounce package frozen chopped broccoli, thawed
- ¾ cup finely shredded Swiss cheese (3 ounces)
- 1 cup fat-free milk
- ½ cup refrigerated or frozen egg product, thawed, or 2 whole eggs, beaten
- 2 teaspoons snipped fresh dill or 1 teaspoon dried dill
- ¼ teaspoon salt

**1** Preheat oven to 400°. Lightly coat thirty-six 1¾-inch muffin cups with cooking spray. Set aside.

**2** Prepare piecrust mix according to package directions. On a lightly floured surface, roll dough to slightly less than ⅛ inch thick. Using a 2½-inch fluted round biscuit or cookie cutter, cut dough into circles. Reroll scraps, cutting additional circles. Line each muffin cup with a pastry circle.

**3** Drain broccoli well. Pat broccoli dry with paper towels. Divide broccoli and cheese evenly among pastry-lined muffin cups. In a small bowl combine milk, egg product, dill, and salt; spoon about 2 teaspoons of the milk mixture into each muffin cup.

**4** Bake about 25 minutes or until puffed and set. Cool in pans on wire racks for 5 minutes. Loosen and remove from pans. Serve warm.

**PER SERVING:** 123 cal., 7 g total fat (3 g sat. fat), 5 mg chol., 179 mg sodium, 9 g carbo., 0 g fiber, 3 g pro.

Everyone loves a bite of hot pastry with a yummy, cheesy filling. Even when you're trying to eat healthfully, you can still indulge in a tasty treat. These petite vegetable-stuffed quiches save on fat and calories by using skim milk, refrigerated egg product, and just a little bit of cheese for flavor.

These crunchy herbed toasts are delicious with an assortment of cheeses and a chilled dry white wine.

Savory Bites

Macadamia Nut-Turkey Salad on Cucumber Slices

## Savory Bites

**MAKES:** 10 servings **PREP:** 10 minutes
**BAKE:** 15 minutes **OVEN:** 300°

- **1 5¼-ounce package plain melba toast rounds (3 cups)**
- **4 teaspoons olive oil**
- **2 teaspoons white wine Worcestershire sauce**
- **2 teaspoons water**
- **½ teaspoon dried basil, crushed**
- **¼ teaspoon garlic powder**
- **Dash cayenne pepper**

**1** Preheat oven to 300°. Place toast rounds in a medium bowl; set aside. In a small bowl stir together oil, Worcestershire sauce, water, basil, garlic powder, and cayenne pepper. Drizzle oil mixture over toast rounds, tossing to coat. Spread toast rounds in an even layer in a shallow baking pan.

**2** Bake for 15 minutes. Cool in pan on a wire rack. Store in an airtight container at room temperature for up to 1 week.

**PER SERVING:** 70 cal., 2 g total fat (0 g sat. fat), 0 mg chol., 109 mg sodium, 12 g carbo., 1 g fiber, 2 g pro.

## Macadamia Nut-Turkey Salad on Cucumber Slices

**MAKES:** 12 servings **PREP:** 25 minutes **CHILL:** 2 hours

- **1 tablespoon purchased chutney**
- **½ cup finely chopped cooked turkey or chicken (about 3 ounces)**
- **⅓ cup chopped apple**
- **2 tablespoons light mayonnaise or salad dressing**
- **1 tablespoon snipped fresh chives or sliced green onion**
- **½ teaspoon grated fresh ginger or ⅛ teaspoon ground ginger**
- **¼ cup chopped macadamia nuts, cashews, or peanuts**
- **24 ¼-inch cucumber slices**

**1** Cut up any large pieces in chutney. In a small bowl combine chutney, turkey, apple, mayonnaise dressing, chives, and ginger. Cover and chill for 2 hours. Just before serving, stir in 2 tablespoons of the nuts.

**2** To serve, spoon a scant tablespoon turkey mixture onto each cucumber slice. Sprinkle cucumber slices with remaining nuts.

**PER SERVING:** 47 cal., 3 g total fat (1 g sat. fat), 5 mg chol., 28 mg sodium, 3 g carbo., 0 g fiber, 2 g pro.

## Pork Bites with Roasted Pepper-Almond Sauce

**MAKES:** 6 to 8 servings **PREP:** 20 minutes
**MARINATE:** 30 minutes **ROAST:** 15 minutes **OVEN:** 400°

- **2 pounds pork tenderloin, cut into 1½-inch cubes**
- **¼ cup lemon juice**
- **2 tablespoons olive oil**
- **4 cloves garlic, minced**
- **½ teaspoon salt**
- **½ teaspoon ground black pepper**
- **½ cup bottled roasted red sweet peppers, drained**
- **1 tablespoon slivered almonds**
- **2 tablespoons fine dry bread crumbs**
- **2 tablespoons fat-free milk**
- **¼ teaspoon smoked paprika or paprika**

**1** Place pork cubes, lemon juice, oil, garlic, salt, and black pepper in a resealable plastic bag set in a shallow dish; seal bag. Marinate in the refrigerator for 30 minutes.

**2** Preheat oven to 400°. Meanwhile, for sauce, place roasted peppers and almonds in a food processor or blender. Cover and process or blend until finely chopped. Add bread crumbs, milk, and paprika. Cover and process or blend just until combined. Set aside.

**3** Drain pork, discarding marinade. Arrange pork cubes in a single layer in a 13×9×2-inch baking pan. Roast, uncovered, for 15 to 20 minutes or until pork cubes are just slightly pink in centers, stirring once. Serve pork cubes with sauce.

**PER SERVING:** 243 cal., 10 g total fat (2 g sat. fat), 98 mg chol., 318 mg sodium, 5 g carbo., 1 g fiber, 33 g pro.

Chicken Party Kabobs

## Chicken Party Kabobs

**MAKES:** 16 servings **PREP:** 25 minutes
**MARINATE:** 4 hours **GRILL:** 8 minutes

- 4 skinless, boneless chicken breast halves
- 2 tablespoons olive oil
- 2 tablespoons white wine vinegar
- 1 teaspoon finely shredded lemon peel
- 1 tablespoon lemon juice
- 2 cloves garlic, minced
- 1 teaspoon salt
- 1 teaspoon snipped fresh oregano or ¼ teaspoon dried oregano, crushed
- 1 teaspoon snipped fresh thyme or ¼ teaspoon dried thyme, crushed
- ¼ teaspoon ground black pepper
- 1 6-ounce carton plain low-fat yogurt
- 2 tablespoons thinly sliced green onions (1)
- 2 teaspoons grated onion
- ⅛ teaspoon salt

**1** Cut chicken lengthwise into 16 strips. Place chicken in a resealable plastic bag set in a shallow bowl.

**2** For marinade, in a small bowl, combine olive oil, vinegar, lemon peel, lemon juice, garlic, salt, oregano, thyme, and pepper. Pour over chicken; seal bag. Marinate in the refrigerator for 4 to 24 hours, turning bag occasionally.
**3** Drain chicken and discard marinade. Thread chicken, accordion-style, on sixteen 6-inch skewers.*
**4** Grill chicken skewers on the rack of an uncovered grill directly over medium heat for 8 to 10 minutes or until chicken is no longer pink (170°), turning once.
**5** For yogurt sauce, in a small bowl, stir together yogurt, sliced green onion, grated onion, and salt.
**6** To serve, arrange kabobs on a platter and serve warm with yogurt sauce.
***Note:** If using wooden skewers, soak them in water for 30 minutes; drain before using.

**PER SERVING:** 45 cal., 1 g total fat (0 g sat. fat), 13 mg chol., 114 mg sodium, 3 g carbo., 0 g fiber, 6 g pro.

## Nacho Pizzas 

**MAKES:** 8 servings **PREP:** 10 minutes
**BAKE:** 6 minutes **OVEN:** 450°

- Nonstick cooking spray
- 4 5- to 6-inch flour tortillas
- ½ of a 16-ounce can (¾ cup) refried beans
- ⅔ cup chopped roma tomatoes (2 medium)
- ¾ cup shredded cheddar cheese or Monterey Jack cheese with jalapeño peppers (3 ounces)
- ¾ cup purchased guacamole
- Desired toppers (such as sour cream, snipped fresh cilantro, pickled jalapeño chile pepper slices, and/or salsa)

**1** Preheat oven to 450°. Line a baking sheet with foil. Lightly coat foil with cooking spray. Arrange tortillas on prepared baking sheet in a single layer. Bake for 2 to 3 minutes or until just beginning to brown. Remove from oven. Cool slightly.
**2** Spread beans evenly over baked tortillas. Top with tomatoes and cheese. Bake for 4 to 5 minutes more or until cheese is melted.
**3** Cut each pizza into six wedges. Top each wedge with some of the guacamole. Serve with desired toppers.

**PER SERVING:** 156 cal., 8 g total fat (3 g sat. fat), 13 mg chol., 286 mg sodium, 15 g carbo., 4 g fiber, 6 g pro.

## Zesty Turkey Meatballs

**MAKES:** 18 (2-meatball) servings **PREP:** 15 minutes
**BAKE:** 20 minutes **OVEN:** 375°

- ¾ cup sugar-free apricot preserves
- 12 large cloves garlic, halved
- ¼ cup rice vinegar
- 3 tablespoons grated fresh ginger
- 2 teaspoons finely shredded lemon peel
- ½ teaspoon toasted sesame oil
- Several dashed bottled hot pepper sauce
- 1 egg white, beaten
- ⅓ cup finely chopped green or red sweet pepper
- ⅓ cup quick-cooking rolled oats
- ½ teaspoon salt
- 1 pound uncooked lean ground turkey

**1** Preheat oven to 375°. For sauce, in a blender container combine apricot preserves, garlic, vinegar, ginger, lemon peel, oil, and hot pepper sauce. Cover and blend until smooth. Set aside.

**2** In a medium bowl stir together egg white, sweet pepper, oats, and salt. Stir in ⅓ cup of the sauce. Add turkey; mix well. Shape into 1½-inch balls. Arrange meatballs in a 15×10×1-inch baking pan.

**3** Bake, uncovered, for 15 minutes or until no longer pink (165°). Brush with some of the remaining sauce and bake 5 minutes more or until golden and glazed. Remove from oven and drain on paper towels. In a saucepan heat remaining sauce over medium heat until bubbly and slightly thickened. Serve over meatballs.

**PER SERVING:** 58 cal., 2 g total fat (1 g sat. fat), 20 mg chol., 86 mg sodium, 5 g carbo., 0 g fiber, 53 g pro.

## Fruit Kabobs ✪

**MAKES:** 8 servings **PREP:** 20 minutes **CHILL:** 30 to 60 minutes

- ¾ cup bite-size cantaloupe chunks
- ¾ cup bite-size honeydew melon chunks
- ¾ cup small fresh strawberries, hulled
- ¾ cup bite-size fresh pineapple chunks
- 1 small banana cut into 1-inch-thick slices
- 1 cup orange juice
- ¼ cup lime juice
- 1 6-ounce carton vanilla low-fat or fat-free yogurt
- 2 tablespoons frozen orange juice concentrate, thawed
- Ground nutmeg or ground cinnamon (optional)

**1** On eight 6-inch skewers,* alternately thread cantaloupe, honeydew melon, strawberries, pineapple, and banana pieces, leaving ¼ inch between pieces. Place kabobs in a glass baking dish. In a small bowl combine orange juice and lime juice; pour evenly over kabobs. Cover and chill for 30 to 60 minutes, turning occasionally.

**2** Meanwhile, for dip, in a small bowl stir together yogurt and orange juice concentrate. Cover and chill until ready to serve.

**3** To serve, arrange kabobs on a serving platter; discard juice mixture. If desired, sprinkle kabobs with nutmeg. Serve with dip.

***Note:** If using wooden skewers, soak them in water for 30 minutes; drain before using.

**PER SERVING:** 62 cal., 0 g total fat, 1 mg chol., 20 mg sodium, 14 g carbo., 1 g fiber, 2 g pro.

Fruit Kabobs

Hot Cider Surprise Punch

Star anise has a flavor that is similar to anise seed, but it's stronger and more pungent. Star anise differs from many spices in that it is actually the fruit, (not the seed) of a tree native to China and Vietnam. Each section of a star anise is a seedpod. Not only does it add flavor to this spiced cider, but serves as an eye-catching garnish as well.

## Hot Cider Surprise Punch 

**MAKES:** 10 (8-ounce) servings **PREP:** 10 minutes
**COOK:** 20 minutes

- 4 cups apple cider
- 4 cups cranberry juice
- 2 cups pomegranate juice
- 6 inches stick cinnamon
- 3 pieces whole star anise
- 2 2- to 3-inch-long strips orange peel*
- 1 2- to 3-inch-long strip lemon peel*
- Apple wedges and/or star anise

**1** In a 4- to 5-quart Dutch oven combine apple cider, cranberry juice, pomegranate juice, cinnamon, star anise, orange peel, and lemon peel. Bring to boiling; reduce heat. Simmer, covered, for 20 minutes.
**2** Using a slotted spoon, remove and discard cinnamon, star anise, orange peel, and lemon peel. Serve punch warm in mugs. Garnish with apple wedges and/or star anise.
***Note:** When cutting orange peel and lemon peel, avoid any white pith because it will add bitterness to the punch.

**PER SERVING:** 122 cal., 0 g total fat, 0 mg chol., 20 mg sodium, 31 g carbo., 0 g fiber, 0 g pro.

## Chocolate-Peppermint Frappé

**MAKES:** 4 servings **START TO FINISH:** 5 minutes

- 3 small round peppermint candies (¾ ounce total)
- 4 ice cubes, crushed
- 2 cups cold fat-free milk
- 1½ cups fat-free coffee frozen yogurt or fat-free chocolate frozen yogurt
- ⅓ cup chocolate syrup
- Peppermint sticks (optional)

**1** Place peppermint candies in a blender. Cover and blend until the candies are finely crushed. Add the ice, milk, frozen yogurt, and chocolate syrup to blender. Cover and with on/off pulses blend until the mixture is thick and smooth.
**2** Pour into four chilled tall glasses. If desired, garnish with peppermint sticks.

**PER SERVING:** 194 cal., 1 g total fat (1 g sat. fat), 3 mg chol., 135 mg sodium, 42 g carbo., 2 g fiber, 9 g pro.

## Punchy Sangria

**MAKES:** about 10 (6-ounce) servings
**START TO FINISH:** 15 minutes

- **4½ cups rosé wine, chilled**
- **1 12-ounce can frozen pink lemonade concentrate, thawed**
- **⅓ cup lime juice**
- **2 cups club soda, chilled**
- **1 lemon, thinly sliced**
- **1 orange, thinly sliced**
- **Ice cubes**

**1** In a very large pitcher stir together wine, lemonade concentrate, and lime juice. Slowly stir in the club soda. Add lemon and orange slices. Serve over ice.

**PER SERVING:** 147 cal., 0 g total fat, 0 mg chol., 17 mg sodium, 21 g carbo., 1 g fiber, 1 g pro.

## Watermelon-Limeade Cooler

**MAKES:** 8 (about 8-ounce) servings
**PREP:** 30 minutes **CHILL:** 2 hours

- **11 cups peeled and cubed seedless watermelon**
- **1 12-ounce can frozen limeade concentrate, thawed**
- **Ice**
- **Fresh mint sprigs (optional)**

**1** Place one-third of the watermelon in a food processor or blender. Cover and process or blend until smooth. Place watermelon puree in a large pitcher. Repeat twice more with remaining watermelon. Stir limeade concentrate into watermelon. Cover and chill for 2 hours. Serve over ice. If desired, garnish with mint.

**PER SERVING:** 168 cal., 0 g total fat, 0 mg chol., 3 mg sodium, 42 g carbo., 1 g fiber, 1 g pro.

## Madeline's Lemonade

**MAKES:** 8 to 9 servings **PREP:** 15 minutes **CHILL:** 8 to 24 hours

- **6 cups water**
- **1½ cups lemon juice (about 8 lemons)**
- **1 cup sugar**
- **⅓ cup lime juice (about 3 limes)**
- **1 cup fresh raspberries**
- **Ice cubes**
- **Lemon and/or lime slices**

**1** In a 2-quart pitcher combine the water, lemon juice, sugar, and lime juice, stirring to dissolve sugar. Add raspberries; cover and chill 8 to 24 hours. Serve over ice. Garnish with lemon and/or lime slices.

**PER SERVING:** 121 cal., 0 g total fat, 0 mg chol., 6 mg sodium, 33 g carbo., 2 g fiber, 0 g pro.

Madeline's Lemonade

page 52
page 45

# Better &

# Breakfasts Brunches

Bacon, Mushroom, and Tomato Scrambled Eggs

## Bacon, Mushroom, and Tomato Scrambled Eggs

**MAKES:** 4 servings **START TO FINISH:** 20 minutes

- Nonstick cooking spray
- ½ cup sliced fresh mushrooms
- ¼ cup thinly sliced green onions (2)
- 1 teaspoon vegetable oil
- 1 8-ounce carton refrigerated or frozen egg product, thawed, or 4 eggs, beaten
- ¼ cup fat-free milk
- ⅛ teaspoon ground black pepper
- ½ cup shredded reduced-fat cheddar cheese (2 ounces) or ¼ cup crumbled feta or blue cheese (1 ounce)
- 1 slice turkey bacon or bacon, crisp-cooked, drained, and crumbled
- 8 grape or cherry tomatoes, halved

**1** Coat an unheated large nonstick skillet with cooking spray. Preheat skillet over medium heat. Add mushrooms and green onions. Cook and stir for 5 to 7 minutes or until vegetables are tender. Stir in oil.

**2** Meanwhile, in a medium bowl combine egg product, milk, and pepper. Pour egg mixture over vegetables in skillet. Cook, without stirring, until mixture begins to set on the bottom and around edges. With a large spoon or spatula, lift and fold the partially cooked egg mixture so that the uncooked portion flows underneath.

**3** Sprinkle with cheese and bacon. Continue cooking over medium heat for 2 to 3 minutes or until egg mixture is cooked through but is still glossy and moist. Immediately remove from heat. (Be careful not to overcook the egg mixture.) Top with tomatoes.

**PER SERVING:** 102 cal., 5 g total fat (2 g sat. fat), 13 mg chol., 286 mg sodium, 5 g carbo., 1 g fiber, 11 g pro.

## Baked Brie Strata

**MAKES:** 6 servings **PREP:** 20 minutes **CHILL:** 4 hours
**BAKE:** 55 minutes **STAND:** 10 minutes **OVEN:** 325°

- 2 small zucchini, cut into ¼-inch slices
- ⅛ teaspoon kosher salt
- ⅛ teaspoon freshly ground black pepper
- Nonstick cooking spray
- 6 cups 1-inch cubes whole wheat or crusty sourdough bread (6 ounces)
- 1 4.4-ounce package Brie cheese, cut into ½-inch cubes
- 1 cup halved grape or cherry tomatoes
- 4 eggs, lightly beaten
- ⅔ cup evaporated fat-free milk
- ⅓ cup sliced green onions (5)
- 3 tablespoons snipped fresh dill
- ½ teaspoon kosher salt
- ⅛ teaspoon freshly ground black pepper

**1** In a covered medium saucepan cook zucchini in a small amount of boiling, lightly salted water for 2 to 3 minutes or just until tender; drain. Transfer zucchini to a medium bowl. Season with the ⅛ teaspoon salt and ⅛ teaspoon pepper; set aside.

**2** Lightly coat a 2-quart rectangular baking dish with cooking spray. Arrange 4 cups of the bread cubes in the prepared baking dish. If desired, remove and discard rind from Brie cheese. Sprinkle cheese evenly over bread in baking dish. Top with zucchini and tomatoes. Sprinkle with the remaining 2 cups of bread cubes.

**3** In a medium bowl combine eggs, milk, green onions, dill, the ½ teaspoon salt, and the ⅛ teaspoon pepper. Pour egg mixture evenly over bread mixture in baking dish. Using the back of a spoon, gently press down on layers. Cover and chill in the refrigerator for 4 to 24 hours.

**4** Preheat oven to 325°. Bake, covered, for 30 minutes. Uncover; bake for 25 to 30 minutes more or until a knife inserted near the center comes out clean. Let stand for 10 minutes before serving.

**PER SERVING:** 216 cal., 10 g total fat (5 g sat. fat), 163 mg chol., 549 mg sodium, 18 g carbo., 3 g fiber, 14 g pro.

With creamy Brie cheese, herbs, and lots of fresh vegetables, this make-ahead strata is a great start to your day.

Baked Brie Strata

# Menu

Breakfast Fruit Medley
[page 61]

Cheesy Spinach Quiche
[right]

Grilled ham steak

Whole wheat toast

Cheesy Spinach Quiche

## Cheesy Spinach Quiche

**MAKES:** 10 servings **PREP:** 30 minutes **BAKE:** 50 minutes **STAND:** 10 minutes **OVEN:** 450°/350°

- **1 recipe Baked Oil Pastry Shell**
- **3 ounces Gruèyre or Swiss cheese**
- **2½ cups refrigerated or frozen egg product, thawed, or 10 eggs, lightly beaten**
- **1 cup chopped fresh spinach**
- **½ cup fat-free half-and-half or fat-free milk**
- **1 tablespoon snipped fresh thyme or 1 teaspoon dried thyme, crushed**
- **¼ teaspoon ground black pepper**

**1** Prepare Baked Oil Pastry Shell; set aside. Reduce oven temperature to 350°.
**2** Shred the Gruèyre cheese; you should have ¾ cup. Set aside 2 tablespoons of the cheese.
**3** In a large bowl whisk together the remaining cheese, the egg product, spinach, half-and-half, thyme, and pepper. Pour egg mixture into pastry shell.
**4** Bake for 40 minutes. Sprinkle with the reserved 2 tablespoons cheese. If necessary to prevent overbrowing, cover edge of quiche with foil. Bake about 10 minutes more or until a knife inserted near center comes out clean. Let stand on a wire rack for 10 minutes before serving.

**Baked Oil Pastry Shell:** Preheat oven to 450°. In a medium bowl stir together 1⅓ cups all-purpose flour and ¼ teaspoon salt. Add ⅓ cup vegetable oil and 3 tablespoons fat-free milk all at once. Stir lightly with a fork until combined. Form pastry into a ball. On a well-floured surface, use your hands to slightly flatten the pastry ball. Roll pastry from center to edges into a circle 12 inches in diameter (press any cracks back together). To transfer pastry, wrap it around the rolling pin; unroll pastry into a 9-inch pie plate. Ease pastry into pie plate without stretching it. Trim pastry ½ inch beyond edge of pie plate. Fold under pastry. Crimp edge as desired. Do not prick pastry. Line pastry with a double thickness of foil. Bake for 8 minutes. Remove foil. Bake for 5 to 6 minutes more or until crust is golden. Cool on a wire rack. Makes 1 piecrust.

**PER SERVING:** 199 cal., 10 g total fat (3 g sat. fat), 9 mg chol., 218 mg sodium, 15 g carbo., 1 g fiber, 11 g pro.

## Eggs Benedict Strata

**MAKES:** 6 servings **PREP:** 20 minutes **STAND:** 8 hours + 10 minutes **CHILL:** 2 hours **BAKE:** 55 minutes **OVEN:** 325°

- **8 slices whole wheat or whole grain white bread**
- **Nonstick cooking spray**
- **6 cups baby spinach leaves or torn fresh kale**
- **2 teaspoons canola oil**
- **4 ounces Canadian-style bacon, torn into bite-size pieces (about 7 slices)**
- **4 eggs, lightly beaten**
- **2 egg whites, lightly beaten**
- **¼ cup light sour cream**
- **2 tablespoons all-purpose flour**
- **1 teaspoon finely shredded lemon peel**
- **1 teaspoon dry mustard**
- **¼ teaspoon ground black pepper**
- **1⅔ cups fat-free milk**
- **⅓ cup light sour cream**
- **1 to 2 tablespoons fat-free milk**
- **2 teaspoons Dijon-style mustard**
- **Fresh thyme sprigs (optional)**

**1** Place bread slices in a single layer on a wire rack; cover loosely with a clean kitchen or paper towel and let stand 8 to 12 hours or until dried. (Or place in a 15×10×1-inch baking pan; bake in a preheated 300° oven for 10 to 15 minutes or until dry, turning once.) Tear slices into large pieces.
**2** Lightly coat a 2-quart rectangular baking dish with cooking spray; set aside. In an extra-large nonstick skillet cook spinach in hot oil over medium heat for 1 to 2 minutes or just until wilted, turning frequently with tongs. (If using kale, cook for 6 to 8 minutes or just until tender.) Coarsely chop spinach or kale.
**3** In prepared baking dish arrange half of the bread pieces. Top with the spinach and the Canadian-style bacon. Top with remaining bread pieces.
**4** In a medium bowl whisk together the eggs, egg whites, the ¼ cup sour cream, flour, lemon peel, dry mustard, and pepper. Stir in the 1⅔ cups milk. Pour egg mixture evenly over the layers in dish. Cover and chill in the refrigerator for 2 to 24 hours.
**5** Preheat oven to 325°. Bake, uncovered, for 55 to 60 minutes or until a knife inserted near center comes out clean. Let stand for 10 minutes before serving.
**6** For sauce, in a small bowl combine the ⅓ cup sour cream, 1 to 2 tablespoons milk, and Dijon-style mustard to make sauce a drizzling consistency. To serve, drizzle sauce over strata. Garnish with fresh thyme, if desired.

**PER SERVING:** 241 cal., 9 g total fat (3 g sat. fat), 158 mg chol., 521 mg sodium, 23 g carbo., 3 g fiber, 17 g pro.

## Brunch Blintzes

**MAKES:** 15 blintzes **PREP:** 30 minutes **BAKE:** 15 minutes
**OVEN:** 350°

- Nonstick cooking spray
- 1½ cups fat-free milk
- 1 cup all-purpose flour
- 1 egg
- 1 15-ounce carton light ricotta cheese
- 2 tablespoons low-sugar orange marmalade
- ⅛ teaspoon ground cinnamon
- 1 8-ounce carton light sour cream
- Shredded orange peel (optional)
- 1½ cups fresh raspberries and/or blueberries

**1** Lightly coat an unheated 6-inch skillet or crepe pan with cooking spray.
**2** For crepes, in a medium bowl beat milk, flour, and egg with a rotary beater or wire whisk until smooth. Heat prepared skillet over medium heat. Remove skillet from heat and spoon in 2 tablespoons of the batter; lift and tilt skillet to spread batter evenly. Return skillet to heat; cook for 30 to 60 seconds or until brown on bottom. (Or cook on a crepe maker according to manufacturer's directions.)
**3** Invert pan over paper towels; remove crepe from pan. Repeat with remaining batter, making 15 crepes total. (Adjust heat as necessary during cooking. When necessary, coat skillet with additional cooking spray, removing skillet from heat before coating.)
**4** Preheat oven to 350°. Lightly coat a 15×10×1-inch baking pan with cooking spray. Set aside.
**5** For filling, in a medium bowl combine ricotta cheese, orange marmalade, and cinnamon. Spread about 2 tablespoons of the filling on the unbrowned side of a crepe. Fold the crepe in half. Fold in half again, forming a triangle. Place in the prepared pan. Repeat with remaining filling and crepes, overlapping as necessary to fit in pan.
**7** Bake for 15 to 20 minutes or until heated through. To serve, spoon sour cream onto blintzes. If desired, sprinkle with orange peel. Top with raspberries.

**PER BLINTZ:** 101 cal., 3 g total fat (2 g sat. fat), 27 mg chol., 51 mg sodium, 12 g carbo., 1 g fiber, 5 g pro.

## Breakfast Burritos ✪

**MAKES:** 6 servings **START TO FINISH:** 20 minutes

- 2 cups frozen or refrigerated egg product, thawed, or 8 eggs, lightly beaten
- ⅓ cup fat-free milk
- ½ teaspoon garlic salt
- 8 ounces uncooked bulk turkey sausage
- ½ cup chopped green sweet pepper (1 small)
- ½ cup chopped fresh mushrooms
- ¼ cup chopped onion
- ¾ cup bottled chunky salsa
- ½ cup chopped romaine
- 2 tablespoons finely chopped fresh jalapeño chile pepper (optional)(see note, page 182)
- 6 8- to 10-inch whole wheat tortillas, warmed
- ¾ cup shredded reduced-fat cheddar cheese
- Bottled chunky salsa (optional)
- Grapes (optional)

**1** In a medium bowl combine egg product, milk, and garlic salt; set aside.
**2** In a large skillet cook and stir sausage, sweet pepper, mushrooms, and onion over medium heat until sausage is brown and vegetables are tender; drain off fat. Add egg mixture to skillet. Cook, without stirring, until mixture begins to set on the bottom and around edges.
**3** With a spatula or a large spoon, lift and fold the partially cooked egg mixture so that the uncooked portion flows underneath. Continue cooking over medium heat for 2 to 3 minutes or until egg mixture is cooked through but is still glossy and moist.
**4** Immediately remove skillet from heat. Stir in the ¾ cup salsa, romaine, and, if desired, jalapeño pepper. Divide egg mixture among warm tortillas; top each with cheese. Fold bottom edge of each tortilla up and over the filling. Fold opposite sides in. Roll up from bottom. If desired, serve with additional salsa and serve with grapes.

**PER SERVING:** 325 cal., 11 g total fat (3 g sat. fat), 37 mg chol., 1,038 mg sodium, 30 g carbo., 3 g fiber, 26 g pro.

Breakfast Burritos

# Any of these hearty egg dishes

Ranch Eggs

## Ranch Eggs

**MAKES:** 6 servings **PREP:** 20 minutes **BAKE:** 20 minutes
**STAND:** 5 minutes **OVEN:** 400°

- **Nonstick cooking spray**
- **1 large onion, halved lengthwise and thinly sliced**
- **1 14.5-ounce can diced tomatoes, drained**
- **1 fresh jalapeño chile pepper, seeded and chopped** **(see note, page 182)**
- **1 clove garlic, minced**
- **½ teaspoon chili powder**
- **6 eggs**
- **¼ teaspoon salt**
- **⅛ teaspoon black pepper**
- **⅓ cup reduced-fat shredded Monterey Jack or cheddar cheese**
- **6 6-inch corn tortillas, warmed according to package directions (optional)**

**1** Preheat oven to 400°. Coat an unheated large ovenproof skillet with cooking spray. Preheat skillet over medium-high heat. Add onion to hot skillet. Cook about 5 minutes or until tender, stirring occasionally. Remove skillet from heat.
**2** In a small bowl combine the drained tomatoes, jalapeño pepper, garlic, and chili powder. Pour tomato mixture over onion in skillet; spread evenly. Break one of the eggs into a measuring cup or custard cup. Carefully slide egg onto tomato mixture. Repeat with remaining eggs, spacing eggs as evenly as possible. Sprinkle eggs with salt and black pepper.
**3** Bake, uncovered, about 20 minutes or until eggs are set. Remove from oven; sprinkle with cheese. Let stand for 5 minutes before serving. If desired, serve with warmed tortillas.

**PER SERVING:** 121 cal., 7 g total fat (3 g sat. fat), 217 mg chol., 367 mg sodium, 7 g carbo., 2 g fiber, 9 g pro.

## Vegetable Frittata (30)

**MAKES:** 8 servings **START TO FINISH:** 25 minutes

- **1 cup broccoli florets (about 3 ounces)**
- **1 cup water**
- **½ cup finely chopped carrot (1 medium)**
- **¼ cup sliced green onions (2)**
- **Kosher salt**
- **Freshly ground black pepper**
- **Nonstick olive oil cooking spray**
- **¾ cup shredded reduced-fat cheddar or Swiss cheese (3 ounces)**
- **8 eggs, lightly beaten**
- **1 tablespoon chopped fresh basil or 1 teaspoon dried basil, crushed**
- **1 tablespoon Dijon-style mustard**
- **¼ teaspoon freshly ground black pepper**
- **Tomato slices (optional)**

**1** In a medium saucepan combine broccoli, the water, carrot, and green onions. Bring to boiling; reduce heat. Simmer, covered, for 6 to 8 minutes or until vegetables are crisp-tender. Drain well. Transfer drained vegetables to a medium bowl; season lightly with salt and pepper.
**2** Coat an unheated large nonstick skillet with cooking spray. Spread the cooked vegetables in the bottom of the skillet. Sprinkle with half of the cheese.
**3** In a medium bowl whisk together eggs, basil, mustard, and the ¼ teaspoon pepper. Pour egg mixture over vegetable mixture in skillet. Cook over medium heat. As mixture sets, run a spatula around the skillet edge, lifting egg mixture so uncooked portion flows underneath. Continue cooking and lifting edges until egg mixture is almost set (surface will be moist). Reduce heat as necessary to prevent overcooking. Remove from heat. Cover and let stand for 3 to 4 minutes or until top is set.
**4** To serve, cut the frittata into 8 wedges. Sprinkle with the remaining cheese. If desired, garnish with tomato slices.

**PER SERVING:** 114 cal., 7 g total fat (3 g sat. fat), 219 mg chol., 245 mg sodium, 3 g carbo., 1 g fiber, 10 g pro.

satisfies at suppertime too.

## Salmon and Eggs Benedict

**MAKES:** 6 servings **PREP:** 20 minutes
**BAKE:** 15 minutes **OVEN:** 350°

- 1 1.1-ounce or 0.9-ounce envelope hollandaise sauce mix (to make about 1¼ cups sauce)
- 2 tablespoons capers, rinsed and drained
- ½ teaspoon finely shredded lemon peel
- 3 English muffins, split and toasted
- 6 ounces thinly sliced smoked salmon (lox-style) or Canadian-style bacon
- 6 eggs
- ¼ cup milk
- ⅛ teaspoon ground black pepper
- 2 tablespoons butter or margarine
- ¾ cup soft bread crumbs (1 slice)
- Snipped fresh chives (optional)

**1** Preheat oven to 350°. For sauce, prepare hollandaise mix according to package directions. Stir in capers and lemon peel. Spread about ½ cup of the sauce over bottom of a 2-quart rectangular baking dish. Cover remaining sauce; set aside.
**2** Arrange muffins, cut sides up, on top of sauce in dish. Divide salmon into six equal portions. Place salmon, folding as necessary, on top of each muffin half.
**3** For scrambled eggs, in a medium bowl beat together eggs, milk, and pepper with a rotary beater. In a large nonstick skillet melt 1 tablespoon of the butter over medium heat; pour in egg mixture. Cook over medium heat, without stirring, until mixture begins to set on the bottom and around edges.
**4** With a spatula or a large spoon, lift and fold the partially cooked egg mixture so that the uncooked portion flows underneath. Continue cooking over medium heat for 2 to 3 minutes or until egg mixture is cooked but is still glossy and moist. Immediately remove from heat.
**5** Spoon scrambled eggs on top of muffin stacks, dividing evenly. Spoon remaining sauce over eggs.
**6** For crumb topping, melt the remaining 1 tablespoon butter. Add bread crumbs, tossing lightly to coat. Sprinkle over egg stacks.
**7** Bake, uncovered, for 15 to 20 minutes or until heated through. If desired, sprinkle with snipped chives.
**Note:** To make ahead, prepare sauce, egg mixture, and bread crumbs. Cover and chill the three mixtures in separate containers overnight. Assemble egg stacks as directed. Sprinkle eggs with crumb topping. Bake in a 350° oven for 20 to 25 minutes or until heated through. Serve as directed.

**PER SERVING:** 400 cal., 27 g total fat (15 g sat. fat), 273 mg chol., 1,210 mg sodium, 22 g carbo., 1 g fiber, 16 g pro.

Salmon and Eggs Benedict

Here's how to make perfect scrambled eggs: First, before cooking, beat as much air as you can into the eggs. More air means lighter, fluffier eggs. Use a nonstick pan, if possible, to avoid sticking. And last, stir as little as possible when cooking to keep the curds large. Large curds stay moist and tender.

Swiss-Potato Breakfast Casserole

Sectioned grapefruit

Swiss-Potato Breakfast Casserole [below]

Morning Glory Muffins [page 50]

Green tea

## Swiss-Potato Breakfast Casserole

**MAKES:** 6 servings **PREP:** 20 minutes **BAKE:** 35 minutes **STAND:** 5 minutes **OVEN:** 350°

- **1 pound tiny new potatoes, cut into ¼-inch slices**
- **Nonstick cooking spray**
- **⅓ cup thinly sliced leek**
- **¾ cup diced cooked ham (3½ ounces)**
- **3 ounces Swiss cheese, cut into small pieces**
- **1¼ cups fat-free milk**
- **1 tablespoon all-purpose flour**
- **3 eggs, lightly beaten**
- **½ teaspoon dried thyme, crushed**
- **¼ teaspoon salt**
- **¼ teaspoon ground black pepper**

**1** Preheat oven to 350°. In a large saucepan cook potatoes in a small amount of boiling, lightly salted water about 10 minutes or just until tender, adding leek during the last 5 minutes of cooking. Drain well.
**2** Lightly coat a 2-quart rectangular baking dish with cooking spray. Arrange cooked potatoes and leek evenly in the prepared dish. Sprinkle with ham and cheese.
**3** In a medium bowl whisk together milk and flour. Whisk in eggs, thyme, salt, and pepper. Pour the egg mixture over layers in dish.
**4** Bake, uncovered, for 35 to 40 minutes or until a knife inserted near the center comes out clean. Let stand 5 minutes before serving.

**PER SERVING:** 207 cal., 9 g total fat (4 g sat. fat), 132 mg chol., 409 mg sodium, 18 g carbo., 2 g fiber, 13 g pro.

## Breakfast Tacos  

**MAKES:** 10 pancake tacos **PREP:** 20 minutes **BAKE:** 10 minutes **OVEN:** 350°

- **Nonstick cooking spray**
- **⅓ cup chopped celery**
- **⅓ cup chopped green sweet pepper**
- **2 teaspoons butter or margarine**
- **1 cup shredded cheddar cheese (4 ounces)**
- **1 cup diced fully cooked ham**
- **1 8-ounce can crushed pineapple (juice pack), well drained, or ¾ cup finely chopped apple**
- **1 egg, lightly beaten**
- **1⅓ cups packaged complete buttermilk pancake mix**
- **1 cup water**

**1** Preheat oven to 350°. Lightly coat a 2-quart rectangular baking dish with cooking spray; set aside.
**2** For filling, in a small nonstick skillet cook celery and sweet pepper in hot butter over medium heat until tender. Remove from heat. Stir in ¾ cup of the cheese, the ham, and drained pineapple. Set filling aside.
**3** For pancakes, in a medium bowl combine egg, pancake mix, and the water.
**4** For each pancake, pour about ¼ cup batter onto the hot, lightly greased griddle or heavy skillet, spreading batter into a circle about 4 inches in diameter. Cook over medium heat for 1 to 2 minutes on each side or until pancakes are golden brown, turning to cook second sides when pancakes have bubbly surfaces and edges are slightly dry.
**5** Place about ¼ cup filling in the center of each cooked pancake. Bring up the sides of each pancake; stand pancake shells upright in prepared baking pan (to keep pancakes upright, wedge each pancake against the pancake next to it).
**6** Bake for 10 to 12 minutes or until heated through. Remove from oven. Sprinkle with the remaining ¼ cup cheese.

**PER PANCAKE TACO:** 137 cal., 5 g total fat (2 g sat. fat), 37 mg chol., 472 mg sodium, 16 g carbo., 1 g fiber, 8 g pro.

Turkey-Pork Sausage Patties

Ground turkey is a great low-fat substitute for ground beef or pork, but you have to know what you're getting. Ground turkey made from breast is the leanest, at about 3% fat. Regular ground turkey, made from both light and dark meat and skin, is about 10% fat; frozen ground turkey, made from dark meat and skin, is about 15% fat.

## Turkey-Pork Sausage Patties 30

**MAKES:** 6 servings **START TO FINISH:** 25 minutes

**12 ounces lean ground turkey**
**3 ounces ground pork**
**1 teaspoon dried sage, crushed**
**½ teaspoon garlic powder**
**½ teaspoon onion powder**
**½ teaspoon cumin seeds, lightly toasted**
**½ teaspoon freshly ground black pepper**
**¼ teaspoon crushed red pepper**
**¼ teaspoon dried oregano, crushed**
**¼ teaspoon dried tarragon, crushed**
**Nonstick olive oil cooking spray**

**1** In a bowl combine turkey, pork, sage, garlic powder, onion powder, cumin, black pepper, red pepper, oregano, and tarragon. Shape mixture into six 3- to 4-inch round patties.
**2** Lightly coat an unheated extra-large nonstick skillet with cooking spray. Heat the skillet over medium heat. Place patties in skillet and cook about 8 minutes or until no longer pink (165°), turning once halfway through cooking.

**PER SERVING:** 126 cal., 8 g total fat (2 g sat. fat), 55 mg chol., 62 mg sodium, 1 g carbo., 0 g fiber, 12 g pro.

## Cheesy Grits and Sausage 30

**MAKES:** 4 servings **START TO FINISH:** 20 minutes

**4 cups water**
**1 cup quick-cooking grits**
**4 ounces uncooked bulk turkey sausage, cooked**
**2 tablespoons sliced green onion (1)**
**4 teaspoons finely chopped, seeded fresh jalapeño chile pepper (see note, page 182)**
**½ teaspoon garlic salt**
**⅛ teaspoon ground black pepper**
**¼ cup shredded reduced-fat cheddar cheese**

**1** In a medium saucepan bring the water to boiling. Slowly add grits, stirring constantly. Return to boiling; reduce heat. Cook and stir over low heat for 5 to 7 minutes or until the water is absorbed and mixture is thickened.
**2** Remove saucepan from heat. Stir in the turkey sausage, green onion, jalapeño chile pepper, garlic salt, and black pepper. Sprinkle each serving with cheese.

**PER SERVING:** 226 cal., 7 g total fat (2 g sat. fat), 42 mg chol., 444 mg sodium, 30 g carbo., 2 g fiber, 12 g pro.

Apple-Cherry-Filled Rolls

## Apple-Cherry-Filled Rolls ✪

**MAKES:** 16 rolls **PREP:** 15 minutes **RISE:** 30 minutes
**BAKE:** 13 minutes **OVEN:** 375°

- Nonstick cooking spray
- 1 16-ounce package hot roll mix
- 1 cup chopped, peeled apple
- ¼ cup dried tart cherries
- 2 tablespoons packed brown sugar
- ½ teaspoon ground cinnamon
- 1 recipe Orange Icing

**1** Lightly coat 2 baking sheets with cooking spray; set aside. Prepare hot roll mix according to package directions through the resting step.

**2** For filling, in a small bowl stir together apple, dried cherries, brown sugar, and cinnamon.

**3** Divide dough into 16 pieces. Flatten or roll each piece into a 4-inch circle. Spoon a rounded teaspoon of the filling into center of each dough circle. Bring sides of dough up around filling; pinch edges of dough to seal. Place dough balls, seam sides down, on prepared baking sheet. Cover; let rolls rise in a warm place until nearly double in size (about 30 minutes).

**4** Preheat oven to 375°. Bake for 13 to 15 minutes or until tops are golden brown. Cool slightly on a wire rack. Drizzle with Orange Icing. Serve warm.

**Orange Icing:** In a small bowl combine 1 cup powdered sugar and enough orange juice (1 to 2 tablespoons) to make icing a drizzling consistency.

**PER ROLL:** 165 cal., 2 g total fat (0 g sat. fat), 13 mg chol., 186 mg sodium, 33 g carbo., 0 g fiber, 4 g pro.

Slimmed-Down Cinnamon Rolls

## Menu

Cooked turkey bacon or turkey sausage

Poached eggs

Slimmed-Down Cinnamon Rolls [below]

Mixed Fruit with Pineapple Yogurt [page 62]

### Slimmed-Down Cinnamon Rolls ✪

**MAKES:** 18 rolls **PREP:** 35 minutes **RISE:** 1½ hours
**STAND:** 10 minutes **BAKE:** 20 minutes **COOL:** 5 minutes
**OVEN:** 375°

- **2¾ to 3¼ cups all-purpose flour**
- **1 package active dry yeast**
- **1 cup fat-free milk**
- **⅓ cup granulated sugar**
- **3 tablespoons vegetable oil**
- **¼ teaspoon salt**
- **¼ cup refrigerated or frozen egg product, thawed, or 2 slightly beaten egg whites**
- **1 cup whole wheat flour or all-purpose flour**
- **Nonstick cooking spray**
- **⅓ cup packed brown sugar**
- **1 teaspoon ground cinnamon**
- **1 cup powdered sugar**
- **1 to 2 tablespoons orange juice**

**1** In a large mixing bowl combine 2 cups of the all-purpose flour and the yeast; set aside. In a small saucepan heat and stir the milk, granulated sugar, oil, and salt just until warm (120° to 130°).

**2** Add milk mixture to flour mixture along with egg product. Beat with an electric mixer on low to medium speed for 30 seconds, scraping the sides of the bowl. Beat on high speed for 3 minutes more. Using a wooden spoon, stir in the 1 cup of whole wheat or all-purpose flour, plus as much of the remaining all-purpose flour as you can.

**3** Turn dough out onto a floured surface. Knead in enough remaining all-purpose flour to make a moderately soft dough that is smooth and elastic (3 to 5 minutes total). Shape into a ball.

**4** Coat a large bowl with cooking spray. Place dough in bowl; turn once to grease surface of the dough. Cover and let rise in a warm place until double in size (about 1 hour). Punch dough down. Turn onto a lightly floured surface. Divide in half. Cover and let rest for 10 minutes.

**5** In a small bowl combine brown sugar and cinnamon; set aside. Coat two 8×1½-inch round baking pans with cooking spray; set aside.

**6** On a lightly floured surface, roll each dough half into a 12×8-inch rectangle. Brush lightly with a little water. Sprinkle the brown sugar-cinnamon mixture over dough, leaving 1 inch unfilled along one of the long sides. Roll up each rectangle, starting from the filled long side. Pinch dough to seal seams. Slice each roll into 9 equal pieces. Arrange pieces in prepared pans. Cover and let rise in a warm place until nearly double in size (about 30 minutes).

**7** Preheat oven to 375°. Bake for 20 to 25 minutes or until golden. Cool about 5 minutes; remove pans.

**8** For icing, stir together powdered sugar and 1 tablespoon of the juice. Stir in additional juice, 1 teaspoon at a time, until the icing is of a drizzling consistency. Drizzle the powdered sugar icing over the rolls. If desired, serve warm.

**PER ROLL:** 167 cal., 3 g total fat (0 g sat. fat), 0 mg chol., 45 mg sodium, 32 g carbo., 1 g fiber, 4 g pro.

You almost feel virtuous eating one of these sweet rolls. Just a few ingredient swaps from traditional rolls make a huge difference in the nutritional value. This version uses fat-free milk in place of 2% or whole milk, a few tablespoons of vegetable oil for the traditional butter, and a cup of whole-wheat flour to boost the fiber content.

# Raspberries and cream cheese

Raspberry-Cheese Coffee Cake

is a luscious combination.

## Raspberry-Cheese Coffee Cake

**MAKES:** 10 servings **PREP:** 15 minutes **BAKE:** 35 minutes
**COOL:** 10 minutes **OVEN:** 375°

- Nonstick cooking spray
- 1¼ cups all-purpose flour
- 1¼ teaspoons baking powder
- 1 teaspoon finely shredded lemon or orange peel
- ¼ teaspoon baking soda
- ¼ teaspoon salt
- 1 cup granulated sugar
- 3 tablespoons butter, softened
- ¼ cup refrigerated or frozen egg product, thawed
- 1 teaspoon vanilla
- ½ cup buttermilk
- 2 ounces reduced-fat cream cheese (Neufchâtel)
- 2 tablespoons refrigerated or frozen egg product, thawed
- 1 cup fresh or frozen raspberries
- Powdered sugar
- Raspberries (optional)

**1** Preheat oven to 375°. Lightly coat a 9-inch round baking pan with cooking spray; set aside. In a medium bowl stir together flour, baking powder, lemon peel, baking soda, and salt.

**2** In a medium mixing bowl beat ¾ cup of the granulated sugar and the butter with an electric mixer on medium to high speed until combined. Add the ¼ cup egg product and the vanilla. Beat on low to medium speed for 1 minute. Alternately add flour mixture and buttermilk to beaten egg mixture, beating just until combined after each addition. Pour batter into prepared pan.

**3** In a small mixing bowl beat cream cheese and the remaining ¼ cup granulated sugar on medium to high speed until combined. Add the 2 tablespoons egg product; beat until combined. Sprinkle the 1 cup raspberries over the batter in pan. Spoon cream cheese mixture over raspberries, allowing some of the berries to show.

**4** Bake about 35 minutes or until a toothpick inserted near the center comes out clean. Cool in pan for 10 minutes. Sprinkle with powdered sugar. Serve warm. If desired, garnish with additional raspberries.

**PER SERVING:** 195 cal., 5 g total fat (3 g sat. fat), 14 mg chol., 223 mg sodium, 33 g carbo., 1 g fiber, 4 g pro.

## Apricot-Filled Muffins (30)

**MAKES:** 12 muffins **PREP:** 10 minutes **BAKE:** 15 minutes
**COOL:** 5 minutes **OVEN:** 400°

- Nonstick cooking spray
- 1 cup all-purpose flour or whole wheat pastry flour
- ½ cup soy flour
- ½ cup sugar
- 1 teaspoon baking powder
- 1 teaspoon ground cinnamon
- ¼ teaspoon baking soda
- ⅛ teaspoon salt
- ¾ cup buttermilk
- ¼ cup refrigerated or frozen egg product, thawed, or 1 egg
- 3 tablespoons cooking oil
- ¼ cup apricot, peach, or raspberry spreadable fruit

**1** Preheat oven to 400°. Lightly coat twelve 2½-inch muffin cups with cooking spray; set aside. In a medium bowl combine all-purpose flour, soy flour, sugar, baking powder, cinnamon, baking soda, and salt. Make a well in the center of the flour mixture; set aside.

**2** In a small bowl combine buttermilk, egg product, and oil. Add buttermilk mixture to flour mixture all at once; stir just until moistened (batter should be lumpy).

**3** Spoon about half of batter into prepared muffin cups, filling each about one-third full. Place about 1 teaspoon of the spreadable fruit in the center of batter in each cup (if necessary, make an indentation in batter with back of spoon). Top with remaining batter, dividing equally. Muffin cups will be about two-thirds full.

**4** Bake for 15 to 18 minutes or until tops are golden. Cool in muffin cups on a wire rack for 5 minutes. Remove muffins from cups. Serve warm.

**Note:** To make ahead, store baked muffins at room temperature, wrapped tightly in heavy foil, for up to 3 days or freeze for up to 3 months. To reheat, bake in a 300° preheated oven for 15 to 18 minutes.

**PER MUFFIN:** 125 cal., 4 g total fat (1 g sat. fat), 1 mg chol., 101 mg sodium, 21 g carbo., 0 g fiber, 2 g pro.

Lemon Poppy Seed Muffins

## Lemon Poppy Seed Muffins ✪

**MAKES:** 12 muffins **PREP:** 10 minutes **BAKE:** 20 minutes
**COOL:** 5 minutes **OVEN:** 375°

- **Nonstick cooking spray**
- **1¾ cups all-purpose flour**
- **½ cup granulated sugar**
- **1 tablespoon poppy seeds**
- **1 tablespoon finely shredded lemon peel**
- **2 teaspoons baking powder**
- **½ teaspoon salt**
- **¾ cup fat-free milk**
- **¼ cup refrigerated or frozen egg product, thawed, or 1 egg, beaten**
- **¼ cup cooking oil**
- **2 tablespoons coarse sugar**

**1** Preheat oven to 375°. Lightly coat twelve 2½-inch muffin cups with cooking spray, or line with paper bake cups. Set muffin cups aside.
**2** In a medium bowl combine flour, granulated sugar, the poppy seeds, lemon peel, baking powder, and salt. Make a well in the center of flour mixture.
**3** In another medium bowl combine milk, egg product, and oil. Add egg mixture all at once to flour mixture. Stir just until moistened (batter will be lumpy). Spoon batter into the prepared muffin cups, filling each two-thirds full. Sprinkle tops with coarse sugar.
**4** Bake for 20 to 25 minutes or until tops are golden. Cool in muffin cups on a wire rack for 5 minutes. Remove from pans. Serve warm.

**PER MUFFIN:** 159 cal., 5 g total fat (1 g sat. fat), 0 mg chol., 153 mg sodium, 25 g carbo., 1 g fiber, 3 g pro.

## Maple Bran Muffins

**MAKES:** 12 to 16 muffins **PREP:** 20 minutes **STAND:** 10 minutes
**BAKE:** 25 minutes **COOL:** 5 minutes **OVEN:** 350°

- **Nonstick cooking spray**
- **1⅔ cups buttermilk**
- **2 cups whole bran cereal**
- **1 cup whole wheat flour**
- **1¾ teaspoons baking powder**
- **½ teaspoon ground cinnamon**
- **¼ teaspoon baking soda**
- **½ cup refrigerated or frozen egg product, thawed, or 2 eggs, lightly beaten**
- **⅓ cup packed brown sugar**
- **¼ cup pure maple syrup or maple-flavor syrup**
- **3 tablespoons canola oil**
- **¾ cup mixed dried fruit bits and/or raisins**
- **1 recipe Maple Icing (optional)**

**1** Preheat oven to 350°. Lightly coat twelve to sixteen 2½-inch muffin cups with cooking spray; set aside.
**2** In a large bowl stir buttermilk into bran cereal; let stand for 5 to 10 minutes or until cereal is softened. In a small bowl stir together flour, baking powder, cinnamon, and baking soda; set aside.
**3** Stir the egg product, brown sugar, syrup, and oil into bran mixture. Add flour mixture to bran mixture; stir just until combined. Stir in dried fruit bits. Spoon batter evenly into prepared muffin cups, filling each three-fourths full.
**4** Bake for 25 to 30 minutes or until tops spring back when touched and a toothpick inserted in centers comes out clean. Cool in muffin cups on a wire rack for 5 minutes. Remove from muffin cups. If desired, drizzle with Maple Icing. Serve warm.

**PER MUFFIN:** 173 cal., 4 g total fat (0 g sat. fat), 1 mg chol., 152 mg sodium, 33 g carbo., 5 g fiber, 5 g pro.

**Maple Icing:** In a small bowl combine ⅓ cup powdered sugar and ¼ teaspoon maple flavoring. Stir in fat-free milk, 1 teaspoon at a time, until the icing is of a drizzling consistency.

Maple Bran Muffins

## Morning Glory Muffins

**MAKES:** 18 muffins **PREP:** 10 minutes **BAKE:** 18 minutes
**COOL:** 5 minutes **OVEN:** 375°

- **2 cups all-purpose flour**
- **1¼ cups packed brown sugar**
- **2 teaspoons baking soda**
- **2 teaspoons ground cinnamon**
- **½ teaspoon salt**
- **1⅓ cups chopped, peeled apples (2 medium)**
- **1¼ cups finely shredded carrots (2 medium)**
- **½ cup raisins**
- **3 eggs, lightly beaten**
- **1 8-ounce can crushed pineapple (juice pack), undrained**
- **⅔ cup vegetable oil**
- **½ teaspoon vanilla**

**1** Preheat oven to 375°. Line eighteen 2½-inch muffin cups with paper bake cups; set aside.
**2** In a large bowl combine flour, brown sugar, baking soda, cinnamon, and salt. Stir in apples, carrots, and raisins. Make a well in the center of the flour mixture.
**3** In a medium bowl combine eggs, the undrained pineapple, oil, and vanilla. Add pineapple mixture to flour mixture. Stir just until moistened (batter should be lumpy). Spoon batter into prepared muffin cups.

Morning Glory Muffins

**4** Bake about 18 minutes or until a wooden toothpick inserted in centers comes out clean. Cool in muffin cups on a wire rack for 5 minutes. Remove from muffin cups. Serve warm.

**PER MUFFIN:** 221 cal., 9 g total fat (1 g sat. fat), 35 mg chol., 225 mg sodium, 33 g carbo., 1 g fiber, 3 g pro.

## Pear-Cheddar Quick Bread

**MAKES:** 1 loaf (16 slices) **PREP:** 15 minutes **BAKE:** 55 minutes
**COOL:** 10 minutes **OVEN:** 350°

- **Nonstick cooking spray**
- **1⅓ cups all-purpose flour**
- **½ cup whole wheat pastry flour or whole wheat flour**
- **¼ cup flaxseed meal or toasted wheat germ**
- **2 teaspoons baking powder**
- **¼ teaspoon salt**
- **2 cups shredded firm pears (2 medium)**
- **½ cup refrigerated or frozen egg product, thawed, or 2 eggs, lightly beaten**
- **½ cup sugar**
- **⅓ cup canola oil**
- **¼ cup buttermilk**
- **¼ cup honey**
- **1 teaspoon vanilla**
- **½ cup shredded white cheddar cheese (2 ounces)**

**1** Preheat oven to 350°. Lightly coat the bottom and ½ inch up the sides of one 9×5×3-inch loaf pan or two 7×3½×2-inch loaf pans with cooking spray; set aside. In a large bowl combine all-purpose flour, whole wheat pastry flour, flaxseed meal, baking powder, and salt. Make a well in center of the flour mixture.
**2** In a medium bowl combine pear, egg product, sugar, oil, buttermilk, honey, and vanilla. Add pear mixture to flour mixture all at once. Stir just until combined. Fold in cheese. Spoon batter in prepared pan.
**3** Bake for 55 to 60 minutes (45 to 50 minutes for the smaller pans) or until a wooden toothpick inserted near center comes out clean. Cool in pan on a wire rack for 10 minutes. Remove from pan. Cool completely on a wire rack. Wrap and store overnight before slicing.

**PER SLICE:** 163 cal., 6 g total fat (1 g sat. fat), 4 mg chol., 107 mg sodium, 24 g carbo., 2 g fiber, 4 g pro.

## Menu

Pear-Cheddar Quick Bread [left]

Vegetable Frittata [page 38]

Pomegranate or cranberry juice

Pear-Cheddar Quick Bread

Multigrain Orange-Kissed Waffles

## Multigrain Orange-Kissed Waffles

**MAKES:** 12 to 16 (4-inch) waffles **PREP:** 10 minutes
**BAKE:** per waffle baker directions

- **1½ cups all-purpose flour**
- **½ cup whole wheat flour**
- **½ cup oat flour**
- **1 tablespoon baking powder**
- **1 tablespoon packed brown sugar**
- **½ teaspoon baking soda**
- **¼ teaspoon salt**
- **1¾ cups fat-free milk or light vanilla soymilk**
- **½ cup refrigerated or frozen egg product, thawed, or 2 eggs, lightly beaten**
- **½ cup canola oil**
- **1 tablespoon finely shredded orange peel**
- **½ cup low-sugar orange marmalade**
- **1½ cups fresh blueberries, raspberries, and/or sliced strawberries**

**1** In a large bowl combine all-purpose flour, whole wheat flour, oat flour, baking powder, brown sugar, baking soda, and salt. Make a well in the center of flour mixture.
**2** In a medium bowl combine milk, egg product, oil, and orange peel. Add egg mixture to flour mixture all at once. Stir just until moistened (batter should be slightly lumpy).
**3** Pour ⅔ to 1 cup batter onto grids of a preheated, lightly greased waffle baker (use a regular or Belgian waffle baker). Close lid quickly; do not open until done. Bake according to manufacturer's directions. When done, use a fork to lift waffle off grid. Repeat with remaining batter.
**4** For sauce, in a small saucepan heat marmalade until melted. Stir in blueberries; heat through. Spoon sauce over warm waffles.

**PER WAFFLE:** 221 cal., 10 g total fat (1 g sat. fat), 1 mg chol., 226 mg sodium, 28 g carbo., 2 g fiber, 5 g pro.

## Baked Orange French Toast

**MAKES:** 6 servings **PREP:** 10 minutes **BAKE:** 35 minutes
**STAND:** 10 minutes **OVEN:** 325°

- ¼ cup sugar
- 1 teaspoon ground cinnamon
- 6 eggs, lightly beaten
- 1¾ cups milk
- ⅓ cup orange marmalade
- ½ teaspoon vanilla
- 6 cups 1-inch cubes whole wheat bread (6 ounces)
- ⅓ cup raisins
- 1 recipe Marmalade Sauce

**1** Preheat oven to 325°. In a medium bowl whisk together sugar and cinnamon. Whisk in eggs, milk, orange marmalade, and vanilla.
**2** Place bread cubes in an ungreased 2-quart rectangular baking pan. Sprinkle with raisins. Pour egg mixture evenly over the bread. Using the back of a spoon, gently press down on layers.
**3** Bake, uncovered, for 35 to 40 minutes (center may appear slightly wet but will set during standing). Let stand for 10 minutes before serving. Serve warm with Marmalade Sauce.
**Marmalade Sauce:** In a small saucepan combine 1 tablespoon cornstarch and 1/2 teaspoon finely shredded orange peel. Stir in 3/4 cup orange juice and 1/3 cup orange marmalade. Cook and stir over medium-low heat until thickened and bubbly. Remove from heat. If desired, stir in 2 teaspoons butter. Serve warm. Makes 1 cup.

**PER SERVING:** 342 cal., 7 g total fat (3 g sat. fat), 217 mg chol., 254 mg sodium, 59 g carbo., 3 g fiber, 13 g pro.

Banana Waffle Stacks

Bananas turn brown quickly when exposed to air—a process called oxidation that also affects apples, pears, and potatoes. Prevent that from happening by tossing the banana slices in a teaspoon or two of fresh lemon juice. It doesn't have much impact on flavor—just on the color.

## Banana Waffle Stacks ✪

**MAKES:** 8 servings (3 mini waffles per serving) **PREP:** 10 minutes
**BAKE:** per waffle baker directions

- Nonstick cooking spray
- 1¾ cups all-purpose flour
- 1 tablespoon sugar
- 1 tablespoon baking powder
- ¼ teaspoon salt
- ¼ teaspoon ground cinnamon
- 1 egg, lightly beaten
- 1½ cups fat-free milk
- ⅔ cup mashed ripe banana
- 2 tablespoons vegetable oil
- 2 cups bias-sliced bananas
- ½ cup frozen light whipped dessert topping, thawed
- 8 maraschino cherries

**1** Lightly coat the grids of a waffle baker with cooking spray. Preheat waffle baker according to manufacturers directions.
**2** In a bowl combine flour, sugar, baking powder, salt, and cinnamon. Make a well in the center of the flour mixture.
**3** In another medium bowl combine egg, milk, mashed banana, and oil. Add egg mixture to flour mixture all at once. Stir just until moistened (batter should be slightly lumpy).
**4** Pour about 2 tablespoons of the batter onto each quarter of the preheated waffle baker. Close lid quickly; do not open until done. Bake according to manufacturer's directions. When done, use a fork to lift waffle off grid. Repeat with remaining batter.
**5** For each serving, stack 3 of the waffles on each plate. Top each with banana slices, dessert topping, and a maraschino cherry.

**PER SERVING:** 228 cal., 5 g total fat (1 g sat. fat), 27 mg chol., 257 mg sodium, 41 g carbo., 2 g fiber, 6 g pro.

## Banana-Oat Breakfast Cookies ✪

**MAKES:** 12 breakfast cookies **PREP:** 10 minutes
**BAKE:** 14 minutes per batch **COOL:** 1 minute **OVEN:** 350°

- Nonstick cooking spray
- ½ cup mashed banana
- ½ cup chunky natural peanut butter (unsalted and unsweetened) or regular chunky peanut butter
- ½ cup honey
- 1 teaspoon vanilla
- 1 cup rolled oats
- ½ cup whole wheat flour
- ¼ cup nonfat dry milk powder
- 2 teaspoons ground cinnamon
- ¼ teaspoon baking soda
- 1 cup dried cranberries or raisins

**1** Preheat oven to 350°. Lightly coat two cookie sheets with cooking spray; set aside. In a large bowl combine banana, peanut butter, honey, and vanilla.
**2** In a small bowl combine oats, flour, milk powder, cinnamon, and baking soda. Stir the oat mixture into the banana mixture until combined. Stir in dried cranberries.
**3** Using a ¼-cup measure, drop mounds of dough about 3 inches apart onto prepared baking sheets. With a thin metal or small plastic spatula dipped in water, flatten and spread each mound of dough to a 2¾-inch round, about ½ inch thick.
**4** Bake, one sheet at a time, for 14 to 16 minutes or until edges are light brown and centers are set. Cool on cookie sheets for 1 minute. Transfer to wire racks and let cool.
**Note:** Store cookies in an airtight container or resealable plastic bag for up to 3 days or freeze for up to 2 months; thaw before serving.

**PER BREAKFAST COOKIE:** 227 cal., 6 g total fat (1 g sat. fat), 0 mg chol., 77 mg sodium, 37 g carbo., 4 g fiber, 6 g pro.

## Breakfast Fruit and Nut Cookies

**MAKES:** 10 cookies **PREP:** 10 minutes
**BAKE:** 12 minutes per batch **COOL:** 1 minute **OVEN:** 350°

- ¾ cup packed brown sugar
- ½ cup frozen or refrigerated egg product, thawed, or 2 eggs, lightly beaten
- 3 tablespoons butter, melted
- 1 teaspoon vanilla
- ⅓ cup finely snipped dried dates, dried apricots, or dried figs
- 1 cup all-purpose flour
- ½ cup whole wheat flour
- ⅓ cup oat bran
- 2 tablespoons ground flaxseed
- ½ teaspoon baking soda
- ½ teaspoon ground cinnamon
- ⅓ cup chopped pecans or walnuts or sliced almonds

**1** Preheat oven to 350°. Line two cookie sheets with parchment paper; set aside. In a large bowl combine brown sugar, the egg product, butter, and vanilla. Stir in dates; set aside.
**2** In a medium bowl combine all-purpose flour, whole wheat flour, oat bran, flaxseed, baking soda, and cinnamon. Add flour mixture to date mixture, stirring until moist. Stir in pecans.
**3** Use a scant ¼ cup measure or scoop to drop mounds of dough about 2 inches apart onto prepared cookie sheets.
**4** Bake, one sheet at a time, about 12 minutes or until edges are golden. Cool on cookie sheets for 1 minute. Transfer to a wire rack and cool completely.

**PER COOKIE:** 232 cal., 8 g total fat (3 g sat. fat), 51 mg chol., 109 mg sodium, 38 g carbo., 3 g fiber, 5 g pro.

Here's one smart cookie: Hearty oats, fresh and dried fruits, and peanut butter for protein—a tasty on-the-go breakfast treat.

Banana-Oat Breakfast Cookies

Blueberry Breakfast Scones

# Menu

Cubed melon

Bacon, Mushroom, and Tomato Scrambled Eggs [page 32]

Blueberry Breakfast Scones [right]

## Blueberry Breakfast Scones 

**MAKES:** 10 scones **PREP:** 15 minutes **BAKE:** 15 minutes
**OVEN:** 400°

- **Nonstick cooking spray**
- **1½ cups all-purpose flour**
- **½ cup white whole wheat flour or whole wheat flour**
- **¼ cup sugar**
- **1 tablespoon baking powder**
- **1 tablespoon finely shredded orange peel**
- **¼ teaspoon baking soda**
- **¼ teaspoon salt**
- **¼ cup cold butter**
- **1 egg, lightly beaten**
- **½ cup buttermilk**
- **1 teaspoon vanilla**
- **1 cup fresh or frozen blueberries**
- **1 recipe Orange Glaze (optional)**

**1** Preheat oven to 400°. Lightly coat a baking sheet with cooking spray; set aside. In a large bowl combine all-purpose flour, whole wheat flour, sugar, baking powder, orange peel, baking soda, and salt. Using a pastry blender, cut in butter until mixture resembles coarse crumbs. Make a well in the center of the flour mixture.
**2** In a small bowl combine egg, buttermilk, and vanilla. Add egg mixture to flour mixture all at once. Using a fork, stir just until moistened. Gently stir in blueberries. (Do not thaw frozen blueberries; thawed berries will discolor the dough.) (Mixture will not completely come together in a ball.)
**3** Turn dough out onto a lightly floured surface. Knead dough by folding and gently pressing it for 10 to 12 strokes or until dough is nearly smooth.
**4** Transfer dough to the prepared baking sheet; pat or lightly roll dough into a 7-inch circle. Cut circle into 10 wedges. Separate wedges so they are about 1 inch apart.
**5** Bake about 15 minutes or until golden. Remove scones from baking sheet. Cool slightly on a wire rack. If desired, drizzle scones with Orange Glaze. Serve warm.

**PER SCONE:** 171 cal., 5 g total fat (3 g sat. fat), 34 mg chol., 215 mg sodium, 27 g carbo., 1 g fiber, 4 g pro.

**Orange Glaze:** In a small bowl combine ¾ cup powdered sugar and ¼ teaspoon finely shredded orange peel. Stir in orange juice or fat-free milk, 1 teaspoon at a time, until the icing is of a drizzling consistency.

## Fruited Granola

**MAKES:** 10 (½-cup) servings **PREP:** 5 minutes
**BAKE:** 38 minutes **OVEN:** 325°

- **Nonstick cooking spray**
- **2½ cups regular rolled oats**
- **1 cup whole bran cereal**
- **½ cup toasted wheat germ**
- **¼ cup sliced almonds**
- **½ cup raspberry applesauce or applesauce**
- **⅓ cup honey**
- **¼ teaspoon ground cinnamon**
- **⅓ cup dried cherries and mixed berries**
- **Vanilla low-fat yogurt (optional)**
- **Fresh apricot halves (optional)**

**1** Preheat oven to 325°. Spray a 15×10×1-inch baking pan with cooking spray; set aside.
**2** In a large bowl combine oats, bran, wheat germ, and almonds. In a small bowl combine applesauce, honey, and cinnamon. Stir applesauce mixture into cereal mixture. Spread granola evenly onto prepared pan.
**3** Bake for 35 minutes, stirring occasionally. Carefully stir in dried cherries and mixed berries. Bake for 3 to 5 minutes more or until golden brown.
**4** Spread granola onto greased foil; cool completely. Store granola in an airtight container or a large resealable plastic bag for up to 2 weeks.
**5** If desired, top granola with yogurt and apricots.

**PER SERVING:** 108 cal., 2 g total fat (1 g sat. fat), 0 mg chol., 9 mg sodium, 21 g carbo., 3 g fiber, 4 g pro.

Some granola deserves its "healthy" designation and some doesn't. Many commercial granolas are made with high-fructose corn syrup and hydrogenated fats. Others—if they contain a lot of nuts—may have a high total fat content but also a lot of the "good" fat and very little or no saturated fat. At just 2 grams of fat for a ½-cup serving, this homemade version has earned the designation.

## Fruit and Grain Cereal Mix (30)

**MAKES:** 5 servings **PREP:** 5 minutes **COOK:** 15 minutes **COOL:** 3 minutes

- **1½ cups cracked wheat cereal**
- **¾ cup quick-cooking brown rice**
- **½ cup mixed dried fruit bits**
- **½ teaspoon ground cinnamon**
- **¼ teaspoon salt**
- **3⅓ cups water**
- **2½ cups milk**
- **Stick cinnamon (optional)**

**1** In a resealable plastic bag combine wheat cereal, rice, dried fruit bits, cinnamon, and salt. Mix thoroughly to evenly distribute fruit and seasonings. (You may have to use your hands to separate fruit bits.) Seal bag and store in refrigerator for up to 1 month.

**2** For five servings, in a large saucepan combine the water and milk. Bring to boiling; reduce heat. Stir in cereal mixture. (For one serving, in a small saucepan bring ⅔ cup water and ½ cup milk to boiling; reduce heat. Stir in ½ cup of the cereal mix.)

**3** Simmer, uncovered, for 15 to 20 minutes or until most of the liquid is absorbed, mixture is creamy, and wheat is just tender,* stirring occasionally. Remove saucepan from heat. Cool for 3 to 5 minutes before serving. If desired, garnish with stick cinnamon.

***Note:** If mixture is dry before wheat is tender, stir in additional water.

**PER SERVING:** 291 cal., 3 g total fat (2 g sat. fat), 10 mg chol., 199 mg sodium, 58 g carbo., 9 g fiber, 11 g pro.

## Fruit and Yogurt Oatmeal

**MAKES:** 8 servings **PREP:** 5 minutes **CHILL:** 1 hour

- **3** **6-ounce cartons plain fat-free yogurt**
- **1** **cup quick-cooking rolled oats**
- **2** **medium bananas, sliced**
- **1** **8-ounce can pineapple chunks (juice pack), undrained**
- **⅔** **cup sliced almonds, toasted**
- **½** **cup dried cranberries**
- **½** **cup dried apricots, snipped**
- **1** **teaspoon vanilla or ¾ teaspoon almond extract**
- **Fat-free milk (optional)**

**1** In a large bowl combine yogurt, oats, bananas, undrained pineapple, almonds, cranberries, apricots, and vanilla. Cover and chill in the refrigerator for at least 1 hour or up to 24 hours. If necessary, thin with milk just before serving.

**PER SERVING:** 212 cal., 6 g total fat (1 g sat. fat), 1 mg chol., 52 mg sodium, 36 g carbo., 4 g fiber, 8 g pro.

Cranberry-Almond Cereal Mix

## Cranberry-Almond Cereal Mix

**MAKES:** 14 (about ⅓-cup) servings **PREP:** 10 minutes **COOK:** 12 minutes

- **1** **cup regular rolled oats**
- **1** **cup quick-cooking barley**
- **1** **cup bulgur or cracked wheat**
- **1** **cup dried cranberries, raisins, and/or snipped dried apricots**
- **¾** **cup sliced almonds, toasted**
- **⅓** **cup sugar**
- **1** **tablespoon ground cinnamon**
- **¼** **teaspoon salt**
- **Fat-free milk (optional)**

**1** In an airtight container stir together oats, barley, bulgur, cranberries, almonds, sugar, cinnamon, and salt. Seal and store at room temperature for up to 2 months or freeze for up to 6 months.

**2** For two servings, in a small saucepan bring 1⅓ cups water to boiling. Stir cereal mix before measuring; add ⅔ cup of the cereal mix to the boiling water. Reduce heat. Simmer, covered, for 12 to 15 minutes or until cereal reaches desired consistency. If desired, serve with milk.

With so many commercial cereals touting their whole grain content, it is easy to be confused about what is whole grain and what isn't. Whole grains contain the entire grain kernel—the bran, germ, and endosperm. This hot cereal mix has three types—oats, barley, and bulgur.

**PER SERVING:** 168 cal., 3 g total fat (0 g sat. fat), 0 mg chol., 44 mg sodium, 33 g carbo., 5 g fiber, 4 g pro.

**Microwave method:** For one breakfast serving, stir cereal mix before measuring. In a microwave-safe 1-quart bowl combine ¾ cup water and ⅓ cup cereal mix. Microwave, uncovered, on 50 percent power (medium) for 8 to 11 minutes or until cereal reaches desired consistency, stirring once. Stir before serving. If desired, serve with milk.

# Rice pudding may taste like

Peachy Rice Pudding

## Peachy Rice Pudding (30)

**MAKES:** 5 servings **START TO FINISH:** 25 minutes

- **1⅓ cups water**
- **⅔ cup uncooked long grain rice**
- **½ of a 12-ounce can (¾ cup) evaporated fat-free milk**
- **⅓ cup mixed dried fruit bits**
- **2 teaspoons honey**
- **¼ teaspoon pumpkin pie spice or ground cinnamon**
- **⅛ teaspoon salt**
- **1 cup sliced, peeled peach (1 medium) or frozen sliced peaches, thawed**
- **¼ cup vanilla fat-free yogurt**
- **Pumpkin pie spice or ground cinnamon (optional)**

**1** In a medium saucepan bring water to boiling. Stir in rice; reduce heat. Simmer, covered, for 15 to 20 minutes or until rice is tender.
**2** Stir the ¾ cup evaporated milk, fruit bits, honey, the ¼ teaspoon pumpkin pie spice, and the salt into cooked rice. Bring just to boiling; reduce heat to medium-low. Simmer, uncovered, about 5 minutes or until mixture is thick and creamy, stirring frequently.
**3** To serve, top warm pudding with peach and yogurt. If desired, sprinkle with additional pumpkin pie spice.

**PER SERVING:** 175 cal., 0 g total fat, 2 mg chol., 120 mg sodium, 47 g carbo., 1 g fiber, 6 g pro.

## Baked Grapefruit Halves (30)

**MAKES:** 6 servings **PREP:** 15 minutes **BAKE:** 12 minutes
**OVEN:** 450°

- **3 red grapefruits**
- **1 medium orange, peeled and sectioned**
- **1 medium banana, sliced**
- **⅓ cup dried cherries**
- **2 tablespoons orange liqueur or orange juice**
- **1 tablespoon canola oil**
- **2 tablespoons packed brown sugar**
- **½ teaspoon ground cinnamon**

**1** Preheat oven to 450°. Cut each grapefruit in half horizontally; cut a very thin slice from the bottom of each half so grapefruits will sit flat. Using a grapefruit knife or a small serrated knife, cut around the outer edge to loosen fruit from shell. Cut between one segment and the membrane, slicing to the grapefruit's center. Turn the knife and slide it up the other side of the section alongside the membrane. Repeat with remaining sections. Place grapefruit halves, cut sides up, in a 3-quart rectangular baking dish.
**2** In a medium bowl combine orange sections, banana slices, cherries, and orange liqueur. Mound the orange mixture on top of grapefruit halves. Drizzle with oil. In a small bowl combine brown sugar and cinnamon; sprinkle over orange mixture.
**3** Bake about 12 minutes or until grapefruits are warm and topping is heated through.

**PER SERVING:** 154 cal., 3 g total fat (0 g sat. fat), 0 mg chol., 4 mg sodium, 32 g carbo., 3 g fiber, 2 g pro.

## Ginger-Fruit Compote

**MAKES:** 6 servings **PREP:** 15 minutes **CHILL:** 7 hours

- **¾ cup water**
- **½ cup sugar**
- **4 teaspoons lemon juice**
- **3 to 4 teaspoons finely chopped crystallized ginger**
- **4 cups assorted fruit (such as sliced kiwifruit, orange sections, chopped apple, sliced banana, blueberries, raspberries, and/or seedless red grapes)**

**1** For syrup, in a small saucepan combine the water, sugar, lemon juice, and ginger. Bring mixture to boiling; reduce

dessert, but it fortifies for the day.

heat. Simmer, covered, for 5 minutes. Transfer mixture to a bowl; cool. Cover and chill in the refrigerator for at least 1 hour or until cold.

**2** In a large serving bowl combine assorted fruit. Pour chilled syrup over fruit, tossing gently to coat. Cover and chill for up to 6 hours.

**3** To serve, spoon fruit and syrup into dessert dishes.

**Note:** To make ahead, prepare the syrup mixture. Cover and chill for up to 24 hours. Mix syrup with fruit and chill as directed.

**PER SERVING:** 132 cal., 0 g total fat, 0 mg chol., 3 mg sodium, 34 g carbo., 2 g fiber, 1 g pro.

Breakfast Fruit Medley

## Breakfast Fruit Medley (30)

**MAKES:** 8 to 10 servings **START TO FINISH:** 20 minutes

- **½ cup dried tart cherries**
- **¼ cup honey**
- **½ teaspoon finely shredded lime peel**
- **1 to 2 tablespoons lime juice**
- **1 cup seedless green grapes, halved**
- **1 cup seedless red grapes, halved**
- **1 Granny Smith apple, cored and cut into bite-size pieces**
- **1 Red Delicious apple, cored and cut into bite-size pieces**
- **2 kiwifruits, peeled and cut into wedges**

**1** Place dried cherries in a small bowl; add enough boiling water to cover cherries. Let stand about 15 minutes or until cherries are plump; drain.

**2** In a large bowl combine honey, lime peel, and lime juice. Stir in the drained cherries, grapes, apples, and kiwifruits. Serve immediately or cover and chill in the refrigerator for up to 2 hours before serving.

**PER SERVING:** 116 cal., 0 g total fat, 0 mg chol., 2 mg sodium, 30 g carbo., 2 g fiber, 1 g pro.

## Honeyed Orange Slices

**MAKES:** 2 servings **START TO FINISH:** 15 minutes

- 1 medium orange
- 1 medium blood orange or orange
- 2 tablespoons honey
- 2 tablespoons orange juice
- 1½ teaspoons brandy (optional)
- Dash ground cinnamon

**1** Peel oranges; trim off bitter white pith. Slice each orange crosswise into 4 to 5 slices. Divide between two dessert dishes; set aside.
**2** For syrup, in a small saucepan combine honey, orange juice, brandy (if using), and cinnamon. Heat and stir over medium heat until bubbly. Boil, uncovered, for 2 minutes. Remove saucepan from heat.
**3** Spoon the hot syrup over orange slices. Serve at room temperature or cover and chill in the refrigerator.

**PER SERVING:** 133 cal., 0 g total fat, 0 mg chol., 1 mg sodium, 34 g carbo., 3 g fiber, 1 g pro.

Honeyed Orange Slices

## Mixed Fruit with Pineapple Yogurt

**MAKES:** 8 servings **PREP:** 10 minutes **CHILL:** 1 hour

- 2 cups plain low-fat yogurt
- 1 8-ounce can crushed pineapple (juice pack), undrained
- 2 teaspoons vanilla
- 5 cups assorted fruit (such as fresh or canned pineapple chunks, seedless grapes, sliced fresh strawberries, raspberries, and/or blueberries)

**1** In a medium bowl combine yogurt, undrained crushed pineapple, and vanilla. Cover and chill in the refrigerator for 1 hour or up to 2 days.
**2** To serve, spoon ¼ cup of the yogurt mixture into each of 8 dessert dishes. Add about ⅔ cup of the assorted fruit to each and top with remaining yogurt mixture.

**PER SERVING:** 104 cal., 1 g total fat (1 g sat. fat), 3 mg chol., 42 mg sodium, 21 g carbo., 2 g fiber, 4 g pro.

## Peach Sunrise Refresher

**MAKES:** 4 servings **START TO FINISH:** 5 minutes

- 2 cups crushed ice
- 1⅓ cups pomegranate juice
- 1⅓ cups peach nectar
- Mint sprigs (optional)
- Quartered orange slices (optional)

**1** Place ½ cup ice into each glass; pour in ⅓ cup pomegranate juice and slowly fill with ⅓ cup peach nectar. If desired, garnish with mint sprigs and orange slices.

**PER SERVING:** 95 cal., 0 g total fat, 0 mg chol., 9 mg sodium, 24 g carbo., 0 g fiber, 0 g pro.

Strawberry-Mango Smoothies

## Peanut Butter-Chocolate Smoothies 

**MAKES:** 4 (6-ounce) servings **PREP:** 10 minutes
**FREEZE:** 1½ hours

- **1 medium banana, peeled**
- **1½ cups vanilla frozen yogurt**
- **1 cup fat-free chocolate milk or light chocolate soy milk**
- **2 tablespoons creamy peanut butter**

**1** Cut banana into 1-inch pieces; place in a single layer on a baking sheet. Cover and freeze about 1½ hours or until frozen.

**2** In a blender combine frozen banana pieces, frozen yogurt, milk, and peanut butter. Cover and blend until smooth. Serve immediately.

**PER SERVING:** 188 cal., 7 g total fat (2 g sat. fat), 9 mg chol., 98 mg sodium, 28 g carbo., 2 g fiber, 6 g pro.

## Strawberry-Mango Smoothies

**MAKES:** 6 (6-ounce) servings **START TO FINISH:** 10 minutes

- **2 cups fresh strawberries, halved and chilled**
- **1 cup chopped fresh pineapple, chilled**
- **¾ cup chopped bottled or fresh mango, chilled**
- **⅓ cup unsweetened pineapple juice, chilled**
- **2 cups ice cubes**
- **Fresh strawberries and/or mango chunks (optional)**

**1** In a blender combine strawberries, pineapple, mango, and pineapple juice. Cover and blend until smooth. With blender running, gradually add ice cubes through opening in lid. Blend until smooth after each addition. Serve immediately in chilled glasses. If desired, garnish with strawberries.

**PER SERVING:** 48 cal., 0 g total fat, 0 mg chol., 1 mg sodium, 12 g carbo., 2 g fiber, 1 g pro.

page 93
page 68

# Fresh Fish

& Seafood

Pecan-Crusted Fish
with Peppers and Squash

## Pecan-Crusted Fish with Peppers and Squash

**MAKES:** 4 servings **PREP:** 15 minutes **BAKE:** 20 minutes
**OVEN:** 425°

- **1 pound fresh or frozen skinless catfish, white fish, or cod fillets, about ½ inch thick**
- **Nonstick cooking spray**
- **2 small red and/or orange sweet peppers, seeded and cut into 1-inch strips**
- **2 medium zucchini and/or yellow summer squash, halved lengthwise and cut into ½-inch diagonal slices**
- **2 teaspoons vegetable oil**
- **½ teaspoon seasoned salt**
- **½ cup yellow cornmeal**
- **⅓ cup finely chopped pecans**
- **½ teaspoon salt**
- **¼ cup all-purpose flour**
- **¼ teaspoon cayenne pepper**
- **1 egg, lightly beaten**
- **1 tablespoon water**
- **2 cups hot cooked brown rice**

**1** Preheat oven to 425°. Thaw fish, if frozen. Rinse fish; pat dry with paper towels. Cut fish into four serving-size pieces; set aside. Line a 15×10×1-inch baking pan with foil. Lightly coat the foil with cooking spray; set aside.
**2** In a large bowl combine sweet peppers and zucchini. Add oil and seasoned salt; toss to coat. Arrange vegetable mixture in prepared pan. Bake, uncovered, for 10 minutes.
**3** Meanwhile, in a shallow dish combine cornmeal, pecans, and salt. In another shallow dish combine flour and cayenne pepper. In a third shallow dish combine egg and the water. Dip fish in flour mixture to coat lightly, shaking off any excess. Dip fish in egg mixture, then in cornmeal mixture to coat all sides. Lightly coat fish piece with cooking spray.
**4** Push vegetables to one side of the pan; place fish in a single layer in baking pan next to partially baked vegetables. Bake, uncovered, for 10 to 15 minutes or until fish begins to flake easily when tested with a fork and vegetables are crisp-tender. Serve with hot cooked brown rice.

**PER SERVING:** 471 cal., 20 g total fat (4 g sat. fat), 106 mg chol., 485 mg sodium, 47 g carbo., 6 g fiber, 26 g pro.

## Lemony Cod with Asparagus (30)

**MAKES:** 4 servings **PREP:** 10 minutes **BROIL:** 4 minutes

- **1 pound fresh or frozen skinless cod or flounder fillets, ½ inch thick**
- **4 soft breadsticks**
- **2 tablespoons butter or margarine, melted**
- **¼ teaspoon garlic salt**
- **12 ounces fresh asparagus spears, trimmed**
- **1 tablespoon lemon juice**
- **½ teaspoon dried thyme, crushed**
- **⅛ teaspoon ground black pepper**
- **Lemon wedges (optional)**

**1** Thaw fish, if frozen. Preheat broiler. Place breadsticks on the unheated rack of a broiler pan. Brush with 1 tablespoon of the melted butter and sprinkle with garlic salt. Broil 4 inches from heat for 1 to 2 minutes or until golden, turning breadsticks once. Remove from pan and keep warm.
**2** Meanwhile, rinse fish; pat dry with paper towels. Place fish and arrange asparagus in a single layer on the same broiler pan rack.
**3** In a small bowl stir together the remaining 1 tablespoon butter and the lemon juice. Drizzle butter mixture over fish and brush over asparagus. Sprinkle fish and asparagus with thyme and pepper.
**4** Broil 4 inches from heat for 4 to 6 minutes or until fish begins to flake easily when tested with a fork and asparagus is crisp-tender, turning asparagus once. Serve fish and asparagus with breadsticks and, if desired, lemon wedges.

**PER SERVING:** 293 cal., 8 g total fat (4 g sat. fat), 64 mg chol., 454 mg sodium, 29 g carbo., 3 g fiber, 27 g pro.

Lemony Cod with Asparagus

# Fish and fresh vegetables

Grouper with Summer Vegetables

## Grouper with Summer Vegetables (30)

**MAKES:** 4 servings **PREP:** 20 minutes
**BAKE:** 4 to 6 minutes per ½-inch thickness **OVEN:** 450°

- **1 pound fresh or frozen skinless grouper or catfish fillets, ½ to ¾ inch thick**
- **Salt**
- **Ground black pepper**
- **2 tablespoons lemon juice**
- **2 tablespoons olive oil**
- **1 small zucchini, halved lengthwise and thinly sliced**
- **½ of a medium yellow or red sweet pepper, cut into 1-inch strips**
- **1 clove garlic, minced**
- **4 teaspoons snipped fresh marjoram or basil**
- **Salt**
- **Ground black pepper**

**1** Thaw fish, if frozen. Preheat oven to 450°. Rinse fish; pat dry with paper towels. Measure thickness of fish. Cut into 4 serving-size pieces, if necessary. Place fish in a 2-quart rectangular baking dish; sprinkle with salt and black pepper. Set aside.
**2** In a small bowl stir together lemon juice and 1 tablespoon of the oil. Drizzle lemon mixture over fish pieces. Bake, uncovered, for 4 to 6 minutes per ½-inch thickness of fish or until fish begins to flake easily when tested with a fork.
**3** Meanwhile, in a large skillet cook and stir zucchini, sweet pepper, and garlic in the remaining 1 tablespoon hot oil until crisp-tender. Stir in 2 teaspoons of the marjoram. Season to taste with salt and black pepper. Sprinkle fish with the remaining 2 teaspoons marjoram and serve with vegetables.

**PER SERVING:** 178 cal., 8 g total fat (1 g sat. fat), 42 mg chol., 209 mg sodium, 3 g carbo., 1 g fiber, 23 g pro.

## Halibut with Pepper Salsa

**MAKES:** 4 servings **PREP:** 15 minutes
**BROIL:** 4 to 6 minutes per ½-inch thickness **CHILL:** 1 hour

- **3 tablespoons rice vinegar**
- **2 tablespoons soy sauce**
- **½ teaspoon grated fresh ginger**
- **⅛ teaspoon ground black pepper**
- **¾ cup coarsely chopped red and/or yellow sweet pepper (1 medium)**
- **½ cup chopped cucumber (½ of a small)**
- **2 tablespoons thinly sliced green onion (1)**
- **2 tablespoons snipped fresh cilantro**
- **½ of a small fresh jalapeño chile pepper, seeded and finely chopped (see note, page 182)**
- **4 4-ounce fresh or frozen skinless halibut or swordfish steaks, ¾ to 1 inch thick**
- **1 teaspoon sesame seeds**
- **Napa cabbage leaves (optional)**

**1** For pepper salsa, in a small bowl combine vinegar, soy sauce, and ginger. In another small bowl combine 2 tablespoons of the vinegar mixture and the black pepper; set aside. To the remaining vinegar mixture, add sweet pepper, cucumber, green onion, cilantro, and jalapeño pepper; toss to coat. Cover and chill salsa in the refrigerator up to 1 hour.
**2** Thaw fish, if frozen. Preheat broiler. Rinse fish steaks; pat dry with paper towels. Measure thickness of fish. Place fish on the greased unheated rack of a broiler pan. Brush fish with the reserved 2 tablespoons vinegar mixture. Sprinkle fish with sesame seeds.
**3** Broil 4 inches from heat for 4 to 6 minutes per ½-inch thickness of fish or until fish begins to flake easily when tested with a fork, turning once halfway through cooking if fish is 1 inch thick.
**4** To serve, if desired, line 4 plates with cabbage leaves. Place fish on cabbage leaves and serve with pepper salsa.

**PER SERVING:** 150 cal., 3 g total fat (0 g sat. fat), 36 mg chol., 525 mg sodium, 3 g carbo., 1 g fiber, 25 g pro.

are tasty and healthful.

Halibut with Pepper Salsa

Lemon-Parsley Fish

The best way to thaw fish is to place it in the refrigerator and allow it to defrost overnight. To speed the thawing process, place the wrapped package of fish under cold running water for 1 to 2 minutes. Don't thaw fish or shellfish in warm water or at room temperature and do not refreeze; doing so is unsafe.

## Lemon-Parsley Fish

**MAKES:** 4 servings **PREP:** 15 minutes **MARINATE:** 30 minutes **BROIL:** 8 minutes

- **1 pound fresh or frozen skinless halibut, swordfish, or salmon steaks, 1 inch thick**
- **1 teaspoon finely shredded lemon peel**
- **3 tablespoons lemon juice**
- **2 tablespoons snipped fresh Italian (flat-leaf) parsley**
- **2 tablespoons olive oil**
- **2 cloves garlic, minced**
- **Salt**
- **Ground black pepper**
- **Fresh basil sprigs (optional)**
- **Lemon wedges (optional)**

**1** Thaw fish, if frozen. Rinse fish; pat dry with paper towels. Cut into 4 serving-size pieces, if necessary. Place fish in a resealable plastic bag set in a shallow dish.

**2** For marinade, in a small bowl combine lemon peel, lemon juice, parsley, oil, and garlic. Pour marinade over fish. Seal bag; turn to coat fish. Marinate in the refrigerator for 30 minutes to 2 hours, turning bag occasionally.

**3** Preheat broiler. Drain fish, reserving marinade. Place fish on the greased unheated rack of a broiler pan. Sprinkle with salt and pepper.

**4** Broil 4 inches from the heat for 8 to 12 minutes or until fish begins to flake easily when tested with a fork, turning once halfway through cooking and brushing with marinade. Discard any remaining marinade. If desired, sprinkle with fresh basil and serve with lemon wedges.

**PER SERVING:** 190 cal., 9 g total fat (1 g sat. fat), 36 mg chol., 208 mg sodium, 2 g carbo., 0 g fiber, 24 g pro.

## Mediterranean Halibut and Squash (30)

**MAKES:** 4 servings **PREP:** 10 minutes **COOK:** 35 minutes

- **1 pound fresh or frozen skinless halibut steaks, 1 inch thick**
- **Salt**
- **Ground black pepper**
- **1 3- to 3½-pound spaghetti squash, halved lengthwise and seeded**
- **¼ teaspoon salt**
- **¼ cup water**
- **½ cup chopped onion (1 medium)**
- **2 cloves garlic, minced**
- **1 tablespoon olive oil**
- **2 cups sliced fresh mushrooms**
- **1 14.5-ounce can diced tomatoes with basil, garlic, and oregano, undrained**
- **¼ cup pitted kalamata or Greek black olives, chopped**
- **¼ cup snipped fresh Italian (flat-leaf) parsley**

**1** Thaw fish steaks, if frozen. Rinse fish; pat dry with paper towels. Cut into four serving-size pieces, if necessary. Season with salt and pepper.

**2** Wrap and refrigerate 1 squash half for another use. Sprinkle remaining squash half with the ¼ teaspoon salt. Place, cut side down, in a 2-quart microwave-safe baking dish with the water. Cover dish with plastic wrap, turning back corner of wrap to allow steam to escape. Microwave on 100 percent power (high) for 20 to 22 minutes or until tender, turning dish once. Cool slightly. Using a fork, scrape stringy squash pulp from shell onto a serving platter; cover and keep warm.

**3** Meanwhile, for sauce, in a large skillet cook and stir onion and garlic in hot oil for 2 minutes. Add mushrooms; cook and stir until onion is tender. Stir in undrained tomatoes, olives, and 2 tablespoons of the parsley. Bring to boiling; reduce heat. Place fish on top of sauce. Cook, covered, 8 to 12 minutes or until fish begins to flake easily when tested with fork.

**4** To serve, place fish on top of warm squash. Spoon tomato sauce around and on top of fish. Sprinkle with the remaining 2 tablespoons of parsley.

**PER SERVING:** 250 cal., 8 g total fat (10 g sat. fat), 36 mg chol., 991 mg sodium, 18 g carbo., 2 g fiber, 28 g pro.

Stir-fried vegetables sprinkled with herbs

Whole wheat ciabatta rolls

Crispy Oven-Fried Fish [below]

Tartar sauce

## Crispy Oven-Fried Fish

**MAKES:** 4 servings **PREP:** 15 minutes
**BAKE:** 4 to 6 minutes per ½-inch thickness **OVEN:** 450°

- **1 pound fresh or frozen skinless cod or white fish fillets, ½ to ¾ inch thick**
- **¼ cup milk**
- **⅓ cup all-purpose flour**
- **⅓ cup fine dry bread crumbs**
- **¼ cup grated Parmesan cheese**
- **½ teaspoon dried dill**
- **⅛ teaspoon ground black pepper**
- **2 tablespoons butter or margarine, melted**

**1** Thaw fish, if frozen. Preheat oven to 450°. Rinse fish; pat dry with paper towels. Cut into 4 serving-size pieces, if necessary. Measure thickness of fish.
**2** Place milk in a shallow dish. Place flour in a second shallow dish. In a third shallow dish combine bread crumbs, Parmesan cheese, dill, and pepper; stir in melted butter.
**3** Dip fish in milk; coat with flour. Dip again in milk, then in crumb mixture to coat all sides. Place fish on a greased baking sheet.
**4** Bake, uncovered, for 4 to 6 minutes per ½-inch thickness of fish or until fish begins to flake when tested with a fork.

**PER SERVING:** 242 cal., 9 g total fat (5 g sat. fat), 71 mg chol., 423 mg sodium, 13 g carbo., 1 g fiber, 25 g pro.

## Sweet Mustard Halibut 

**MAKES:** 4 servings **PREP:** 10 minutes
**BAKE:** 8 minutes **OVEN:** 450°

- **1 to 1¼ pounds fresh or frozen skinless halibut steaks, ¾ inch thick**
- **½ cup chunky salsa**
- **2 tablespoons honey**
- **2 tablespoons Dijon-style mustard**

**1** Thaw fish, if frozen. Preheat oven to 450°. Rinse fish; pat dry with paper towels. Arrange fish steaks in a 2-quart rectangular baking dish.
**2** Bake, uncovered, about 6 minutes or until fish begins to flake when tested with a fork. Drain liquid from baking dish.
**3** In a bowl stir together salsa and honey. Spread mustard over fish; spoon salsa mixture on top of mustard. Bake for 2 to 3 minutes more or until salsa mixture is heated through.

**PER SERVING:** 176 cal., 4 g total fat (0 g sat. fat), 36 mg chol., 362 mg sodium, 11 g carbo., 0 g fiber, 24 g pro.

## Cilantro-Lime Orange Roughy 

**MAKES:** 4 servings **PREP:** 10 minutes
**BROIL:** 4 to 6 minutes per ½-inch thickness

- **1¼ pounds fresh or frozen skinless orange roughy, ocean perch, cod, or haddock fillets, ¾ to 1 inch thick**
- **Salt**
- **Ground black pepper**
- **Nonstick cooking spray**
- **¼ cup snipped fresh cilantro**
- **1 tablespoon butter or margarine, melted**
- **1 teaspoon finely shredded lime peel**
- **1 tablespoon lime juice**

**1** Thaw fish, if frozen. Preheat broiler. Rinse fish; pat dry with paper towels. Sprinkle fish with salt and pepper.
**2** Lightly coat the unheated rack of a broiler pan with cooking spray. Place fish on broiler pan. Broil 4 inches from heat for 4 to 6 minutes per ½-inch thickness of fish or until fish begins to flake easily when tested with a fork, turning once halfway through cooking if fish is 1 inch thick.
**3** For sauce, in a small bowl combine cilantro, melted butter, lime peel, and lime juice. Spoon sauce over fish.

**PER SERVING:** 127 cal., 4 g total fat (2 g sat. fat), 36 mg chol., 259 mg sodium, 1 g carbo., 0 g fiber, 21 g pro.

Flecks of fresh herb add flavor.

Cilantro-Lime Orange Roughy

Fish with Roma Relish

## Fish with Roma Relish

**MAKES:** 4 servings **PREP:** 15 minutes
**COOK:** 4 to 6 minutes per ½-inch thickness

- 1 pound fresh or frozen skinless orange roughy, cod, flounder, catfish, or trout fillets, about ¾ inch thick
- Salt
- Freshly ground black pepper
- 3 tablespoons lemon juice
- Olive oil
- 2 medium roma tomatoes, halved lengthwise
- 1 19-ounce can cannellini beans (white kidney beans), rinsed and drained
- 2 slices thinly sliced prosciutto or thinly sliced cooked ham, cut into thin strips
- 1 tablespoon olive oil
- 1 clove garlic, minced
- 1 teaspoon snipped fresh rosemary or ¼ teaspoon dried rosemary, crushed
- ⅛ teaspoon salt
- Lemon wedges (optional)

**1** Thaw fish, if frozen. Rinse fish; pat dry with paper towels. Measure thickness of fish. Sprinkle fish with salt and pepper and drizzle with 1 tablespoon of the lemon juice; set aside.
**2** Heat a grill pan or an extra-large nonstick skillet over medium heat until hot. Brush tomatoes with oil. Add tomato halves to grill pan, cut sides down. Cook for 6 to 8 minutes or until tomatoes are very tender, turning once halfway through cooking. Remove tomatoes from pan; set aside.
**3** Add fish to grill pan. Cook for 4 to 6 minutes per ½-inch thickness of fish or until fish begins to flake easily when tested with a fork, turning once halfway through cooking.
**4** For relish, coarsely chop tomatoes. In a serving bowl gently toss together tomatoes, the remaining 2 tablespoons lemon juice, the drained beans, prosciutto, the 1 tablespoon olive oil, garlic, rosemary, and the ⅛ teaspoon salt. Serve fish with relish and, if desired, lemon wedges.

**PER SERVING:** 221 cal., 5 g total fat (1 g sat. fat), 74 mg chol., 684 mg sodium, 21 g carbo., 7 g fiber, 29 g pro.

## Simple Salsa Fish 

**MAKES:** 4 servings **PREP:** 15 minutes
**BROIL:** 4 to 6 minutes per ½-inch thickness plus 1 minute

- 1 pound fresh or frozen skinless orange roughy or red snapper fillets, ½ to 1 inch thick
- ⅓ cup salsa
- 1 clove garlic, minced
- 1 14-ounce can vegetable broth
- 1 cup quick-cooking couscous
- ¼ cup thinly sliced green onions (2) or snipped fresh cilantro
- Salt
- Ground black pepper
- Lime or lemon wedges (optional)

**1** Thaw fish, if frozen. Preheat broiler. Rinse fish; pat dry with paper towels. Measure thickness of fish; set aside. In a small bowl combine salsa and garlic; set aside.
**2** In a medium saucepan bring broth to boiling. Stir in couscous; cover and remove saucepan from heat. Let stand about 5 minutes or until liquid is absorbed. Fluff couscous with a fork. Stir in green onions.
**3** Place fish on the greased unheated rack of a broiler pan. Sprinkle fish with salt and pepper. Broil 4 inches from heat for 4 to 6 minutes per ½-inch thickness of fish or until fish begins to flake easily when tested with a fork, turning once halfway through cooking if fish is 1 inch thick.
**4** Spoon salsa mixture over fish; broil about 1 minute more or until salsa is heated through. To serve, arrange fish on couscous mixture. If desired, garnish with lime wedges.

**PER SERVING:** 265 cal., 1 g total fat (0 g sat. fat), 22 mg chol., 529 mg sodium, 39 g carbo., 3 g fiber, 23 g pro.

Simple Salsa Fish

# Menu

Salad of mesclun, pears, walnuts, and dressing

Roasted rosemary-garlic sweet potatoes

Steamed Orange Roughy [below]

Crusty Italian bread

## Steamed Orange Roughy

**MAKES:** 4 servings **START TO FINISH:** 20 minutes

- 1 to 1¼ pounds fresh or frozen skinless orange roughy, ocean perch, or cod fillets
- 1 medium onion, sliced
- ¼ teaspoon garlic salt
- Ground black pepper
- 4 celery stalks, leafy ends only
- 1 recipe Herb Butter, Ginger-Garlic Butter, or salsa (optional)

**1** Thaw fish, if frozen. Rinse fish; pat dry with paper towels. Cut fish into 4 serving-size pieces, if necessary. Measure thickness of fish; set aside.
**2** Fill a large, deep saucepan or wok with water to a depth of 1 inch. Bring water to boiling; reduce heat.
**3** Meanwhile, arrange onion slices in the bottom of a steamer basket. Place fish pieces on top of onion slices. Sprinkle fish with garlic salt and pepper. Place steamer into saucepan over simmering water. Place celery on fish. Simmer gently, covered, for 4 to 6 minutes per ½-inch thickness of fish or until fish begins to flake easily when tested with a fork. Discard vegetables. If desired, serve with Herb Butter.

**PER SERVING:** 92 cal., 1 g total fat (0 g sat. fat), 23 mg chol., 160 mg sodium, 3 g carbo., 1 g fiber, 17 g pro.

**Herb Butter:** In a small bowl combine ¼ cup softened butter and 1 tablespoon snipped fresh tarragon or dill or ¼ teaspoon dried tarragon, crushed, or dried dill.
**Ginger-Garlic Butter:** In a small bowl combine ¼ cup softened butter, 2 tablespoons snipped Italian (flat-leaf) parsley, 2 teaspoons grated fresh ginger, and 1 clove garlic, minced.

## Salmon Salad

**MAKES:** 4 servings **PREP:** 15 minutes **MARINATE:** 30 minutes
**BROIL:** 8 minutes

- 2 tablespoons olive oil
- 5 cloves garlic, thinly sliced
- 2 tablespoons lemon juice
- 1 tablespoon water
- 1 tablespoon Worcestershire sauce
- 1 tablespoon Dijon-style mustard
- ½ teaspoon ground black pepper
- ⅓ cup plain fat-free yogurt
- 12 ounces fresh or frozen skinless salmon fillets, 1 inch thick
- Nonstick cooking spray
- 10 cups torn romaine
- ½ cup thinly sliced red onion
- ¼ cup freshly grated Parmesan cheese
- 1 cup cherry tomatoes, halved
- ½ cup pitted ripe olives, halved (optional)

**1** In a small saucepan heat olive oil over medium-low heat. Cook and stir garlic in hot oil for 30 seconds to 1 minute or until garlic is lightly golden. Transfer garlic to a blender. Add lemon juice, the water, Worcestershire sauce, mustard, and pepper. Cover and blend until combined. Reserve 2 tablespoons of garlic mixture; set aside. Add yogurt to remaining garlic mixture in blender. Cover and blend until smooth. Cover and chill yogurt mixture in the refrigerator until serving time.
**2** Thaw salmon, if frozen. Rinse fish; pat dry with paper towels. Cut into 4 serving size pieces, if necessary. Brush the reserved garlic mixture evenly over salmon. Cover and marinate in the refrigerator for 30 minutes.
**3** Preheat broiler. Lightly coat the unheated rack of a broiler pan with cooking spray. Place salmon on the rack. Broil 4 to 5 inches from heat for 8 to 12 minutes or until salmon begins to flake easily when tested with a fork, turning once halfway through cooking.
**4** Meanwhile, in a large bowl toss romaine, onion, and Parmesan cheese with the chilled yogurt mixture. Divide romaine mixture among 4 plates. Top with a piece of fish, tomatoes, and, if desired, olives.

**PER SERVING:** 234 cal., 13 g total fat (3 g sat. fat), 21 mg chol., 331 mg sodium, 12 g carbo., 4 g fiber, 19 g pro.

Salmon Burgers with Basil Mayonnaise

To make the Basil Mayonnaise more healthful, use reduced-fat mayonnaise in place of the regular mayonnaise. Try the flavored mayo as a dipping sauce for broiled chicken, fish, or steamed vegetables.

## Salmon Burgers with Basil Mayonnaise (30)

**MAKES:** 4 servings **PREP:** 15 minutes **BROIL:** 8 minutes

- 1 egg, lightly beaten
- 1 cup soft whole wheat bread crumbs (1 slice)
- 2 tablespoons milk
- 2 tablespoons snipped fresh basil
- ¼ teaspoon ground black pepper
- 1 8-ounce piece smoked salmon, flaked, with skin and bones removed
- ⅓ cup finely shredded Gruyère or Swiss cheese
- ¼ cup coarsely shredded carrot
- Nonstick cooking spray
- ¼ cup mayonnaise or salad dressing
- 1 teaspoon finely shredded lemon peel
- 8 slices whole wheat or rye bread, toasted
- 4 lettuce leaves
- 4 tomato slices (optional)

**1** Preheat broiler. In a bowl combine the egg, bread crumbs, milk, 4 teaspoons of the basil, and pepper. Add salmon, cheese, and carrot; mix. Form mixture into four ¾-inch thick patties.
**2** Lightly coat a baking sheet with cooking spray. Place salmon patties on prepared baking sheet. Broil 3 inches from the heat about 8 minutes or until 160°, turning once halfway through cooking.
**3** Meanwhile, for the basil mayonnaise, combine the remaining 2 teaspoons basil, mayonnaise, and lemon peel.
**4** Place salmon burgers on 4 of the bread slices. Top with basil mayonnaise, lettuce, tomato slices (if desired), and remaining bread slices.

**PER SERVING:** 391 cal., 21 g total fat (5 g sat. fat), 83 mg chol., 888 mg sodium, 29 g carbo., 3 g fiber, 21 g pro.

## Maple-Balsamic Glazed Fish with Spinach Sauté (30)

**MAKES:** 4 servings **PREP:** 10 minutes **BROIL:** 8 minutes

- 1 pound fresh or frozen skinless sea bass, halibut, salmon, swordfish, or tuna fillets, about 1 inch thick
- 3 tablespoons maple syrup
- 1 tablespoon balsamic vinegar
- 1 to 2 teaspoons Dijon-style mustard
- 1 recipe Spinach Sauté

**1** Thaw fish, if frozen. Preheat broiler. Rinse fish; pat dry with paper towels. Cut fish into 4 serving-size pieces, if necessary.
**2** For glaze, in a small bowl combine syrup, vinegar, and mustard.
**3** Place fish on the greased unheated rack of a broiler pan. Broil 4 inches from the heat for 8 to 12 minutes or until fish begins to flake easily when tested with a fork, turning once halfway through cooking and brushing with glaze during the last 2 to 3 minutes of cooking time. Serve with Spinach Sauté.

**Spinach Sauté:** In a 4-quart Dutch oven heat 1 tablespoon olive oil over medium-high heat. Add 1 pound fresh spinach leaves, trimmed. Cook and stir for 1 to 2 minutes or just until wilted. Remove from heat. Stir in 3 tablespoons chopped toasted walnuts, a dash Worcestershire sauce or soy sauce, ¼ teaspoon salt, and ⅛ teaspoon ground black pepper.

**PER SERVING:** 250 cal., 10 g total fat (1 g sat. fat), 46 mg chol., 386 mg sodium, 17 g carbo., 3 g fiber, 25 g pro.

Smoked Salmon Club Sandwiches

Classic Club salad calls for bacon. The smoky flavor in this triple-stacked sandwich comes from lean smoked salmon.

## Smoked Salmon Club Sandwiches

**MAKES:** 4 servings **START TO FINISH:** 15 minutes

- ½ of an 8-ounce tub light cream cheese (½ cup)
- ½ cup coarsely shredded carrot (1 medium)
- ½ cup finely chopped red or yellow sweet pepper (1 small)
- 1 tablespoon snipped fresh chives
- ½ teaspoon finely shredded lemon peel
- 8 slices whole wheat or rye bread
- 1½ cups fresh baby spinach
- ½ of a medium cucumber, thinly bias-sliced
- 6 ounces thinly sliced smoked salmon (lox-style)

**1** In a small bowl combine cream cheese, carrot, sweet pepper, chives, and lemon peel. Spread mixture on 4 of the bread slices. Top with spinach, cucumber, and salmon. Add the remaining 4 bread slices. Cut each sandwich in half to serve.

**PER SERVING:** 241 cal., 8 g total fat (4 g sat. fat), 23 mg chol., 1,266 mg sodium, 28 g carbo., 5 g fiber, 16 g pro.

## Salmon with Lemon-Dill Garden Rice

**MAKES:** 6 servings **PREP:** 20 minutes **MARINATE:** 1 hour
**STAND:** 5 minutes **COOK:** 26 minutes

- 6 4- to 5-ounce fresh or frozen skinless salmon fillets, 1 inch thick
- ¾ cup dry white wine or dry vermouth
- 4 teaspoons finely shredded lemon peel
- ⅓ cup lemon juice
- 3 tablespoons snipped fresh dill or ¾ teaspoon dried dill
- 3 tablespoons olive oil
- 4 teaspoons Dijon-style mustard
- 3 cloves garlic, minced
- ¾ teaspoon coarsely ground black pepper
- ¼ to ½ teaspoon salt
- 3¾ cups chicken broth
- 2 cups uncooked long grain rice
- ½ cup chicken broth
- 18 ounces fresh asparagus, trimmed and cut into 1½-inch lengths
- 12 ounces fresh snow peas or sugar snap peas, trimmed
- 6 ounces fresh cremini or brown mushrooms, sliced
- 6 green onions, sliced
- 6 radishes, thinly sliced
- Lemon wedges (optional)
- Fresh dill sprigs (optional)
- Cracked black pepper (optional)

**1** Thaw salmon, if frozen. Rinse fish; pat dry with paper towels. Set aside.

**2** For dressing, in a screw-top jar combine wine, lemon peel, lemon juice, dill, olive oil, mustard, garlic, the coarsely ground black pepper, and the salt. Cover and shake well.

**3** In a 3-quart rectangular baking dish place fish in a single layer and pour ⅔ cup of the dressing over fish. Cover and marinate in the refrigerator for 1 hour, turning once. Set the remaining dressing aside.

**4** For rice, in a medium saucepan bring the 3¾ cups chicken broth to boiling. Stir in rice; reduce heat. Simmer, covered, for 15 to 20 minutes or until liquid is absorbed and rice is tender. Remove saucepan from heat. Let stand, covered, for 5 minutes. Fluff with fork. Transfer rice to a large bowl. Set aside.

**5** For vegetables, in a large nonstick skillet bring the ½ cup chicken broth to boiling. Add asparagus, peas, and mushrooms. Return to boiling; reduce heat. Simmer, covered, for 3 to 5 minutes or until vegetables are crisp-tender. Drain vegetables, if necessary.

**6** Add vegetables to rice in large bowl. Shake the remaining dressing well and drizzle over rice-vegetable mixture. Add green onions and radishes; toss to combine. Set aside.

**7** In the same nonstick skillet place fish and marinade. Bring to boiling; reduce heat. Simmer, covered, for 8 to 12 minutes or until fish begins to flake easily when tested with a fork.

**8** To serve, divide rice-vegetable mixture among 6 serving plates. Using a slotted spoon, place fish on top of rice-vegetable mixture. If desired, garnish with lemon wedges, dill sprigs, and the cracked black pepper.

**PER SERVING:** 478 cal., 13 g total fat (2 g sat. fat), 21 mg chol., 856 mg sodium, 57 g carbo., 4 g fiber, 28 g pro.

Meaty tuna steak is healthful,

## Tangy Thyme Fish

**MAKES:** 4 servings **START TO FINISH:** 20 minutes

- **1 pound fresh or frozen skinless salmon, sole, flounder, cod, or orange roughy fillets, ½ to ¾ inch thick**
- **1 cup reduced-sodium chicken broth**
- **¼ cup chopped onion**
- **¼ teaspoon dried thyme or marjoram, crushed**
- **⅛ teaspoon ground black pepper**
- **¼ cup bottled low-carb ranch salad dressing**
- **2 tablespoons snipped fresh parsley**
- **Lemon slices (optional)**

**1** Thaw fish, if frozen. Rinse fish; pat dry with paper towels.
**2** In a large skillet combine broth, onion, thyme, and pepper. Bring to boiling. Place fish in skillet, tucking under any thin edges (to make fish of uniform thickness). Simmer, covered, for 4 to 6 minutes per ½-inch thickness of fish or until fish begins to flake easily when tested with a fork. Using a slotted spatula, transfer fish to a serving platter.
**3** For sauce, stir salad dressing and parsley into cooking liquid. Serve fish with sauce and, if desired, lemon slices.

**PER SERVING:** 245 cal., 16 g total fat (3 g sat. fat), 66 mg chol., 428 mg sodium, 1 g carbo., 0 g fiber, 24 g pro.

## Pan-Seared Tilapia with Black Bean and Papaya Salsa

**MAKES:** 4 servings **PREP:** 10 minutes **CHILL:** 15 minutes
**COOK:** 4 to 6 minutes per ½-inch thickness

- **1 15-ounce can black beans, rinsed and drained**
- **1 small papaya, halved, seeded, and cubed**
- **¼ cup finely chopped red onion**
- **1 small fresh jalapeño chile pepper, seeded and chopped (see note, page 182)**
- **1 teaspoon finely shredded lime peel**
- **1 tablespoon lime juice**
- **4 6-ounce fresh or frozen skinless tilapia, cod, orange roughy, or flounder fillets, ½ to ¾ inch thick**
- **2 teaspoons lemon-pepper seasoning**
- **2 tablespoons olive oil**

**1** For salsa, in a medium bowl combine drained beans, papaya, onion, jalapeño, lime peel, and lime juice. Cover and chill for 15 minutes or until ready to serve.
**2** Thaw fish, if frozen. Rinse fish; pat dry with paper towels. Sprinkle both sides of fish with lemon-pepper seasoning.
**3** In very large skillet heat oil over medium heat. Cook fish for 4 to 6 minutes per ½-inch thickness of fish or until fish begins to flake easily when tested with fork, turning once halfway through cooking.
**4** To serve, stir salsa and spoon over fish just before serving.

**PER SERVING:** 330 cal., 10 g total fat (2 g sat. fat), 85 mg chol., 1,241 mg sodium, 21 g carbo., 6 g fiber, 40 g pro.

## Nutty Fish and Roasted Sweet Potatoes

**MAKES:** 6 servings **PREP:** 15 minutes **BAKE:** 30 minutes plus 4 to 6 minutes per ½-inch thickness **OVEN:** 425°/450°

- **6 3- to 4-ounce fresh or frozen skinless tilapia, cod, orange roughy, or flounder fillets, ½ to ¾ inch thick**
- **Nonstick cooking spray**
- **2 tablespoons packed brown sugar**
- **2 tablespoons water**
- **¼ teaspoon salt**
- **2 large sweet potatoes (about 2 pounds total), peeled and cut into ¼-inch slices**
- **½ cup all-purpose flour**
- **½ cup refrigerated or frozen egg product, thawed,**
- **2 tablespoons water**
- **¾ cup finely chopped pecans**
- **3 tablespoons ground flaxseeds**
- **2 tablespoons packed brown sugar**
- **¼ teaspoon salt**

**1** Thaw fish, if frozen. Preheat the oven to 425°. Rinse fish; pat dry with paper towels. Coat a 3-quart rectangular or oval baking dish and a large baking sheet with cooking spray.
**2** In a bowl combine 2 tablespoons brown sugar, 2 tablespoons water, and ¼ teaspoon salt. Add sweet potatoes, tossing to coat. Layer sweet potato slices in baking dish. Bake, uncovered, 30 minutes or until tender. Remove from oven. Cover to keep warm. Increase oven temperature to 450°.
**3** Place flour in a shallow dish. In another shallow dish combine egg and 2 tablespoons water. In a third shallow dish combine pecans, flaxseeds, 2 tablespoons brown sugar, and ¼ teaspoon salt.
**4** Dip each fish fillet in flour, turning to coat both sides and shaking off excess. Dip in egg mixture; coat with pecan mixture. Place fish fillets on the prepared baking sheet. Bake in a 450° oven for 4 to 6 minutes per ½ inch thickness of fish or until fish begins to flake easily when tested with a fork. Serve fish with sweet potatoes.

**PER SERVING:** 392 cal., 15 g total fat (2 g sat. fat), 43 mg chol., 342 mg sodium, 42 g carbo., 6 g fiber, 24 g pro.

hearty, and satisfying.

Marinated Tuna Steaks

## Marinated Tuna Steaks

**MAKES:** 4 servings **PREP:** 10 minutes **MARINATE:** 1 hour
**GRILL:** 8 minutes

- 4 6-ounce fresh or frozen skinless tuna or swordfish steaks, 1 inch thick
- ⅓ cup dry white wine
- 1 tablespoon lemon juice
- 1 tablespoon olive oil or vegetable oil
- 1 clove garlic, minced
- 2 teaspoons snipped fresh rosemary or ½ teaspoon dried rosemary, crushed
- 1 teaspoon snipped fresh oregano or ¼ teaspoon dried oregano, crushed
- ¼ teaspoon salt
- Lemon slices (optional)
- Fresh rosemary and/or oregano (optional)

**1** Thaw fish, if frozen. Rinse fish; pat dry with paper towels. Place fish in a resealable plastic bag set in a shallow dish.
**2** For marinade, in a small bowl combine wine, lemon juice, oil, garlic, the 2 teaspoons fresh rosemary, the 1 teaspoon fresh oregano, and salt. Pour marinade over fish. Seal bag; turn to coat fish. Marinate in the refrigerator for 1 to 2 hours, turning bag occasionally. Drain fish, discarding marinade.
**3** For a charcoal grill, grill fish on the greased rack of an uncovered grill directly over medium coals for 8 to 12 minutes or until fish begins to flake easily when tested with a fork, turning once halfway through grilling. (For a gas grill, preheat grill. Reduce heat to medium. Place fish on greased grill rack over heat. Cover and grill as above.) If desired, garnish with lemon slices and additional rosemary and/or oregano.

**PER SERVING:** 277 cal., 10 g total fat (2 g sat. fat), 71 mg chol., 106 mg sodium, 0 g carbo., 0 g fiber, 43 g pro.

Pasta with Tuna, Roasted Peppers, and Artichokes

## Pasta with Tuna, Roasted Peppers, and Artichokes

**MAKES:** 6 servings **START TO FINISH:** 20 minutes

- 1 pound dried medium shell macaroni (conchiglie) or medium bow tie (farfalle)
- 1 7-ounce jar roasted red sweet peppers, drained and cut into thin strips
- 1 6.5-ounce can chunk white tuna (water pack), drained and broken into chunks
- 1 6-ounce jar marinated artichoke hearts, drained and halved
- 2 tablespoons olive oil
- 1 tablespoon capers, rinsed and drained
- 1 tablespoon snipped fresh parsley
- 2 teaspoons balsamic vinegar
- 1 teaspoon minced garlic
- ½ teaspoon salt
- ¼ teaspoon freshly ground black pepper

**1** Cook pasta according to package directions. Drain. Return to pot. Cover and keep warm.

**2** Meanwhile, in a large serving bowl combine roasted red peppers, tuna, artichoke hearts, olive oil, capers, parsley, balsamic vinegar, garlic, salt, and black pepper. Add the warm pasta; toss lightly to coat. Serve immediately.

**PER SERVING:** 415 cal., 10 g total fat (2 g sat. fat), 5 mg chol., 476 mg sodium, 61 g carbo., 19 g pro.

## Avocado-Lime Tuna Wraps

**MAKES:** 4 servings **START TO FINISH:** 10 minutes

- 1 ripe avocado, halved, seeded, peeled, and coarsely mashed
- ¼ cup salsa
- ¼ cup chopped green onions (2)
- 1 tablespoon lime juice
- 1 6-ounce can chunk white tuna (water pack), drained and broken into chunks
- 4 8- to 10-inch flour tortillas
- 1¼ cups shredded lettuce
- ½ cup shredded cheddar (2 ounces)

**1** In a medium bowl combine avocado, salsa, green onions, and lime juice. Add the tuna and mix gently to combine.

**2** For each wrap, place some tuna mixture near an edge of tortilla. Top with some of the lettuce and cheese. Fold edge over filling; fold in the sides and roll up. Serve immediately.

**PER SERVING:** 270 cal., 13 g total fat (4 g sat. fat), 38 mg chol., 534 mg sodium, 20 g carbo., 3 g fiber, 18 g pro.

## Broiled Tuna with Rosemary

**MAKES:** 4 servings **PREP:** 10 minutes
**BROIL:** 4 to 6 minutes per ½-inch thickness

- 4 4-ounce fresh or frozen skinless tuna or salmon steaks, ½ to 1 inch thick
- 2 teaspoons olive oil
- 2 teaspoons lemon juice
- ⅛ teaspoon salt
- ⅛ teaspoon ground black pepper
- 2 teaspoons snipped fresh rosemary or tarragon or 1 teaspoon dried rosemary or tarragon, crushed
- 2 cloves garlic, minced
- Nonstick cooking spray
- 1 tablespoon capers, rinsed and drained

**1** Thaw fish, if frozen. Preheat broiler. Rinse fish; pat dry with paper towels. Brush fish with oil and lemon juice; sprinkle with salt and pepper. Top with rosemary and garlic.

**2** Lightly coat the unheated rack of a broiler pan with cooking spray. Place fish on broiler pan. Broil 4 inches from heat for 4 to 6 minutes per ½-inch thickness of fish or until fish begins to flake easily with a fork. Sprinkle with capers.

**PER SERVING:** 145 cal., 3 g total fat (1 g sat. fat), 51 mg chol., 166 mg sodium, 1 g carbo., 0 g fiber, 27 g pro.

## Sicilian Tuna with Capers

**MAKES:** 4 servings **PREP:** 10 minutes **MARINATE:** 15 minutes **BROIL:** 8 minutes

- 4 4- to 5-ounce fresh or frozen skinless tuna steaks, 1 inch thick
- 2 tablespoons red wine vinegar
- 1 tablespoon snipped fresh dill or 1 teaspoon dried dill
- 2 teaspoons olive oil
- ¼ teaspoon salt
- ⅛ teaspoon cayenne pepper
- Nonstick cooking spray
- ½ cup chopped tomato (1 medium)
- 1 tablespoon capers, rinsed and drained
- 1 tablespoon chopped pitted ripe olives
- 1 clove garlic, minced

**1** Thaw fish, if frozen. Rinse fish; pat dry with paper towels. Set aside.

**2** For marinade, in a shallow dish combine vinegar, dill, oil, salt, and half of the cayenne pepper. Add fish to marinade in dish, turning to coat fish. Cover and marinate in the refrigerator for 15 minutes.

**3** Preheat broiler. Lightly coat the unheated rack of a broiler pan with cooking spray. In a small bowl combine tomato, drained capers, olives, garlic, and the remaining cayenne pepper.

**4** Drain fish, reserving marinade. Place fish on prepared rack of a broiler pan. Broil 4 inches from heat for 8 to 12 minutes or until fish begins to flake when tested with a fork, turning once and brushing with reserved marinade halfway through cooking. Serve tuna topped with tomato mixture.

**PER SERVING:** 151 cal., 4 g total fat (0 g sat. fat), 51 mg chol., 271 mg sodium, 1 g carbo., 0 g fiber, 27 g pro.

# Here's a hot, spicy handful!

Thai Tuna Wraps

## Thai Tuna Wraps

**MAKES:** 6 servings **START TO FINISH:** 25 minutes **OVEN:** 350°

- 4 ounces dried thin spaghetti, broken
- 6 8- or 10-inch flour tortillas
- ⅔ cup lime juice
- ⅓ cup Thai fish sauce (nam pla)
- 2 tablespoons sugar
- 2 tablespoons rice vinegar
- 2 tablespoons soy sauce
- ½ cup snipped fresh cilantro
- 2 fresh Thai chile peppers or jalapeño chile peppers, seeded and finely chopped (see note, page 182)
- 1 12- or 12.25-ounce can solid white tuna, drained and broken into chunks
- ⅓ cup coarsely shredded carrot
- 2 cups coarsely chopped romaine leaves

**1** Preheat oven to 350°. Cook pasta according to package directions. Drain pasta in a colander. Rinse under cold running water about 1 minute or until cool; drain well. Set aside.
**2** Wrap tortillas tightly in foil. Heat in oven for 10 minutes to soften.
**3** Meanwhile, in a small bowl combine lime juice, fish sauce, sugar, vinegar, and soy sauce; stir in cilantro and chile peppers. Set aside.
**4** In a large bowl combine well-drained pasta, tuna, carrot, and ¼ cup of the lime juice mixture; toss gently to moisten.
**5** Arrange ⅓ cup of the romaine on each tortilla just below the center. Spoon ½ cup of the tuna-pasta mixture on top of romaine. Fold bottom edges of tortillas up and over filling, just until mixture is covered. Fold in opposite sides of tortillas until they meet. Roll up tortillas from the bottom. Cut in half crosswise. Serve immediately with remaining lime juice mixture as a dipping sauce.

**PER SERVING:** 319 cal., 6 g total fat (1 g sat. fat), 24 mg chol., 1,930 mg sodium, 45 g carbo., 2 g fiber, 21 g pro.

## Tuna-Noodle Casserole

**MAKES:** 6 servings **PREP:** 20 minutes **BAKE:** 25 minutes **OVEN:** 350°

- 4 ounces dried medium noodles (2½ cups)
- 3 tablespoons panko (Japanese-style bread crumbs) or fine dry bread crumbs
- 1 tablespoon butter, melted

Tuna-Noodle Casserole

- 10 ounces fresh green beans, trimmed and cut into 2-inch pieces, or one 10-ounce package frozen cut green beans
- 1 cup sliced fresh mushrooms
- ¾ cup chopped red or green sweet pepper (1 medium)
- ½ cup chopped onion (1 medium)
- ½ cup sliced celery (1 stalk)
- ½ cup water
- 2 cloves garlic, minced
- 1 10.75-ounce can reduced-sodium condensed cream of mushroom soup
- ½ cup fat-free milk
- ½ cup shredded American or process Swiss cheese (2 ounces)
- 2 4.5-ounce cans very low-sodium chunk white tuna (water pack), drained and flaked

**1** Preheat oven to 350°. Cook noodles according to package directions. Drain and set aside. Toss panko with melted butter; set aside.
**2** In a large saucepan combine green beans, mushrooms, red pepper, onion, celery, the water, and garlic. Bring to boiling; reduce heat. Simmer, covered, about 5 minutes or until vegetables are crisp-tender.
**3** Stir soup and milk into vegetable mixture. Cook and stir until heated through. Remove from heat; stir in cheese until melted. Stir in noodles and tuna. Spoon tuna-noodle mixture into a 2-quart casserole. Sprinkle panko mixture around outside edges of casserole.
**4** Bake, uncovered, for 25 to 30 minutes or until tuna mixture is bubbly and panko is golden brown.

**PER SERVING:** 241 cal., 7 g total fat (3 g sat. fat), 53 mg chol., 414 mg sodium, 26 g carbo., 3 g fiber, 18 g pro.

Wasabi-Glazed Whitefish
with Vegetable Slaw

## Fettuccine with Peas and Shrimp

**MAKES:** 2 servings **START TO FINISH:** 25 minutes

- 8 ounces fresh or frozen medium shrimp in shells
- 4 ounces dried whole wheat or spinach fettuccine
- 1 teaspoon olive oil
- 2 cloves garlic, minced
- ½ cup dry white wine or reduced-sodium chicken broth
- ½ cup frozen peas, thawed
- ⅓ cup finely chopped roma tomato (1 medium)
- ½ teaspoon finely shredded lemon peel
- ¼ teaspoon ground nutmeg
- ⅛ teaspoon salt
- 1 teaspoon snipped fresh Italian (flat-leaf) parsley
- Whole grain baguette-style French bread, sliced (optional)

**1** Thaw shrimp, if frozen. Peel and devein shrimp, leaving tails intact if desired. Rinse shrimp; pat dry with paper towels; set aside. Cook pasta according to package directions. Drain. Return to pot. Cover and keep warm.
**2** Meanwhile, in a medium skillet heat oil over medium heat. Add garlic. Cook and stir cook for 30 seconds. Add shrimp and wine to skillet. Cook and stir for 3 to 4 minutes or until shrimp are opaque. Stir in peas, tomato, lemon peel, nutmeg, and salt. Add warm pasta; toss lightly with shrimp mixture to mix. Heat through.
**3** To serve, divide pasta mixture between two shallow soup bowls. Sprinkle with parsley. If desired, serve with bread.

**PER SERVING:** 432 cal., 5 g total fat (1 g sat. fat), 172 mg chol., 340 mg sodium, 54 g carbo., 2 g fiber, 34 g pro.

## Mediterranean Stir-Fry

**MAKES:** 4 servings **START TO FINISH:** 25 minutes

- 1 pound fresh or frozen medium shrimp in shells
- 1 5.8-ounce package roasted garlic-flavored couscous mix
- 2 medium oranges
- 1 tablespoon olive oil
- 2 cloves garlic, minced
- ½ cup sliced green onions (4)
- 4 teaspoons snipped fresh oregano or 1 teaspoon dried oregano, crushed
- ½ teaspoon freshly ground black pepper
- 1⅓ cups chopped roma tomatoes (4 medium)
- ½ cup pitted kalamata or Greek black olives, quartered

**1** Thaw shrimp, if frozen. Peel and devein shrimp, removing tails. Rinse shrimp; pat dry. Set aside. Prepare couscous according to package directions.
**2** Meanwhile, cut peel from oranges. Section oranges over a small bowl to catch juice; set sections aside.
**3** In a large skillet heat oil over medium heat. Add garlic. Cook and stir for 30 seconds. Add shrimp, green onions, oregano, and pepper. Cook and stir for 2 to 3 minutes or until shrimp are opaque. Add tomatoes and olives. Cook and stir 1 minute more. Stir in orange sections and juice; heat through. Serve shrimp mixture with couscous.

**PER SERVING:** 372 cal., 9 g total fat (1 g sat. fat), 172 mg chol., 774 mg sodium, 44 g carbo., 5 g fiber, 31 g pro.

## Sautéed Shrimp with Peppers

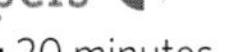

**MAKES:** 2 servings **START TO FINISH:** 20 minutes

- 8 ounces fresh or frozen medium shrimp
- Nonstick cooking spray
- 2 small red and/or green sweet peppers, cut into thin strips
- ¼ cup sliced green onions (2)
- 1 clove garlic, minced
- ½ cup canned sliced water chestnuts
- 2 tablespoons apricot preserves
- 1 tablespoon reduced-sodium soy sauce
- Several dashes bottled hot pepper sauce
- 1 teaspoon sesame seeds, toasted
- 1 cup hot cooked rice or orzo

**1** Thaw shrimp, if frozen. Peel and devein shrimp, removing tails. Rinse shrimp; pat dry with paper towels. Set aside.
**2** Lightly coat an unheated medium skillet with cooking spray. Heat skillet over medium heat. Add peppers, green onions, and garlic. Cook and stir for 3 to 4 minutes or until crisp-tender.
**3** Add shrimp and water chestnuts. Cook and stir for 3 to 4 minutes or until shrimp are opaque. Remove skillet from heat. Stir in apricot preserves, soy sauce, and hot pepper sauce. Sprinkle with sesame seeds. Serve over hot cooked rice.

**PER SERVING:** 220 cal., 2 g total fat (0 g sat. fat), 131 mg chol., 436 mg sodium, 34 g carbo., 1 g fiber, 17 g pro.

For pretty presentation, serve

## Seafood Pizza

**MAKES:** 4 servings **PREP:** 30 minutes **GRILL:** 9 minutes
**STAND:** 5 minutes

- 4 ounces fresh or frozen medium shrimp
- 4 ounces fresh or frozen sea scallops
- 1 large fennel bulb (1 to 1½ pounds)
- 2 teaspoons olive oil
- ½ cup water
- Nonstick cooking spray
- 1 13.8-ounce package refrigerated pizza dough
- ½ of a 10-ounce container (about ½ cup) refrigerated light Alfredo sauce
- ½ teaspoon fennel seeds, crushed (optional)
- 1 cup shredded provolone, scamorza, and/or mozzarella cheese (4 ounces)
- 1 tablespoon snipped fresh fennel leaf (optional)

**1** Thaw shrimp and scallops, if frozen. Peel and devein shrimp, removing tails. Rinse shrimp and scallops; pat dry with paper towels. Halve any large scallops. Set aside.
**2** Cut off and discard stalks and base of the fennel. (If desired, reserve some of the feathery leaves for garnish.) Wash fennel bulb; remove any brown or wilted outer layers. Halve, core, and cut fennel crosswise into thin slices. Set aside.
**3** In a large nonstick skillet heat oil over medium-high heat. Add shrimp and scallops. Cook, stirring frequently, for 2 to 3 minutes or until shrimp and scallops are opaque. Remove shrimp mixture from skillet. Set aside. Add fennel slices and the water to skillet. Bring to boiling; reduce heat. Simmer, covered, for 2 to 3 minutes or just until tender. Drain fennel; set aside.
**4** Coat a 16-inch grill pizza pan or a 12- to 13-inch pizza pan with cooking spray; set aside. Unroll pizza dough; divide into 4 pieces.* If desired, shape each piece into a ball for round pizzas, or leave as rectangles. On a lightly floured surface, roll out each dough piece to ¼-inch thickness. Grilling 2 pizzas at a time, transfer crusts to prepared pizza pan.
**5** For a charcoal grill, grill pizzas in pan on the rack of an uncovered grill directly over medium coals for 6 to 8 minutes or until bottoms of crusts turn slightly golden, giving pan a half turn after 4 minutes. Remove pan from grill; cool about 3 minutes. Carefully turn crusts over. (For a gas grill, preheat grill. Reduce heat to medium. Place pizzas in pan on grill rack over heat. Cover and grill as above.)
**6** Spread Alfredo sauce on pizza crusts to within ½ inch of edge. Top each crust with one-fourth of the shrimp, scallops, and sliced fennel. If desired, sprinkle with fennel seeds. Sprinkle each with one-fourth of the cheese. Return pizzas to grill. Cover and grill for 3 to 4 minutes more or until cheese is melted and bottoms of crusts are golden. (For a gas grill, cover and grill asdirected.)
**7** Remove pizzas from grill. If desired, sprinkle with snipped fennel leaf. Let stand for 5 minutes before serving.
***Note:** Or shape the entire package of dough into one circle about 12 to 15 inches in diameter. Continue as directed.

**PER SERVING:** 420 cal., 18 g total fat (9 g sat. fat), 88 mg chol., 921 mg sodium, 38 g carbo., 4 g fiber, 25 g pro.

## Shrimp and Zucchini with Basil-Chive Cream Sauce

**MAKES:** 4 to 6 servings **PREP:** 25 minutes **GRILL:** 10 minutes

- 1 8-ounce container sour cream
- ½ cup snipped fresh basil
- 3 tablespoons snipped fresh chives
- ¾ teaspoon salt
- ⅛ teaspoon ground black pepper
- 1¼ pounds fresh or frozen large shrimp in shells
- 2 medium zucchini, halved lengthwise and cut into 1-inch slices
- 2 tablespoons olive oil
- ½ teaspoon finely shredded orange or lime peel
- 1 tablespoon orange juice or lime juice
- ¼ teaspoon cayenne pepper
- 5 cups spinach, arugula, and/or romaine

**1** For basil sauce, in a food processor or blender combine sour cream, basil, chives, ½ teaspoon of the salt, and the black pepper. Cover and process or blend until nearly smooth. Cover and chill in the refrigerator until ready to serve.
**2** Thaw shrimp, if frozen. Peel and devein shrimp, leaving tails intact. Rinse shrimp; pat dry with paper towels.
**3** Thread shrimp and zucchini alternately on four to six 8- to 10-inch skewers, leaving about ¼ inch between pieces. In a small bowl combine olive oil, orange peel, orange juice, the remaining ¼ teaspoon salt, and the cayenne pepper; brush evenly on shrimp and zucchini.
**4** For a charcoal grill, grill kabobs on the greased rack of an uncovered grill directly over medium coals about 10 minutes or until shrimp are opaque, turning once halfway through grilling. (For a gas grill, preheat grill. Reduce heat to medium. Cover and grill as above.)
**5** Arrange spinach on a serving platter. Top with kabobs and serve with basil sauce.

**PER SERVING:** 283 cal., 20 g total fat (9 g sat. fat), 174 mg chol., 670 mg sodium, 7 g carbo., 3 g fiber, 20 g pro.

# shrimp and veggies on a skewer.

Shrimp and Zucchini
with Basil-Chive Cream Sauce

page 108
page 129

# Pleasing

Poultry

Rosemary Chicken and Artichokes

Salad of Italian greens, sliced red onion, fresh berries, and dressing

Hot cooked brown rice

Rosemary Chicken and Artichokes [below]

## Rosemary Chicken and Artichokes

**MAKES:** 6 servings **PREP:** 15 minutes
**COOK:** 5 to 5½ hours (low) or 2½ to 3 hours (high) + 30 minutes

- ½ cup chopped onion (1 medium)
- ⅓ cup reduced-sodium chicken broth
- 6 cloves garlic, minced
- 1 tablespoon quick-cooking tapioca
- 2 to 3 teaspoons finely shredded lemon peel
- 2 teaspoons snipped fresh rosemary or 1 teaspoon dried rosemary, crushed
- ¾ teaspoon ground black pepper
- 2½ to 3 pounds chicken thighs, skinned
- ½ teaspoon salt
- 1 8- or 9-ounce package frozen artichoke hearts, thawed
- 1 cup red sweet pepper strips (1 medium)
- Hot cooked brown rice (optional)
- Snipped fresh parsley (optional)
- Fresh rosemary sprigs (optional)

**1** In a 3½- or 4-quart slow cooker combine onion, broth, garlic, tapioca, 1 teaspoon of the lemon peel, the snipped rosemary, and ½ teaspoon of the black pepper. Add chicken. Sprinkle chicken with the salt and the remaining ¼ teaspoon black pepper.
**2** Cover and cook on low-heat setting for 5 to 5½ hours or on high-heat setting for 2½ to 3 hours.
**3** If using low-heat setting, turn cooker to high heat. Add thawed artichokes and sweet pepper strips. Cover and cook for 30 minutes more.
**4** To serve, sprinkle with remaining 1 to 2 teaspoons lemon peel. If desired, serve with hot cooked rice; sprinkle rice with parsley. If desired, garnish with rosemary sprigs.

**PER SERVING:** 168 cal., 4 g total fat (1 g sat. fat), 89 mg chol., 328 mg sodium, 8 g carbo., 3 g fiber, 23 g pro.

## Tex-Mex Sloppy Joes (30)

**MAKES:** 6 sandwiches **START TO FINISH:** 25 minutes

- 2 teaspoons vegetable oil
- 1 cup chopped onion (1 large)
- ¾ cup chopped green sweet pepper (1 medium)
- ½ cup fresh or frozen whole kernel corn
- 2 large cloves garlic, minced
- 1 fresh jalapeño chile pepper, seeded and finely chopped (see note, page 182)
- 1 pound uncooked ground chicken breast or turkey breast
- 1 teaspoon chili powder
- 1 teaspoon ground cumin
- 1 teaspoon dried oregano, crushed
- ¾ cup ketchup
- 4 teaspoons Worcestershire sauce
- 6 whole grain sandwich-style rolls, split
- Dill pickle slices (optional)

**1** In an extra-large nonstick skillet heat oil over medium-high heat. Add onion, sweet pepper, corn, garlic, and jalapeño pepper. Cook for 4 to 5 minutes or until onion is tender, stirring occasionally. Stir in chicken, chili powder, cumin, and oregano. Cook for 5 to 6 minutes more or until chicken is no longer pink. Stir in ketchup and Worcestershire sauce; heat through.
**2** Divide mixture among rolls. If desired, top with pickle slices.

**PER SANDWICH:** 280 cal., 6 g total fat (1 g sat. fat), 44 mg chol., 644 mg sodium, 35 g carbo., 4 g fiber, 23 g pro.

## Spring Chicken with Garlic

**MAKES:** 6 servings **PREP:** 25 minutes **ROAST:** 1¼ hours
**STAND:** 15 minutes **OVEN:** 375°

- 3 heads garlic (about 40 cloves)
- 2 tablespoons olive oil or vegetable oil
- 1 tablespoon snipped fresh lemon thyme, snipped fresh thyme, or 1 teaspoon dried thyme, crushed
- 1 teaspoon cracked black pepper
- ¼ teaspoon salt
- 1 3- to 3½-pound whole broiler-fryer chicken
- 1 medium onion, cut into wedges
- 2 cups fat-free half-and-half or half-and-half
- 2 tablespoons all-purpose flour
- 1 teaspoon snipped fresh lemon thyme, snipped fresh thyme, or ¼ teaspoon dried thyme, crushed
- ¼ teaspoon salt
- ⅛ teaspoon ground black pepper
- Fresh lemon thyme sprigs (optional)

**1** Preheat oven to 375°. Peel away outer papery leaves from heads of garlic, leaving skin of garlic cloves intact. Separate the cloves. (You should have about 40 cloves.) Peel and mince 4 of the cloves. Set aside remaining garlic cloves.
**2** In a small bowl combine minced garlic, 1 tablespoon of the oil, the 1 tablespoon snipped lemon thyme, the cracked black pepper, and ¼ teaspoon salt. Rub mixture over chicken.
**3** Place six garlic cloves into the cavity of the chicken. Tie legs to tail. Twist wing tips under back. Place onion wedges and the remaining garlic cloves in the bottom of a shallow roasting pan. Drizzle the remaining 1 tablespoon oil over onion and garlic.
**4** Place chicken, breast side up, on top of the onion and garlic. Insert meat thermometer into center of an inside thigh muscle. Do not allow thermometer tip to touch bone. Roast, uncovered, for 1¼ to 1½ hours or until drumsticks move easily in their sockets and meat thermometer registers 180°.
**5** Remove chicken from pan. Using a slotted spoon, remove onion wedges and garlic cloves from pan. Reserve 2 or 3 onion wedges for garnish. Cover chicken loosely with foil; let stand for 15 minutes before carving.
**6** For gravy, carefully squeeze 10 cloves of the roasted garlic from skins into a blender container or food processor bowl. Add the remaining roasted onion wedges and ¼ cup of the half-and-half. Cover and blend or process the garlic mixture until smooth. Transfer to a small saucepan. Stir in flour. Add the remaining 1¾ cups half-and-half, the 1 teaspoon snipped lemon thyme, ¼ teaspoon salt, and ground black pepper to mixture in saucepan. Cook and stir over medium heat until slightly thickened and bubbly. Cook and stir for 1 minute more.
**7** Serve chicken with gravy, remaining roasted garlic cloves, and reserved onion wedges. If desired, garnish with fresh lemon thyme sprigs.

**PER SERVING:** 282 cal., 10 g total fat (2 g sat. fat), 67 mg chol., 343 mg sodium, 18 g carbo., 1 g fiber, 26 g pro.

## Oven-Fried Parmesan Chicken 

**MAKES:** 12 servings **PREP:** 30 minutes **BAKE:** 45 minutes
**OVEN:** 375°

- ½ cup refrigerated or frozen egg product, thawed, or 2 eggs, beaten
- ¼ cup fat-free milk
- ¾ cup grated Parmesan cheese
- ¾ cup fine dry bread crumbs
- 2 teaspoons dried oregano, crushed
- 1 teaspoon paprika
- ¼ teaspoon ground black pepper
- 5 pounds meaty chicken pieces (breast halves, thighs, and drumsticks), skinned
- ¼ cup butter or margarine, melted
- Snipped fresh oregano (optional)

**1** Preheat oven to 375°. Grease 2 large shallow baking pans; set aside. In a small bowl combine egg product and milk. In a shallow dish combine Parmesan cheese, bread crumbs, dried oregano, paprika, and pepper.
**2** Dip chicken pieces into egg product mixture; coat with crumb mixture. Arrange chicken pieces in prepared baking pans, making sure pieces do not touch. Drizzle chicken pieces with melted butter.
**3** Bake for 45 to 55 minutes or until chicken is no longer pink (170° for breasts; 180° for thighs and drumsticks). Do not turn chicken pieces during baking. If desired, sprinkle with fresh oregano.

**PER SERVING:** 198 cal., 9 g total fat (4 g sat. fat), 79 mg chol., 363 mg sodium, 6 g carbo., 0 g fiber, 23 g pro.

Italian Chicken and Pasta

## Italian Chicken and Pasta

**MAKES:** 4 servings **PREP:** 15 minutes
**COOK:** 5 to 6 hours (low) or 2½ to 3 hours (high)

- 1 9-ounce package frozen Italian-style green beans
- 1 cup fresh mushrooms, quartered
- 1 small onion, cut into ¼-inch-thick slices
- 12 ounces skinless, boneless chicken thighs, cut into 1-inch pieces
- 1 14.5-ounce can Italian-style stewed tomatoes, undrained
- 1 6-ounce can Italian-style tomato paste
- 1 teaspoon dried Italian seasoning, crushed
- 2 cloves garlic, minced
- 6 ounces dried fettuccine
- Finely shredded or grated Parmesan cheese (optional)

**1** In a 3½- or 4-quart slow cooker stir together frozen beans, mushrooms, and onion. Place chicken on top of vegetables in cooker.
**2** In a small bowl stir together undrained tomatoes, tomato paste, Italian seasoning, and garlic. Pour over chicken.
**3** Cover and cook on low-heat setting for 5 to 6 hours or on high-heat setting for 2½ to 3 hours.
**4** To serve, cook fettuccine according to package directions; drain. Serve chicken mixture over hot cooked fettuccine. If desired, sprinkle with Parmesan cheese.

**PER SERVING:** 405 cal., 7 g total fat (2 g sat. fat), 75 mg chol., 728 mg sodium, 55 g carbo., 4 g fiber, 28 g pro.

Teriyaki and Orange Chicken

## Teriyaki and Orange Chicken

**MAKES:** 4 servings **PREP:** 15 minutes
**COOK:** 4 to 5 hours (low) or 2 to 2½ hours (high)

- 1 16-ounce package frozen broccoli, carrots, and water chestnuts
- 2 tablespoons quick-cooking tapioca
- 1 pound skinless, boneless chicken breast halves or thighs, cut into 1-inch pieces
- ¾ cup reduced-sodium chicken broth
- 3 tablespoons low-sugar orange marmalade
- 2 tablespoons bottled light teriyaki sauce
- 1 teaspoon dry mustard
- ½ teaspoon ground ginger
- 2 cups hot cooked brown rice

**1** In a 3½- or 4-quart slow cooker combine frozen vegetables and tapioca. Add chicken.
**2** In a small bowl combine broth, marmalade, teriyaki sauce, mustard, and ginger. Pour over mixture in cooker.
**3** Cover and cook on low-heat setting for 4 to 5 hours or on high-heat setting for 2 to 2½ hours. Serve with hot cooked rice.

**PER SERVING:** 320 cal., 2 g total fat (1 g sat. fat), 66 mg chol., 432 mg sodium, 41 g carbo., 5 g fiber, 32 g pro.

## Balsamic Chicken

**MAKES:** 4 servings **PREP:** 25 minutes **CHILL:** 2 to 6 hours
**BAKE:** 10 minutes **OVEN:** 450°

- 4 small skinless, boneless chicken breast halves (1 to 1¼ pounds total)
- Nonstick cooking spray
- 1 tablespoon paprika
- 1 tablespoon olive oil
- 2 cloves garlic, minced
- ½ teaspoon snipped fresh rosemary
- ¼ teaspoon ground black pepper
- ¼ cup dry red wine or water
- 3 tablespoons balsamic vinegar
- Fresh rosemary sprigs (optional)

**1** If desired, place each chicken breast half between 2 pieces of plastic wrap and pound with the flat side of a meat mallet to a rectangle that is ¼ to ½ inch thick.
**2** Coat a 13×9×2-inch baking pan with cooking spray; set aside. In a small bowl combine paprika, oil, garlic, the snipped rosemary, and pepper, mixing until mixture forms a paste. Using your fingers, generously coat both sides of chicken pieces with paste. Place coated chicken pieces in prepared pan. Cover and chill for 2 to 6 hours.
**3** Preheat oven to 450°. Drizzle chicken with wine. Bake for 10 to 12 minutes or until chicken is no longer pink (170°), turning once halfway through baking. (If chicken has been pounded, bake about 6 minutes or until chicken is no longer pink and juices run clear, turning once halfway through baking.)
**4** Remove from oven. Immediately drizzle vinegar over chicken in the baking pan. Transfer chicken to dinner plates. Stir the liquid in the baking pan and drizzle over chicken. If desired, garnish with rosemary sprigs.

**PER SERVING:** 181 cal., 5 g total fat (1 g sat. fat), 66 mg chol., 62 mg sodium, 3 g carbo., 1 g fiber, 27 g pro.

Balsamic Chicken

# Chicken is a versatile bird,

## Creamy Chicken with Mushrooms

**MAKES:** 4 servings **START TO FINISH:** 30 minutes

- Nonstick cooking spray
- 4 small skinless, boneless chicken breast halves (about 1 to 1¼ pounds total)
- 1 teaspoon olive oil
- 2 cups sliced fresh mushrooms
- 1 medium red or green sweet pepper, cut into ¾-inch squares
- 1 clove garlic, minced
- ½ cup reduced-sodium chicken broth
- Salt
- Ground black pepper
- ½ cup fat-free sour cream
- 1 tablespoon all-purpose flour
- ⅛ teaspoon ground black pepper
- 2 cups hot cooked white or brown rice

**1** Coat a large nonstick skillet with cooking spray. Preheat skillet. Add chicken. Cook over medium heat about 4 minutes or until browned, turning once halfway through cooking. Remove chicken from skillet.
**2** Carefully add oil to hot skillet. Add mushrooms, sweet pepper, and garlic; cook and stir in hot oil until tender. Remove vegetables from skillet; cover with foil to keep warm.
**3** Carefully stir chicken broth into skillet. Return chicken to skillet. Sprinkle lightly with salt and pepper. Bring to boiling; reduce heat. Simmer, covered, for 5 to 7 minutes or until the chicken is no longer pink (170°). Remove chicken from skillet; cover with foil to keep warm.
**4** For sauce, in a small bowl combine sour cream, flour, and the ⅛ teaspoon pepper until smooth. Add to skillet. Cook and stir until thickened and bubbly. Add chicken and vegetables; heat through. Serve over hot cooked rice.

**PER SERVING:** 291 cal., 4 g total fat (1 g sat. fat), 69 mg chol., 319 mg sodium, 31 g carbo., 2 g fiber, 32 g pro.

Creamy Chicken with Mushrooms

## Chicken Cacciatore

**MAKES:** 4 servings **START TO FINISH:** 40 minutes

- Nonstick cooking spray
- 4 skinless, boneless chicken breast halves (about 1¼ to 1½ pounds total)
- 1 14.5-ounce can stewed tomatoes, undrained
- 1 cup green sweet pepper cut into thin bite-size strips (1 medium)
- ½ cup sliced fresh mushrooms
- ¼ cup chopped onion
- ¼ cup dry red wine or water
- 2 teaspoons dried Italian seasoning, crushed
- ⅛ teaspoon ground black pepper

**1** Coat a large skillet with cooking spray. Preheat over medium heat. Add chicken and cook about 6 minutes or until lightly browned, turning once halfway through cooking.
**2** Stir in undrained tomatoes, sweet pepper, mushrooms, onion, wine, Italian seasoning, and black pepper. Bring to boiling; reduce heat. Simmer, covered, about 15 minutes or until chicken is no longer pink (170°). Remove chicken from skillet; cover chicken to keep warm.
**3** Simmer tomato mixture, uncovered, about 5 minutes more or until desired consistency. Serve with chicken.

**PER SERVING:** 231 cal., 3 g total fat (1 g sat. fat), 82 mg chol., 266 mg sodium, 11 g carbo., 2 g fiber, 35 g pro.

## Curried Chicken Couscous 

**MAKES:** 4 servings **START TO FINISH:** 20 minutes

- ¼ cup bottled mango chutney
- Nonstick cooking spray
- ⅔ cup chopped onion
- 2 teaspoons curry powder
- 1⅓ cups water
- ⅔ cup quick-cooking couscous
- 2 cups cubed cooked chicken breast (about 5 ounces)
- ⅔ cup frozen peas
- ½ cup fat-free mayonnaise dressing or salad dressing
- ½ cup chopped red sweet pepper (1 small)

**1** Cut up any large pieces of chutney. Set aside.
**2** Lightly coat a medium skillet with cooking spray. Preheat skillet over medium heat. Add onion; cook and stir until

crisp-tender. Stir in curry powder; cook for 1 minute more. Add the water and couscous to skillet; bring to boiling. Remove from heat. Stir in chutney, chicken, peas, mayonnaise, and sweet pepper; heat through.

**PER SERVING:** 303 cal., 3 g total fat (1 g sat. fat), 59 mg chol., 365 mg sodium, 39 g carbo., 3 g fiber, 27 g pro.

## Spicy Chicken Breasts with Fruit (30)

**MAKES:** 4 servings **START TO FINISH:** 25 minutes

- 1 tablespoon Jamaican jerk seasoning
- 4 skinless, boneless chicken breast halves (about 1¼ pounds total)
- 1 tablespoon vegetable oil
- 3 green onions, cut into 1-inch pieces
- ½ cup peach nectar
- 1 teaspoon cornstarch
- 2 cups frozen peach slices
- ½ cup frozen pitted dark sweet cherries
- 1 tablespoon packed brown sugar
- ⅛ teaspoon salt
- 1 cup sliced plums
- Hot cooked rice (optional)

**1** Sprinkle jerk seasoning evenly over both sides of chicken pieces; rub in with your fingers. In a large skillet heat oil over medium heat. Add chicken; cook for 8 to 12 minutes or until chicken is no longer pink (170°), turning once halfway through cooking. Add the green onions the last 2 to 3 minutes of cooking. Transfer chicken and green onions to serving platter; cover and keep warm.
**2** Meanwhile, in a small bowl combine nectar and cornstarch. Add peaches, cherries, brown sugar, and salt to skillet. Stir in cornstarch mixture. Cook and stir about 3 minutes or until slightly thickened and bubbly. Stir in plums; cook and stir for 1 minute more.
**3** Spoon fruit mixture over chicken. If desired, serve with hot cooked rice.

**PER SERVING:** 294 cal., 6 g total fat (1 g sat. fat), 82 mg chol., 380 mg sodium, 26 g carbo., 3 g fiber, 34 g pro.

Spicy Chicken Breasts with Fruit

Jamaican jerk seasoning is delicious on chicken and pork. The two most significant ingredients in the sweet-spicy blend are ground allspice and searingly hot Scotch bonnet peppers. The flavor is rounded out by cloves, ginger, cinnamon, nutmeg, thyme, and garlic.

Some of the best things about summer are long days, sun, and the smell and sound of chicken sizzling on the grill.

Lemon-Herb Chicken and Vegetable Kabobs

## Lemon-Herb Chicken and Vegetable Kabobs

**MAKES:** 4 servings **PREP:** 30 minutes **MARINATE:** 2 hours **GRILL:** 10 minutes

- 8 tiny new potatoes, halved
- 1 medium yellow summer squash, cut into 1-inch pieces
- 2 skinless, boneless chicken breast halves (about 10 ounces total), cut into 1-inch pieces
- ⅓ cup lemon juice or lime juice
- 2 tablespoons olive oil or vegetable oil
- 2 tablespoons water
- 3 cloves garlic, minced
- 4 teaspoons snipped fresh basil or oregano or 1 teaspoon dried basil or oregano, crushed
- 2 teaspoons snipped fresh thyme or rosemary or ½ teaspoon dried thyme or rosemary, crushed
- ½ teaspoon salt
- ¼ teaspoon ground black pepper
- 1 large red sweet pepper, cut into 1-inch pieces

**1** In a covered medium saucepan cook potatoes in a small amount of boiling water for 12 minutes. Add squash; cook, covered, for 1 to 2 minutes more or until vegetables are nearly tender. Drain and cool.

**2** Place chicken in a resealable plastic bag set in a medium bowl. For marinade, in a small bowl combine the lemon juice, oil, the water, garlic, basil, thyme, salt, and black pepper. Add potatoes, squash, and sweet pepper to the plastic bag with the chicken. Pour the marinade over chicken and vegetables. Seal bag; turn to coat chicken and vegetables. Marinate in the refrigerator for 2 hours, turning bag occasionally.

**3** Meanwhile, soak 4 long wooden skewers in enough water to cover for 30 minutes; drain. Drain the chicken and vegetables, reserving marinade. On soaked skewers, alternately thread the chicken, potatoes, squash, and sweet pepper, leaving about ¼ inch between pieces.

**4** For charcoal grill, place kabobs on the rack of an uncovered grill directly over medium-hot coals. Grill for 5 minutes, brushing frequently with reserved marinade. Discard any remaining marinade. Turn and grill for 5 to 7 minutes more or until chicken is tender and no longer pink. (For gas grill, preheat grill. Reduce heat to medium-hot. Place kabobs on grill rack over heat. Cover and grill as above.)

**PER SERVING:** 308 cal., 9 g total fat (2 g sat. fat), 82 mg chol., 376 mg sodium, 21 g carbo., 4 g fiber, 36 g pro.

Lemon-Tarragon Chicken Toss

## Lemon-Tarragon Chicken Toss 

**MAKES:** 4 servings **START TO FINISH:** 20 minutes

- 6 ounces dried fettuccine or linguine
- 2 cups broccoli florets or cauliflower florets
- ½ cup reduced-sodium chicken broth
- 3 tablespoons lemon juice
- 1 tablespoon honey
- 2 teaspoons cornstarch
- ¼ teaspoon ground white pepper
- 2 teaspoons olive oil or vegetable oil
- 12 ounces skinless, boneless chicken breasts, cut into bite-size strips
- ½ cup shredded carrot
- 1 tablespoon snipped fresh tarragon or ½ teaspoon dried tarragon, crushed
- Lemon slices, halved (optional)

**1** Cook pasta according to package directions, adding the broccoli for the last 4 minutes of cooking. Drain; return to hot pan. Cover and keep warm.

**2** Meanwhile, in a small bowl combine broth, lemon juice, honey, cornstarch, and white pepper; set aside.

**3** In a large nonstick skillet heat oil over medium heat. Add chicken; cook and stir in hot oil for 3 to 4 minutes or until no longer pink. Stir cornstarch mixture; add to skillet. Cook and stir until thickened and bubbly. Add carrot and tarragon; cook for 1 minute more.

**4** Toss chicken mixture with pasta. If desired, garnish with lemon slices.

**PER SERVING:** 320 cal., 4 g total fat (1 g sat. fat), 49 mg chol., 143 mg sodium, 43 g carbo., 3 g fiber, 27 g pro.

Garlic focaccia wedges

Salad of
baby spinach and frisée
with dressing

Chicken, Long Bean,
and Tomato Stir-Fry
[below]

Gelato with berries

## Chicken, Long Bean, and Tomato Stir-Fry 30

**MAKES:** 2 servings **START TO FINISH:** 30 minutes

- **6 ounces wide rice noodles or dried egg noodles**
- **4 teaspoons vegetable oil**
- **2 cloves garlic, minced**
- **1 pound Chinese long beans or whole green beans, cut into 4-inch pieces**
- **¼ cup water**
- **12 ounces skinless, boneless chicken breast halves, cut into bite-size strips**
- **1½ teaspoons Thai or other spicy seasoning blend**
- **2 medium tomatoes, cut into wedges**
- **2 tablespoons cider vinegar or seasoned rice vinegar**

**1** Cook rice noodles in boiling, lightly salted water for 3 to 5 minutes or until tender. (Or cook egg noodles according to package directions.) Drain noodles; return to pan. Cover and keep warm.
**2** Meanwhile, in a large nonstick skillet heat 2 teaspoons of the oil. Add garlic; cook and stir for 15 seconds. Add beans; cook and stir for 2 minutes. Carefully add the water to skillet; reduce heat to low. Simmer, covered, for 5 to 7 minutes or until beans are crisp-tender. Remove beans from skillet.
**3** Toss chicken with seasoning blend. In the same skillet heat the remaining 2 teaspoons oil over medium-high heat. Add chicken; cook and stir for 3 to 4 minutes or until no longer pink. Add beans, noodles, tomatoes, and vinegar; heat through. Serve immediately.

**PER SERVING:** 321 cal., 7 g total fat (1 g sat. fat), 49 mg chol., 284 mg sodium, 44 g carbo., 3 g fiber, 21 g pro.

## Chicken in Shiitake Mushroom Sauce

**MAKES:** 8 servings **PREP:** 20 minutes **COOK:** 40 minutes

- **3 pounds meaty chicken pieces (breast halves, thighs, and drumsticks), skinned**
- **½ teaspoon salt**
- **¼ teaspoon ground black pepper**
- **Nonstick cooking spray**
- **8 ounces pearl onions**
- **4 medium carrots, cut into 1-inch-long pieces**
- **¼ cup dry vermouth**
- **1 14-ounce can reduced-sodium chicken broth**
- **3 tablespoons snipped fresh parsley**
- **1 tablespoon snipped fresh thyme or 1 teaspoon dried thyme, crushed**
- **1 tablespoon snipped fresh rosemary or 1 teaspoon dried rosemary, crushed**
- **8 ounces fresh shiitake or button mushrooms, halved**
- **Fresh rosemary sprigs (optional)**

**1** Sprinkle chicken with salt and pepper. Coat an extra-large nonstick skillet with cooking spray. Preheat over medium heat. Cook chicken in hot skillet about 10 minutes or until chicken is golden, turning to brown evenly. Remove chicken.
**2** Add pearl onions and carrots to skillet. Cook about 5 minutes or until onions are golden, stirring occasionally. Add vermouth, scraping up any crusty browned bits from bottom of skillet. Return chicken to skillet. Pour broth over chicken; sprinkle with parsley, thyme, and the snipped rosemary.
**3** Bring to boiling; reduce heat. Simmer, covered, about 40 minutes or until chicken is no longer pink (170° for breasts; 180° for thighs and drumsticks), adding mushrooms for the last 10 minutes of cooking. If desired, garnish with rosemary sprigs.

**PER SERVING:** 195 cal., 6 g total fat (2 g sat. fat), 69 mg chol., 350 mg sodium, 10 g carbo., 2 g fiber, 24 g pro.

Chicken in Shiitake Mushroom Sauce

## Spinach Chicken Breast Rolls

**MAKES:** 4 servings **PREP:** 30 minutes **BAKE:** 50 minutes
**STAND:** 10 minutes **OVEN:** 375°

- 4 medium skinless, boneless chicken breast halves (about 1¼ pounds total)
- ½ of a 10-ounce package frozen chopped spinach, thawed and well drained
- 1 cup part-skim mozzarella cheese, shredded (4 ounces)
- ⅓ cup lowf-fat cottage cheese, drained
- 1 egg white
- ½ of a 26-ounce jar light spaghetti sauce with garlic and herbs (1¼ cups)
- 2 tablespoons tomato paste
- 6 ounces dried multigrain spaghetti or whole wheat spaghetti, cooked (optional)

**1** Preheat oven to 375°. Place each chicken breast half between 2 pieces of plastic wrap; lightly pound with the flat side of a meat mallet to about ¼-inch thickness. Set aside.
**2** In a small bowl stir together spinach, ½ cup of the mozzarella cheese, cottage cheese, and the egg white. Spoon spinach mixture over chicken breast halves, leaving a ½-inch border around edges. Roll up breast halves from short ends. Place chicken rolls, seam sides down, in a 2-quart rectangular baking dish. In a small bowl stir together spaghetti sauce and tomato paste; spoon over chicken.
**3** Cover and bake for 25 minutes. Uncover; sprinkle with remaining ½ cup mozzarella cheese. Bake, uncovered, about 25 minutes more or until chicken is no longer pink (170°) and cheese is lightly browned. Let stand for 10 minutes before serving. If desired, serve with hot cooked spaghetti.

**PER SERVING:** 292 cal., 7 g total fat (4 g sat. fat), 101 mg chol., 718 mg sodium, 10 g carbo., 3 g fiber, 46 g pro.

## Chicken Enchilada Casserole 

**MAKES:** 6 servings **PREP:** 30 minutes **BAKE:** 25 minutes
**STAND:** 5 minutes **OVEN:** 350°

- ¾ cup water
- ½ cup chopped onion (1 medium)
- 2 cloves garlic, minced
- ½ teaspoon instant chicken bouillon granules
- ⅛ teaspoon ground black pepper
- ½ cup light sour cream
- 2 tablespoons nonfat dry milk powder
- 1 tablespoon all-purpose flour
- 1½ cups shredded cooked chicken breast or turkey breast (about 8 ounces)
- 1 8-ounce can no-salt-added tomato sauce
- 1 4-ounce can diced green chile peppers, drained, or 1 or 2 canned jalapeño chile peppers, rinsed, seeded, and finely chopped (see note, page 182)
- 2 tablespoons snipped fresh cilantro or ½ teaspoon ground coriander
- Nonstick cooking spray
- 4 6-inch corn tortillas, cut into 1-inch strips
- 1 cup canned black beans or kidney beans, rinsed and drained
- ½ cup shredded reduced-fat Monterey Jack cheese (2 ounces)
- Fresh cilantro leaves (optional)

**1** Preheat oven to 350°. In a medium saucepan combine the water, onion, garlic, bouillon granules, and black pepper. Bring to boiling; reduce heat. Simmer, covered, about 3 minutes or until onion is tender. Do not drain. In a small bowl combine sour cream, milk powder, and flour; add to onion mixture. Cook and stir until thickened and bubbly. Remove from heat; stir in chicken. Set aside.
**2** In another small bowl combine tomato sauce, chile peppers, and the snipped cilantro. Set aside.
**3** Coat a 2-quart baking dish with cooking spray. Arrange tortilla strips in the baking dish. Top with chicken mixture. Top with beans. Top with tomato sauce mixture.
**4** Bake for 25 to 30 minutes or until heated through. Sprinkle with cheese. If desired, garnish with cilantro leaves. Let stand for 5 minutes before serving.

**PER SERVING:** 219 cal., 6 g total fat (3 g sat. fat), 43 mg chol., 420 mg sodium, 23 g carbo., 5 g fiber, 19 g pro.

The taste of creamy chicken enchiladas—in a simple casserole.

Chicken Enchilada Casserole

## Chicken Potpie ★

**MAKES:** 4 servings **PREP:** 30 minutes **BAKE:** 20 minutes
**STAND:** 10 minutes **OVEN:** 425°

- 1 recipe Oil Pastry (below)
- Nonstick cooking spray
- 1½ cups sliced fresh mushrooms
- ½ cup chopped onion (1 medium)
- 1 12-ounce can evaporated fat-free milk
- 3 tablespoons all-purpose flour
- ¼ cup water
- 1 teaspoon instant chicken bouillon granules
- ½ teaspoon dried sage, marjoram, or thyme, crushed
- ⅛ teaspoon ground black pepper
- 1½ cups chopped cooked chicken breast or turkey breast (about 8 ounces)
- 1 cup frozen peas with pearl onions, thawed

**1** Preheat oven to 425°. On a lightly floured surface, flatten Oil Pastry with hands. Roll pastry to ⅛-inch thickness. Using 1- to 1½-inch cookie or hors d'oeuvre cutters, make desired-shape pastry cutouts (do not reroll scraps). Cover pastry; set aside.

**2** Lightly coat an unheated medium saucepan with cooking spray. Preheat over medium heat. Add mushrooms and onion to hot pan; cook and stir about 4 minutes or until the onion is tender.

**3** Meanwhile, set aside 1 tablespoon of the evaporated milk. In a small bowl gradually whisk the remaining evaporated milk into the flour until smooth. Stir milk mixture into mushroom mixture in saucepan. Stir in the water, bouillon granules, sage, and pepper. Cook and stir until thickened and bubbly.

**4** Stir in chicken and frozen peas with pearl onions. Transfer mixture to a 9-inch deep-dish pie plate. Arrange pastry cutouts on top of hot chicken mixture. Brush pastry cutouts with the reserved 1 tablespoon evaporated milk.

**5** Bake for 20 to 25 minutes or until the pastry is golden. Let stand for 10 minutes before serving.

**Oil Pastry:** In a medium bowl stir together ⅔ cup all-purpose flour and ⅛ teaspoon salt. Add 3 tablespoons vegetable oil and 2 tablespoons fat-free milk. Stir lightly with a fork to combine. Form dough into a ball.

**PER SERVING:** 386 cal., 13 g total fat (2 g sat. fat), 48 mg chol., 450 mg sodium, 38 g carbo., 3 g fiber, 28 g pro.

Salad of spring greens, carrots, and almonds with fresh herb vinaigrette

Ginger Chicken Noodle Bowl [below]

Simple Almond Cookies [page 282]

## Ginger Chicken Noodle Bowl

**MAKES:** 4 servings **START TO FINISH:** 25 minutes

- 2 cups dried Chinese egg noodles or fine egg noodles (4 ounces)
- ⅓ cup bottled stir-fry sauce
- ¼ teaspoon ground ginger
- 2 teaspoons peanut oil or vegetable oil
- 1 cup snow pea pods or fresh sugar snap peas, tips and stems removed and cut up
- 1 cup red sweet pepper cut into bite-size strips (1 medium)
- 1 cup cooked chicken breast cut into bite-size strips (about 5 ounces)
- 2 tablespoons coarsely chopped cashews or peanuts or toasted sliced almonds

**1** Cook noodles according to package directions. Drain; set aside. In a small bowl combine stir-fry sauce and ginger; set aside.

**2** In a large skillet heat oil over medium-high heat. Add pea pods and sweet pepper; cook and stir in hot oil for 3 to 5 minutes or until crisp-tender. Add cooked noodles, chicken, stir-fry sauce mixture, and cashews; heat through.

**PER SERVING:** 235 cal., 7 g total fat (1 g sat. fat), 49 mg chol., 540 mg sodium, 24 g carbo., 3 g fiber, 18 g pro.

## Thai-Spiced Chicken Kabobs

**MAKES:** 4 servings **PREP:** 30 minutes **GRILL:** 13 minutes

- 1 small fresh pineapple (3 to 3½ pounds)
- Nonstick cooking spray
- 1 pound skinless, boneless chicken breast halves, cut into 1-inch pieces
- 1 recipe Thai Brushing Sauce
- 1 tablespoon butter or margarine, melted
- 1 tablespoon packed brown sugar (optional)
- Hot cooked rice (optional)
- Fresh basil leaves (optional)
- Fresh whole red chile peppers (optional)

**1** Cut off pineapple ends. Halve pineapple lengthwise; cut each half crosswise into 4 slices. Lightly coat pineapple slices with cooking spray. Set aside.

**2** Thread chicken onto 4 long metal skewers, leaving ¼ inch between pieces. Set aside ¼ cup Thai Brushing sauce for brushing; reserve remaining sauce.

**3** For charcoal grill, place skewers on the rack of an uncovered grill directly over medium heat. Grill for 7 minutes. Turn skewers; brush with the ¼ cup Thai Brushing Sauce, discarding any sauce remaining from brushing. Arrange pineapple slices on grill rack directly over medium heat. Grill chicken and pineapple for 6 to 8 minutes or until chicken is no longer pink and pineapple is heated through, turning once halfway through grilling. (For gas grill, preheat grill. Reduce heat to medium. Place skewers on grill rack over heat. Cover and grill chicken and pineapple as directed above.)

**4** In a small bowl combine the remaining Thai Brushing Sauce, melted butter, and, if desired, brown sugar. Serve with chicken and pineapple. If desired, serve with hot cooked rice. If desired, garnish with basil and chile peppers.

**Thai Brushing Sauce:** In a small bowl combine ⅔ cup sweet-and-sour sauce, 2 tablespoons snipped fresh basil, 1 teaspoon Thai seasoning or five-spice powder, and 1 clove garlic, minced. Makes about ¾ cup.

**Note:** To make ahead, prepare Thai Brushing Sauce, cut pineapple into slices, and thread chicken onto skewers as directed. Cover and store separately in refrigerator for up to 24 hours.

**PER SERVING:** 285 cal., 5 g total fat (2 g sat. fat), 73 mg chol., 332 mg sodium, 34 g carbo., 2 g fiber, 27 g pro.

# Serve pasta in warm bowls.

## Chicken and Mushroom Pasta

**MAKES:** 6 servings **START TO FINISH:** 40 minutes

- **8 ounces dried penne pasta**
- **12 ounces skinless, boneless chicken breast halves, cut into bite-size strips**
- **¼ teaspoon salt**
- **⅛ teaspoon ground black pepper**
- **2 tablespoons olive oil**
- **3 large cloves garlic, minced**
- **3 cups sliced fresh mushrooms**
- **1 medium onion, thinly sliced**
- **½ cup chicken broth**
- **¼ cup dry white wine**
- **1 cup cherry tomatoes, halved**
- **¼ cup shredded fresh basil**
- **3 tablespoons snipped fresh oregano**
- **¼ cup finely shredded Parmesan cheese (1 ounce)**
- **⅛ teaspoon ground black pepper**

**1** Cook pasta according to package directions. Drain pasta; return to saucepan. Cover and keep warm.

**2** Meanwhile, sprinkle chicken with salt and ⅛ teaspoon pepper. In a large skillet heat 1 tablespoon of the oil over medium-high heat. Add chicken and garlic. Cook and stir for 3 to 4 minutes or until chicken is no longer pink. Remove from skillet; cover and keep warm.

**3** Add the remaining 1 tablespoon oil to skillet. Add mushrooms and onion; cook just until tender, stirring occasionally. Carefully add broth and wine. Bring to boiling; reduce heat. Boil gently, uncovered, about 2 minutes or until liquid is reduced by half. Remove skillet from heat.

**4** Add cooked pasta, chicken, tomatoes, basil, and oregano to mushroom mixture; toss gently to combine. Transfer chicken mixture to a serving dish; sprinkle with Parmesan cheese and ⅛ teaspoon pepper.

**PER SERVING:** 299 cal., 8 g total fat (2 g sat. fat), 37 mg chol., 249 mg sodium, 33 g carbo., 2 g fiber, 22 g pro.

Chicken and Mushroom Pasta

## Chicken Lasagna

**MAKES:** 8 to 10 servings **PREP:** 40 minutes **BAKE:** 40 minutes
**STAND:** 10 minutes **OVEN:** 350°

- 1 egg, lightly beaten
- 1 15-ounce carton fat-free ricotta cheese
- 1 10-ounce package frozen chopped spinach, thawed and well drained
- 1 teaspoon dried Italian seasoning, crushed
- 1 tablespoon olive oil
- 1 pound skinless, boneless chicken breast halves, cut into ½-inch pieces
- 8 ounces fresh mushrooms, sliced
- ½ cup chopped onion (1 medium)
- 2 cloves garlic, minced
- 1 teaspoon dried Italian seasoning, crushed
- 2 14.5-ounces cans diced tomatoes with basil, garlic, and oregano, undrained
- 2 cups shredded, peeled carrots (4 medium)
- 1 8-ounce can tomato sauce
- ½ teaspoon ground black pepper
- 9 dried lasagna noodles
- Nonstick cooking spray
- 2 cups shredded mozzarella cheese (8 ounces)
- ¼ cup grated Parmesan cheese

**1** In a small bowl combine egg, ricotta cheese, spinach, and 1 teaspoon Italian seasoning. Cover and chill in the refrigerator until ready to assemble lasagna.

**2** In a large skillet heat oil over medium heat. Add chicken, mushrooms, onion, garlic, and 1 teaspoon Italian seasoning; cook and stir in hot oil for 5 to 7 minutes or until chicken is golden. Stir in undrained tomatoes, carrots, tomato sauce, and pepper. Bring to boiling; reduce heat. Simmer, uncovered, for 15 to 20 minutes or until mixture is slightly thickened.

**3** Meanwhile, cook the lasagna noodles according to package directions. Drain noodles; rinse with cold water. Drain again.

**4** Preheat oven to 350°. Coat a 3-quart rectangular baking dish with cooking spray. Place 3 of the lasagna noodles in prepared dish. Spread half of the ricotta mixture over the noodles. Spread one-third of the chicken mixture over the ricotta; sprinkle with 1/2 cup of the mozzarella cheese and 1 tablespoon of the Parmesan cheese. Repeat layers, ending with noodles. Spoon the remaining chicken mixture over the top. Sprinkle with the remaining 1 cup mozzarella cheese and the remaining 2 tablespoons Parmesan cheese.

**5** Bake, covered, in a 350° oven for 35 minutes. Uncover and bake for 5 to 10 minutes more or until cheese is melted and bubbly. Let stand 10 minutes before serving.

**PER SERVING:** 400 cal., 11 g total fat (5 g sat. fat), 82 mg chol., 1,113 mg sodium, 39 g carbo., 4 g fiber, 37 g pro.

Skillet Lasagna

## Skillet Lasagna

**MAKES:** 6 servings **PREP:** 35 minutes **COOK:** 4 minutes
**STAND:** 10 minutes

- 8 ounces uncooked bulk turkey sausage
- ½ cup chopped onion (1 medium)
- 2 cups bottled spaghetti sauce
- 1 cup water
- 2 cups dried wide noodles
- 1½ cups coarsely chopped zucchini
- ½ cup fat-free ricotta cheese
- 2 tablespoons grated Parmesan or Romano cheese
- 1 tablespoon snipped fresh parsley
- ½ cup shredded reduced-fat mozzarella cheese (2 ounces)

**1** In a large skillet cook sausage and onion until meat is brown and onion is tender. Drain off fat. Stir in spaghetti sauce and the water. Bring to boiling. Stir in uncooked noodles and zucchini. Return to boiling; reduce heat. Simmer, covered, about 12 minutes or until noodles are tender, stirring occasionally.

**2** Meanwhile, in a small bowl stir together ricotta cheese, Parmesan cheese, and parsley. Drop cheese mixture by spoonfuls into 6 mounds over the sausage-noodle mixture in the skillet. Sprinkle mounds with mozzarella cheese. Cover and cook on low heat for 4 to 5 minutes or until cheese mixture is heated through. Let stand for 10 minutes before serving.

**PER SERVING:** 221 cal., 8 g total fat (3 g sat. fat), 35 mg chol., 805 mg sodium, 22 g carbo., 3 g fiber, 17 g pro.

Chicken Lasagna Rolls
with Chive-Cream Sauce

Plain low-fat yogurt is a terrific substitute for sour cream. For the best taste with the fewest fat and calories, try Greek yogurt. Greek yogurt comes in varying fat contents, but even the 0% or fat-free Greek yogurt has a thick and creamy texture and rich flavor that domestic yogurt does not. It's a little more expensive, but worth it.

## Chicken Lasagna Rolls with Chive-Cream Sauce

**MAKES:** 6 servings **PREP:** 40 minutes
**BAKE:** 35 minutes **OVEN:** 350°

- **6 dried lasagna noodles**
- **1 8-ounce package reduced-fat cream cheese (Neufchâtel), softened**
- **½ cup milk**
- **¼ cup grated Romano or Parmesan cheese**
- **1 tablespoon snipped fresh chives**
- **1½ cups chopped cooked chicken**
- **½ of a 10-ounce package frozen chopped broccoli, thawed and drained (1 cup)**
- **½ cup bottled roasted red sweet peppers, drained and sliced**
- **⅛ teaspoon ground black pepper**
- **1 cup purchased marinara or pasta sauce**

**1** Preheat oven to 350°. Cook lasagna noodles according to package directions. Drain noodles; rinse with cold water. Drain again. Cut each in half crosswise; set aside.
**2** Meanwhile, for white sauce, in a medium bowl beat cream cheese with an electric mixer on medium to high speed for 30 seconds. Slowly add milk, beating until smooth. Stir in Romano cheese and chives.
**3** For filling, in a medium bowl stir together ½ cup of the white sauce, the chicken, broccoli, roasted peppers, and black pepper. Place about ¼ cup filling at one end of each cooked noodle piece. Roll up noodles around filling. Arrange rolls, seam sides down, in a 3-quart rectangular baking dish.
**4** Spoon the marinara sauce over the rolls. Spoon remaining white sauce over marinara sauce. Cover with foil. Bake for 35 to 40 minutes or until heated through.

**PER SERVING:** 288 cal., 13 g total fat (7 g sat. fat), 65 mg chol., 412 mg sodium, 22 g carbo., 2 g fiber, 19 g pro.

## Chicken Tostadas 

**MAKES:** 4 servings **START TO FINISH:** 30 minutes **OVEN:** 375°

- **4 6-inch corn tortillas**
- **2 tablespoons vegetable oil**
- **3 skinless, boneless chicken breast halves (about 1 pound)**
- **1 cup bottled thick and chunky salsa**
- **¼ cup snipped fresh cilantro**
- **¼ teaspoon ground cumin**
- **4 cups fresh baby spinach leaves**
- **4 roma tomatoes, diced**
- **½ cup plain low-fat yogurt**
- **¼ cup sliced green onions (2)**
- **1 avocado, halved, seeded, peeled, and sliced**

**1** Preheat oven to 375°. Brush both sides of each tortilla with 1 tablespoon of the oil. Place on a baking sheet. Bake for 10 to 12 minutes or until golden and crisp; set aside.
**2** In a large skillet heat the remaining oil over medium heat. Add chicken. Cook for 10 to 12 minutes or until chicken is no longer pink (170°), turning once halfway through cooking. Remove chicken to a cutting board and chop; set aside. In a medium bowl combine salsa, cilantro, and cumin.
**3** Place toasted tortillas on 4 dinner plates. Top each with spinach, chicken, tomatoes, salsa mixture, yogurt, green onions, and avocado (tostadas will be full).

**PER SERVING:** 382 cal., 17 g total fat (3 g sat. fat), 68 mg chol., 590 mg sodium, 29 g carbo., 7 g fiber, 32 g pro.

Tex-Mex Chicken Tacos

## Tex-Mex Chicken Tacos

**MAKES:** 4 servings **PREP:** 20 minutes **MARINATE:** 1 to 2 hours **COOK:** 15 minutes

- 12 ounces skinless, boneless chicken breast halves, ut into bite-size strips
- ½ cup orange juice
- ¼ cup snipped fresh cilantro
- 1 teaspoon finely shredded lime peel
- 2 tablespoons lime juice
- 1 fresh jalapeño chile pepper, seeded and finely chopped (see note, page 182)
- 3 cloves garlic, minced
- ⅛ teaspoon salt
- ⅛ teaspoon ground black pepper
- 2 teaspoons vegetable oil
- 1 cup thin bite-size red pepper strips (1 medium)
- 1 cup frozen whole kernel corn
- 1½ teaspoons cornstarch
- 8 6-inch corn tortillas
- ½ cup light sour cream

**1** Place chicken in a resealable plastic bag set in a shallow dish. For marinade, in a small bowl combine orange juice, cilantro, lime peel, lime juice, jalapeño pepper, garlic, salt, and black pepper. Pour over chicken; seal bag. Marinate in the refrigerator for 1 to 2 hours, turning bag occasionally.

**2** Drain chicken, reserving marinade. In a large nonstick skillet heat oil over medium-high heat. Add sweet pepper strips; cook and stir until crisp-tender. Remove sweet pepper strips from skillet.

**3** Add chicken to skillet. Cook and stir for 3 to 4 minutes or until chicken is no longer pink. Stir in corn; heat through. Combine the marinade and cornstarch; add to chicken mixture. Cook and stir until thickened and bubbly. Cook and stir for 2 minutes more. Return sweet pepper strips to skillet, stirring to combine.

**4** Wrap tortillas in microwave-safe paper towels. Microwave on 100 percent power (high) for 45 to 60 seconds or until warm. Divide the chicken mixture among tortillas and top with sour cream. Fold the tortillas over chicken mixture.

**PER SERVING:** 362 cal., 9 g total fat (3 g sat. fat), 61 mg chol., 138 mg sodium, 47 g carbo., 4 g fiber, 26 g pro.

## Chicken-Salsa Pizza

**MAKES:** 6 servings **PREP:** 25 minutes **BAKE:** 13 minutes
**OVEN:** 400°

- **2 teaspoons vegetable oil**
- **12 ounces skinless, boneless chicken breasts, cut into thin bite-size strips**
- **1 cup thin bite-size red sweet pepper strips (1 medium)**
- **½ of a medium red onion, thinly sliced**
- **Nonstick cooking spray**
- **1 13.8-ounce package refrigerated pizza dough**
- **½ cup bottled mild picante sauce**
- **½ cup shredded sharp cheddar cheese (2 ounces)**

**1** Preheat oven to 400°. In a large nonstick skillet heat oil over medium-high heat. Add chicken; cook in hot oil about 5 minutes or until no longer pink. Remove from skillet. Add sweet pepper and red onion to skillet; cook and stir about 5 minutes or until tender. Remove from skillet; set aside.
**2** Coat a 15×10×1-inch baking pan with cooking spray. Unroll pizza dough into pan; press with fingers to form a 12×8-inch rectangle. Pinch edges of dough to form crust.
**3** Spread crust with picante sauce. Top with chicken and vegetables; sprinkle with cheddar cheese. Bake for 13 to 18 minutes or until crust is brown and cheese is melted.

**PER SERVING:** 305 cal., 9 g total fat (3 g sat. fat), 43 mg chol., 527 mg sodium, 34 g carbo., 2 g fiber, 21 g pro.

Chicken-Salsa Pizza

## Springtime Spinach-and-Chicken Salad

**MAKES:** 6 servings **START TO FINISH:** 35 minutes

- **1 2- to 2¼-pound purchased roasted chicken or 3 cups chopped cooked turkey**
- **8 cups torn fresh spinach**
- **1 medium red onion, thinly sliced and separated into rings**
- **½ of a small jicama, peeled and cut into thin strips (about 2 cups)**
- **½ cup sliced radishes**
- **¼ cup sliced almonds, toasted**
- **3 tablespoons olive oil**
- **2 tablespoons lemon juice**
- **2 tablespoons pure maple syrup or maple-flavored syrup**

**1** Remove and discard skin and bones from chicken. Chop chicken. In a large salad bowl combine chicken, spinach, red onion, jicama, radishes, and almonds; set aside.
**2** For dressing, in a screw-top jar combine oil, lemon juice, and maple syrup. Cover and shake well.
**3** Pour dressing over spinach mixture. Toss gently to coat. Serve immediately.

**PER SERVING:** 294 cal., 20 g total fat (5 g sat. fat), 75 mg chol., 528 mg sodium, 14 g carbo., 4 g fiber, 18 g pro.

# Your supermarket rotisserie is a

concentrate, thawed; and ¼ teaspoon ground black pepper. Makes about ¾ cup.

**PER SERVING:** 193 cal., 6 g total fat (2 g sat. fat), 514 mg sodium, 11 g carbo., 6 g fiber, 23 g pro.

## Chicken-Zucchini Salad

**MAKES:** 6 servings **PREP:** 25 minutes **CHILL:** 4 to 24 hours

- **3 cups shredded cooked chicken (1 pound)**
- **1¼ cups chopped zucchini or yellow summer squash (1 medium)**
- **1¼ cups chopped fennel or kohlrabi**
- **½ cup chopped celery (1 stalk)**
- **½ cup sliced green onions (4)**
- **½ cup chopped carrot (1 medium)**
- **2 tablespoons snipped dried apricots (optional)**
- **1 recipe Herbed Mustard Mayonnaise**
- **Torn mixed salad greens**
- **Salt**
- **Ground black pepper**
- **Orange slices**

**1** In a large bowl combine chicken, zucchini, fennel, celery, green onions, carrot, and apricots (if using). Stir in Herbed Mustard Mayonnaise until mixture is evenly coated. Cover and chill for 4 to 24 hours.

**2** To serve, line 6 dinner plates with greens. Stir chicken mixture; season to taste with salt and pepper. Place on top of greens. Garnish with orange slices.

**Herbed Mustard Mayonnaise:** In a small bowl combine ⅔ cup fat-free mayonnaise dressing or salad dressing; 4 teaspoons Dijon-style mustard; 1 teaspoon finely shredded lemon peel; 1 tablespoon lemon juice; 1 tablespoon snipped fresh dill or tarragon; 1 tablespoon frozen orange juice

## Sesame Chicken Kabob Salad

**MAKES:** 4 servings **PREP:** 30 minutes **GRILL:** 10 minutes

- **4 skinless, boneless chicken breast halves (about 1¼ pounds total)**
- **16 fresh pineapple chunks (1 cup)**
- **1 medium yellow sweet pepper, cut into 1-inch pieces**
- **3 tablespoons rice vinegar or white wine vinegar**
- **2 tablespoons water**
- **1 tablespoon vegetable oil**
- **1 tablespoon soy sauce**
- **1 teaspoon toasted sesame oil**
- **½ teaspoon dry mustard**
- **1 tablespoon plum sauce or chili sauce**
- **2 cups chopped red cabbage**
- **2 cups chopped bok choy or iceberg lettuce**
- **½ cup sliced fresh mushrooms**
- **¼ cup sliced radishes**

**1** Cut each chicken breast half into 4 lengthwise strips. On eight 6-inch skewers,* alternately thread chicken, pineapple, and sweet pepper, leaving ¼ inch between pieces.

**2** For dressing, in screw-top jar combine vinegar, the water, vegetable oil, soy sauce, sesame oil, and mustard. Cover and shake well. Remove 2 tablespoons of the dressing. Cover and chill remaining dressing until needed. In small bowl stir together the 2 tablespoons reserved dressing and plum sauce. Brush over kabobs.

**3** For charcoal grill, place kabobs on rack of uncovered grill directly over medium coals; grill for 10 to 12 minutes or until chicken is tender and no longer pink, turning once halfway through grilling. (For gas grill, preheat grill. Reduce heat to medium. Place kabobs on grill rack over heat. Cover and grill as above.)

**4** In medium bowl combine cabbage, bok choy, mushrooms, and radishes. Divide mixture among 4 dinner plates. Top with kabobs. Shake the reserved dressing; drizzle over salads.

***Note:** If using wooden skewers, soak in water for 30 minutes; drain before using.

**PER SERVING:** 290 cal., 8 g total fat (1 g sat. fat), 82 mg chol., 390 mg sodium, 19 g carbo., 3 g fiber, 36 g pro.

## Grilled Mushroom-Turkey Burgers

**MAKES:** 4 burgers **PREP:** 15 minutes **STAND:** 20 minutes **GRILL:** 14 minutes

- 2 tablespoons dried porcini or shiitake mushrooms
- 1 cup boiling water
- 12 ounces uncooked ground turkey breast
- ½ cup bottled salsa
- ½ cup finely snipped onion (1 medium)
- 2 tablespoons snipped fresh Italian (flat-leaf) parsley
- 6 cloves garlic, minced
- 2 teaspoons chopped fresh sage
- ¼ teaspoon kosher salt
- ⅛ teaspoon ground black pepper
- 4 whole wheat hamburger buns, split and toasted (optional)
- Lettuce leaves, bottled salsa, sliced red onion, sliced avocado, and/or sliced tomato (optional)

**1** Rinse mushrooms well. Place mushrooms in a small bowl; add the boiling water. Let stand about 20 minutes or until soft. Drain the mushrooms well; finely chop.
**2** In a medium bowl combine mushrooms, turkey, the ½ cup salsa, onion, parsley, garlic, sage, kosher salt, and pepper. Shape mixture into four ¾-inch-thick patties.
**3** For a charcoal grill, grease the rack of an uncovered grill. Place patties on the rack directly over medium coals. Grill for 14 to 18 minutes or until internal temperature of each burger registers 165°, turning once halfway through grilling. (For a gas grill, preheat grill. Grease grill rack. Reduce heat to medium. Place burgers on grill rack over heat. Cover and grill as above.)
**4** If desired, serve burgers on whole wheat buns with lettuce, additional salsa, red onion, avocado, and/or tomato.

**PER BURGER:** 119 cal., 1 g total fat (0 g sat. fat), 34 mg chol., 281 mg sodium, 7 g carbo., 1 g fiber, 21 g pro.

## Mexi-Turkey Burgers

**MAKES:** 4 burgers **PREP:** 25 minutes **GRILL:** 14 minutes

- 1 cup radishes, chopped
- 6 green onions, chopped
- 1 cup snipped fresh cilantro
- ¼ teaspoon salt
- 1 pound uncooked ground turkey
- 1 4-ounce can whole green chile peppers, drained
- 4 1-ounce slices Monterey Jack cheese
- 4 large hamburger buns, split and toasted
- 1 cup shredded lettuce
- 4 tomato slices
- ½ cup bottled salsa

**1** In a bowl combine radishes, green onions, cilantro, and salt. Add ground turkey. Shape into four ¾-inch patties.
**2** For a charcoal grill, grease the rack of an uncovered grill. Place patties on the rack directly over medium coals. Grill for 14 to 18 minutes or until internal temperature of each burger registers 165°, turning once halfway through grilling. Top burgers with chile peppers and cheese during the last 1 minute of grilling. (For a gas grill, preheat grill. Grease grill rack. Reduce heat to medium. Place patties on grill rack over heat. Cover; grill as above.)
**3** Serve burgers in buns with lettuce, tomato, and salsa.

**PER BURGER:** 431 cal., 21 g total fat (8 g sat. fat), 115 mg chol., 908 mg sodium, 29 g carbo., 3 g fiber, 33 g pro.

## Turkey Reubens 30

**MAKES:** 4 sandwiches **PREP:** 15 minutes **COOK:** 4 minutes per batch

- 2 cups packaged shredded cabbage with carrot (coleslaw mix)
- 2 tablespoons bottled reduced-calorie clear Italian salad dressing or white wine vinaigrette salad dressing
- 2 tablespoons bottled reduced-calorie Thousand Island salad dressing
- 8 ½-inch-thick slices rye bread
- 8 ounces sliced cooked turkey breast
- 4 slices provolone cheese (4 ounces)
- 1 medium tomato, sliced
- Cucumber spears (optional)

**1** In a medium bowl combine cabbage with carrot and Italian salad dressing; set aside.
**2** Spread Thousand Island salad dressing on 1 side of each bread slice. Top with turkey, cheese, tomato, and cabbage mixture. Top with remaining bread slices.
**3** Preheat a large skillet over medium heat. Reduce heat to medium-low. Cook sandwiches, half at a time, for 4 to 6 minutes or until the bread is toasted and the cheese is melted, turning once halfway through cooking. If desired, serve with cucumber spears.

**PER SANDWICH:** 379 cal., 11 g total fat (5 g sat. fat), 67 mg chol., 884 mg sodium, 38 g carbo., 5 g fiber, 31 g pro.

## Turkey-Spinach Calzones

**MAKES:** 4 calzones **PREP:** 20 minutes **BAKE:** 18 minutes
**OVEN:** 375°

- Nonstick cooking spray
- 2 cups packaged fresh baby spinach leaves
- 1½ cups chopped cooked turkey breast (about 8 ounces)
- ½ cup shredded reduced-fat Italian-blend cheese (2 ounces)
- ¼ cup purchased pizza sauce
- 1 13.8-ounce package refrigerated pizza dough
- Fat-free milk
- Grated Parmesan or Romano cheese (optional)
- Purchased pizza sauce, warmed (optional)

**1** Preheat oven to 375°. Line a baking sheet with foil and lightly coat with cooking spray; set aside.
**2** In a large bowl combine spinach, turkey, Italian blend cheese, and the ¼ cup pizza sauce. On a lightly floured surface, roll out the pizza dough to a 12-inch square. Cut dough into four 6-inch squares.
**3** Divide the turkey mixture among dough squares, placing mixture on one-half of the dough and spreading to within about ½ inch of edges. Moisten edges of dough with water; fold dough over, carefully stretching dough to cover turkey mixture to form a rectangle or triangle. Pinch or press edges with tines of a fork to seal. Prick tops of calzones with a fork; brush with milk. Place on prepared baking sheet.
**4** If desired, sprinkle tops of calzones with Parmesan cheese. Bake about 18 minutes or until golden. If desired, serve with additional warmed pizza sauce.

**PER CALZONE:** 378 cal., 6 g total fat (2 g sat. fat), 55 mg chol., 777 mg sodium, 48 g carbo., 2 g fiber, 30 g pro.

## Spaghetti Pie ✪

**MAKES:** 6 servings **PREP:** 35 minutes **BAKE:** 25 minutes
**STAND:** 15 minutes **OVEN:** 350°

- Nonstick cooking spray
- 4 ounces dried spaghetti
- 2 egg whites, lightly beaten
- ⅓ cup grated Parmesan cheese
- 1 tablespoon olive oil
- 2 egg whites, lightly beaten
- 1 12-ounce container low-fat cottage cheese, drained (1¼ cups)
- 8 ounces uncooked ground turkey breast or lean ground beef
- 1 cup sliced fresh mushrooms
- ½ cup chopped onion (1 medium)
- ½ cup chopped green or red sweet pepper (1 small)
- 2 cloves garlic, minced
- 1 8-ounce can no-salt-added tomato sauce
- 1½ teaspoons dried Italian seasoning, crushed
- ⅛ teaspoon salt
- ½ cup shredded part-skim mozzarella cheese (2 ounces)

**1** Preheat oven to 350°. Coat a 9-inch pie plate with cooking spray; set aside. For crust, cook spaghetti according to package directions, except omit the oil and salt. Meanwhile, in a medium bowl stir together 2 egg whites, the Parmesan cheese, and oil. Drain spaghetti well; add to egg white mixture and toss to coat. Press spaghetti mixture evenly into the bottom and up the side of the prepared pie plate; set aside.
**2** In a small bowl stir together 2 egg whites and drained cottage cheese. Spread the cottage cheese mixture over the crust in pie plate. Set aside.
**3** In a large skillet cook turkey, mushrooms, onion, sweet pepper, and garlic until meat is browned. Drain off fat. Stir tomato sauce, Italian seasoning, and salt into meat mixture in skillet. Spoon over cottage cheese mixture in crust.
**4** Bake about 20 minutes or until heated through. Sprinkle with mozzarella cheese. Bake about 5 minutes more or until the cheese is melted. Let stand for 15 minutes before serving. Cut into wedges to serve.

**PER SERVING:** 256 cal., 7 g total fat (3 g sat. fat), 27 mg chol., 479 mg sodium, 23 g carbo., 2 g fiber, 26 g pro.

Kids love this fun-to-make, fun-to-eat main-dish pie.

Spaghetti Pie

## Greek Meatballs and Orzo Pilaf

**MAKES:** 4 servings (8 meatballs each) **PREP:** 20 minutes **BAKE:** 40 minutes **COOK:** 22 minutes **OVEN:** 350°

- **1 pound ground turkey**
- **½ pound white button mushrooms, cleaned and finely chopped**
- **½ cup fat-free plain yogurt**
- **3 tablespoons chopped fresh mint**
- **1½ teaspoons dried oregano**
- **¾ teaspoon lemon-pepper seasoning**
- **¾ teaspoon salt**
- **1 tablespoon olive oil**
- **½ small onion, chopped**
- **2 large cloves garlic, chopped**
- **¾ cup uncooked orzo**
- **1 can (14.5 ounces) chicken broth**
- **¼ teaspoon salt**
- **⅛ teaspoon black pepper**
- **1 bag (6 ounces) baby spinach**
- **½ cup cherry tomatoes (about 8), each cut into quarters**
- **2 tablespoons chopped fresh mint, plus more for garnish (optional)**

**1** Preheat oven to 350°. Line 15×11×1-inch jelly-roll pan with aluminum foil.
**2** In large bowl mix together turkey, mushrooms, yogurt, mint, oregano, lemon-pepper seasoning and salt. Shape into 28 meatballs, using 1 slightly rounded tablespoon for each. Place meatballs on prepared baking sheet.
**3** Bake about 40 minutes or until browned and internal temperature registers 165° on instant-read thermometer.
**4** For the Orzo Pilaf, while meatballs are baking, in medium-size saucepan heat olive oil over medium heat. Add onion; cook, stirring, 3 minutes or until slightly softened. Add garlic and orzo; cook, stirring, 3 minutes more or until orzo is coated and onion is softened. Add broth, salt and pepper. Simmer, covered, 15 minutes or until orzo is tender. Stir in the spinach, tomatoes, and mint; cook about 1 minute until spinach is wilted and tomatoes are heated through.
**5** Serve meatballs with orzo. If desired, garnish with additional mint.

**PER SERVING:** 342 cal., 13 g total fat (3 g sat. fat), 90 mg chol., 999 mg sodium, 28 g carbo., 3 g fiber, 27 g pro.

## Shepherd's Pie

**MAKES:** 4 servings **PREP:** 45 minutes **BAKE:** 20 minutes **OVEN:** 375°

- **2 medium potatoes, peeled and quartered (about 10 ounces total)**
- **1 medium parsnip, peeled and cut up**
- **¼ cup plain low-fat yogurt**
- **⅛ teaspoon salt**
- **12 ounces uncooked ground turkey breast**
- **½ cup chopped onion (1 medium)**
- **1 10-ounce package frozen mixed vegetables**
- **¼ cup water**
- **1 14.5-ounce can no-salt-added stewed tomatoes, undrained**
- **½ of a 6-ounce can (⅓ cup) no-salt-added tomato paste**
- **1 tablespoon snipped fresh thyme or sage or ¾ teaspoon dried thyme or sage, crushed**
- **1 tablespoon Worcestershire sauce**
- **¼ teaspoon ground black pepper**

**1** Preheat oven to 375°. In a covered medium saucepan cook potatoes and parsnip in enough boiling water to cover about 20 minutes or until tender. Drain well. Mash with a potato masher or with an electric mixer on low speed. Gradually add yogurt and salt, mashing or beating to make potato mixture light and fluffy. Cover and keep warm.
**2** Meanwhile, in a large skillet cook turkey and onion over medium heat until turkey is brown. Drain well. Stir frozen mixed vegetables and the water into turkey mixture. Bring to boiling; reduce heat. Simmer, covered, for 5 to 10 minutes or until vegetables are tender.
**3** Stir in undrained stewed tomatoes, tomato paste, thyme, Worcestershire sauce, and pepper. Heat through.
**4** Divide turkey mixture among four 12- to 16-ounce casseroles or ramekins, or transfer mixture to a 1½-quart casserole. Pipe or drop mashed potato mixture in mounds on top of hot turkey mixture.
**5** Bake for 20 to 25 minutes or until potatoes are heated through.

**PER SERVING:** 279 cal., 2 g total fat (1 g sat. fat), 35 mg chol., 287 mg sodium, 41 g carbo., 7 g fiber, 25 g pro.

Shepherd's Pie

page 146
page 159

# Marvelous Meats

## Mama's Amazing Ziti

**MAKES:** 6 servings **PREP:** 20 minutes **COOK:** 25 minutes

- **1 pound extra-lean ground beef**
- **2 cups shredded carrots (4 medium)**
- **2 10.75-ounce cans reduced-fat and reduced-sodium condensed tomato soup**
- **2½ cups water**
- **8 ounces dried cut ziti pasta (about 2½ cups)**
- **2 tablespoons snipped fresh basil or 2 teaspoons dried basil, crushed**
- **1 teaspoon onion powder**
- **1 teaspoon garlic powder**
- **1 cup shredded part-skim mozzarella cheese (4 ounces)**
- **¼ cup shredded Parmesan cheese (1 ounce)**

**1** In a 4-quart Dutch oven cook ground beef and shredded carrots over medium heat until meat is brown. Drain off fat. Stir tomato soup, the water, uncooked ziti, dried basil (if using), onion powder, and garlic powder into meat mixture in Dutch oven.

**2** Bring mixture to boiling; reduce heat. Cover and cook about 25 minutes or until ziti is tender, stirring occasionally. Stir in fresh basil (if using) and mozzarella cheese. To serve, sprinkle with Parmesan cheese.

**PER SERVING:** 420 cal., 11 g total fat (4 g sat. fat), 73 mg chol., 649 mg sodium, 49 g carbo., 2 g fiber, 32 g pro.

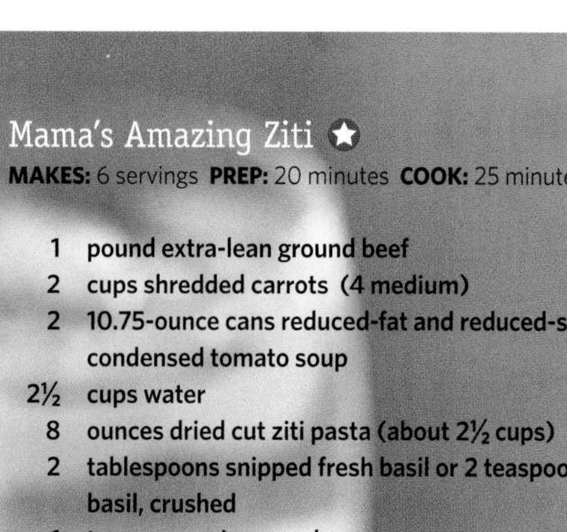

## Italian Casserole 

**MAKES:** 4 or 6 servings **PREP:** 35 minutes **BAKE:** 23 minutes
**OVEN:** 350°

- 2 cups dried multigrain or whole grain penne pasta (about 6 ounces)
- 1 pound lean ground beef
- ½ cup chopped onion (1 medium)
- ¼ cup chopped green sweet pepper or sliced pitted ripe olives (optional)
- 1 14.5-ounce can diced tomatoes with basil, garlic, and oregano, undrained, cut up
- 1 8-ounce can no-salt-added tomato sauce
- ¼ teaspoon salt
- ¼ teaspoon ground black pepper
- 3 tablespoons snipped fresh oregano
- 3 tablespoons snipped fresh basil
- ½ cup shredded part-skim mozzarella cheese (2 ounces)

**1** Cook pasta according to package directions. Drain and set aside.
**2** Meanwhile, in a large skillet cook ground beef, onion, and sweet pepper (if using) until meat is brown. Drain off fat. Stir undrained stewed tomatoes, tomato sauce, salt, and black pepper into meat mixture in skillet. Bring to boiling; reduce heat. Simmer, covered, for 10 minutes. Stir in cooked pasta, oregano, basil, and olives (if using).
**3** Preheat oven to 350°. Spoon the pasta mixture into four or six 10- to 14-ounce individual casseroles.* Place casseroles on a large baking sheet. Bake, covered, about 20 minutes or until heated through. Uncover and sprinkle with cheese. Bake, uncovered, for 3 to 4 minutes more or until cheese is melted.
***Note:** If you do not have individual casseroles, spoon pasta mixture into a 2-quart square baking dish. Bake, covered, for 30 to 35 minutes or until heated through. Uncover and sprinkle with cheese. Bake, uncovered, for 3 to 4 minutes more or until cheese is melted.

**PER SERVING:** 433 cal., 15 g total fat (6 g sat. fat), 83 mg chol., 534 mg sodium, 45 g carbo., 7 g fiber, 33 g pro.

## Spaghetti with Beef and Mushroom Sauce

**MAKES:** 6 servings **PREP:** 15 minutes **COOK:** 20 minutes

- 1 pound lean ground beef
- ½ cup chopped onion (1 medium)
- 1 10.75-ounce can condensed cream of mushroom soup
- 1 15-ounce can tomato sauce
- 1 4-ounce can sliced mushrooms, drained (optional)
- 1 teaspoon dried Italian seasoning, crushed
- ¼ teaspoon ground black pepper
- 12 ounces dried spaghetti
- Grated Parmesan cheese (optional)

**1** In a large saucepan cook meat and onion until meat is brown and onion is tender. Drain off fat. Stir mushroom soup, tomato sauce, mushrooms (if using), Italian seasoning, and pepper into meat mixture in saucepan. Bring to boiling; reduce heat. Simmer, covered, for 20 minutes, stirring occasionally.
**2** Meanwhile, cook spaghetti according to package directions. Drain. Serve sauce over hot spaghetti. If desired, sprinkle with Parmesan cheese.

**PER SERVING:** 398 cal., 11 g total fat (4 g sat. fat), 49 mg chol., 711 mg sodium, 51 g carbo., 3 g fiber, 22 g pro.

## Taco Lover's Pasta 

**MAKES:** 6 servings **START TO FINISH:** 35 minutes

- 8 ounces lean ground beef
- 1 cup chopped onion (1 large)
- ¾ cup chopped green, red, or yellow sweet pepper (1 medium)
- 2 cloves garlic, minced
- 1 15-ounce can tomato sauce
- 1 14.5-ounce can diced tomatoes, undrained
- 1½ teaspoons chili powder
- ¼ teaspoon ground cumin
- Salt
- Ground black pepper
- 10 ounces dried pasta
- 2 tablespoons snipped fresh cilantro
- ½ cup shredded Monterey Jack or cheddar cheese (2 ounces)

**1** In a large saucepan cook ground beef, onion, sweet pepper, and garlic over medium heat until meat is browned. Drain off fat. Stir in tomato sauce, undrained tomatoes, chili powder, and cumin. Bring to boiling; reduce heat. Simmer, uncovered, for 10 to 15 minutes or until desired consistency, stirring occasionally. Season to taste with salt and black pepper.
**2** Meanwhile, cook pasta according to package directions; drain. Just before serving, stir cilantro into meat mixture. Serve over hot cooked pasta. Sprinkle with cheese.

**PER SERVING:** 325 cal., 7 g total fat (3 g sat. fat), 32 mg chol., 562 mg sodium, 47 g carbo., 3 g fiber, 17 g pro.

## Beef and Black Bean Wraps (30)

**MAKES:** 6 servings **START TO FINISH:** 30 minutes

- **8 ounces lean ground beef**
- **1 cup chopped onion (1 large)**
- **2 cloves garlic, minced**
- **1½ teaspoons ground cumin**
- **1 teaspoon chili powder**
- **½ teaspoon ground coriander**
- **1 15-ounce can black beans, rinsed and drained**
- **1 large tomato, chopped**
- **¼ teaspoon salt**
- **¼ teaspoon ground black pepper**
- **6 8-inch whole wheat flour tortillas**
- **1½ cups shredded lettuce**
- **1 to 1½ cups shredded cheddar or Monterey Jack cheese (4 to 6 ounces)**
- **Salsa (optional)**

**1** In a large skillet cook ground beef, onion, and garlic about 5 minutes or until meat is brown. Drain off fat. Stir cumin, chili powder, and coriander into meat mixture in skillet. Cook and stir for 1 minute. Stir in black beans, tomato, salt, and black pepper. Cook, covered, for 5 minutes more, stirring occasionally.

**2** To serve, spoon some of the meat mixture down the center of each tortilla. Sprinkle with lettuce and cheese. Roll up. If desired, serve with salsa.

**PER SERVING:** 267 cal., 10 g total fat (5 g sat. fat), 44 mg chol., 593 mg sodium, 27 g carbo., 14 g fiber, 19 g pro.

## Grilled Taco Meat Loaves

**MAKES:** 8 servings (2 servings per loaf) **PREP:** 30 minutes **GRILL:** 35 minutes **STAND:** 15 minutes

- **1¼ cups soft bread crumbs**
- **¼ cup milk**
- **1 egg, lightly beaten**
- **1 cup shredded taco cheese (4 ounces)**
- **½ cup shredded carrot (1 medium)**
- **¼ cup taco sauce**
- **½ teaspoon seasoned salt**
- **½ teaspoon ground black pepper**
- **1½ pounds lean ground beef**
- **Shredded taco cheese, shredded lettuce, and/or chopped tomato (optional)**

**1** In a large bowl combine bread crumbs, milk, and egg. Add the 1 cup cheese, the carrot, 2 tablespoons of the taco sauce, the seasoned salt, and pepper. Add ground beef; mix well.

**2** Shape meat mixture into 4 mini loaves, each about 4½ inches long and 2 inches wide. Fold a 24×18-inch piece of heavy foil in half crosswise. Trim to a 12-inch square. Cut several large slits in the foil. Place loaves on foil.

**3** For a charcoal grill, arrange medium coals around a drip pan. Test for medium-low heat above pan. Place foil with meat loaves on grill rack over drip pan. Cover and grill for 35 to 40 minutes or until internal temperature of each loaf registers 160° on an instant-read thermometer, brushing with the remaining 2 tablespoons taco sauce during the last 5 minutes of grilling. (For a gas grill, preheat grill. Reduce heat to medium-low. Adjust for indirect cooking. Grill as above.)

**4** Carefully remove meat loaves from grill. Cover with foil; let stand for 15 minutes before serving. If desired, serve with additional cheese, lettuce, and/or tomato.

**PER SERVING:** 230 cal., 10 g total fat (6 g sat. fat), 94 mg chol., 346 mg sodium, 5 g carbo., 0 g fiber, 19 g pro.

*Serve these Mexican-style mini meat loaves with warm tortillas, salsa, and sour cream.*

## Ketchup-Glazed Meat Loaves ✪

**MAKES:** 6 servings **PREP:** 20 minutes **BAKE:** 30 minutes
**STAND:** 10 minutes **OVEN:** 350°

- **1½ pounds lean ground beef or ground pork**
- **2 eggs**
- **1 envelope (½ of a 2-ounce package) onion soup mix**
- **⅔ cup ketchup or hot-style ketchup**
- **⅓ cup fine dry bread crumbs**
- **3 cloves garlic, minced**

**1** Preheat oven to 350°. In a large resealable plastic bag combine meat, eggs, dry onion soup mix, 1/3 cup of the ketchup, the bread crumbs, and garlic; seal bag. Use hands to knead mixture until well mixed. Form mixture into 6 mini loaves, each about 4 inches long and 2 1/2 inches wide.* Arrange loaves in a foil-lined 15×10×1-inch baking pan.

**2** Bake, uncovered, about 30 minutes or until internal temperature of each loaf registers 160° on an instant-read thermometer. Remove from oven. Spoon about 1 tablespoon of the remaining ketchup over each meat loaf. Let stand for 10 minutes before serving.

***Note:** To form loaves, shape meat mixture into a 5-inch square on the foil-lined baking pan. Use a knife to cut square into 6 equal portions and then shape into individual loaves. To make one large meat loaf, prepare as directed, except lightly pat meat mixture into an 8×4×2-inch loaf pan. Bake, uncovered, for 1 to 1 1/4 hours or until internal temperature registers 160° on an instant-read thermometer. Remove from oven. Carefully drain off excess fat. Spoon on the remaining 1/3 cup ketchup. Let stand for 10 minutes before carefully lifting from pan.

**PER SERVING:** 271 cal., 13 g total fat (5 g sat. fat), 142 mg chol., 928 mg sodium, 14 g carbo., 0 g fiber, 24 g pro.

Spaghetti Squash with Chili

Sweet Onion and Spinach Burgers

## Spaghetti Squash with Chili

**MAKES:** 4 servings **PREP:** 30 minutes **BAKE:** 45 minutes
**OVEN:** 350°

- **1** **2-pound spaghetti squash**
- **8** **ounces lean ground beef**
- **½** **cup chopped onion (1 medium)**
- **1** **clove garlic, minced**
- **1** **14.5-ounce can diced tomatoes and green chiles, undrained**
- **1** **11-ounce can no-salt-added corn, drained**
- **1** **8-ounce can no-salt-added tomato sauce**
- **2** **tablespoons no-salt-added tomato paste**
- **2** **teaspoons chili powder**
- **½** **teaspoon dried oregano, crushed**
- **Fresh oregano leaves (optional)**

**1** Preheat oven to 350°. Halve the spaghetti squash lengthwise and remove seeds and membranes. Place squash halves, cut sides down, on a baking sheet. Bake for 45 to 50 minutes or until tender.* Cool slightly. Using a fork, shred and separate the spaghetti squash into strands.
**2** Meanwhile, for sauce, in a medium saucepan cook ground beef, onion, and garlic until meat is brown and onion is tender. Drain off fat.
**3** Stir undrained tomatoes and green chiles, drained corn, tomato sauce, tomato paste, chili powder, and dried oregano into meat mixture in saucepan. Bring to boiling; reduce heat. Simmer, uncovered, about 10 minutes or until desired consistency.
**4** Serve meat sauce with spaghetti squash. If desired, sprinkle with fresh oregano.
***Note:** To cook the squash in the microwave, place one squash half, cut side down, in a microwave-safe baking dish with 1/4 cup water. Cover and microwave on 100 percent power (high) for 5 to 8 minutes or until tender; remove and keep warm. Repeat with second half. Continue as directed.

**PER SERVING:** 326 cal., 13 g total fat (5 g sat. fat), 43 mg chol., 395 mg sodium, 38 g carbo., 6 g fiber, 16 g pro.

## Sweet Onion and Spinach Burgers

**MAKES:** 6 servings **PREP:** 35 minutes **BROIL:** 10 minutes

- **1** **egg, beaten**
- **¼** **cup rolled oats**
- **2** **tablespoons water**
- **½** **teaspoon salt**
- **¼** **teaspoon ground black pepper**
- **1** **pound lean ground veal or lean ground beef**
- **1** **tablespoon butter or margarine**
- **1** **cup sweet onion, sliced (1 small)**
- **2** **teaspoons packed brown sugar**
- **½** **teaspoon dry mustard**
- **2** **cups loosely packed fresh baby spinach leaves or fresh spinach leaves, coarsely chopped**
- **6** **tablespoons light semisoft cheese with garlic and herbs**
- **3** **whole wheat pita bread rounds, halved**

**1** Preheat broiler. In a medium bowl stir together egg, oats, the water, salt, and pepper. Add ground meat; mix well. Shape mixture into six 1/2-inch oval patties. Place patties on the unheated rack of a broiler pan. Broil 3 to 4 inches from heat for 10 to 12 minutes or until internal temperature of each burger registers 160° on an instant-read meat thermometer, turning once halfway through broiling.
**2** Meanwhile, in a medium nonstick skillet melt butter over medium-low heat. Add onion. Cook, covered, for 13 to 15 minutes or until onion is tender. Add brown sugar and mustard. Cook and stir, uncovered, for 3 to 4 minutes or until onions are golden. Stir in spinach. Toss lightly to coat; heat through.
**3** Spread 1 tablespoon of the cheese on 1side of the inside of each pita bread half. Fill each pita bread half with a patty and some of the onion-spinach mixture.

**PER SERVING:** 281 cal., 12 g total fat (5 g sat. fat), 113 mg chol., 557 mg sodium, 24 g carbo., 4 g fiber, 21 g pro.

## Taco Salad Bowls ✪

**MAKES:** 4 servings **PREP:** 35 minutes **BAKE:** 10 minutes
**OVEN:** 350°

- **4** 6- to 8-inch whole wheat or plain flour tortillas
  Nonstick cooking spray
- **12** ounces lean ground beef or uncooked ground turkey
- **½** cup chopped onion (1 medium)
- **1** clove garlic, minced
- **1** 8-ounce can tomato sauce
- **1** tablespoon cider vinegar
- **½** teaspoon ground cumin
- **¼** teaspoon crushed red pepper
- **4** cups shredded lettuce
- **¼** cup shredded reduced-fat cheddar cheese (1 ounce)
- **¼** cup chopped green or red sweet pepper (optional)
- **12** cherry tomatoes, quartered

**1** Preheat oven to 350°. For tortilla bowls, wrap tortillas in foil. Heat in oven for 10 minutes. Coat four 10-ounce custard cups with cooking spray. Carefully press 1 tortilla into each cup. Bake for 10 to 15 minutes or until golden and crisp.* Cool in custard cups on wire rack; remove bowls from custard cups.

**2** Meanwhile, in a large skillet cook ground beef, onion, and garlic until meat is brown and onion is tender. Drain off fat.

**3** Stir tomato sauce, vinegar, cumin, and crushed red pepper into mixture in skillet. Bring to boiling; reduce heat. Simmer, uncovered, for 10 minutes.

**4** Place tortilla bowls on 4 dinner plates. Spoon meat mixture into bowls. Sprinkle with lettuce, cheese, sweet pepper, if using, and tomatoes.

***Note:** To make tortilla bowls ahead, prepare and cool as directed in Step 1. Place in large freezer container with paper towels between bowls and crumpled around the sides of bowls for protection. Seal, label, and freeze for up to 1 month.

**PER SERVING:** 297 cal., 13 g total fat (4 g sat. fat), 59 mg chol., 575 mg sodium, 23 g carbo., 3 g fiber, 22 g pro.

Three-Herb Steaks

## Three-Herb Steaks

**MAKES:** 6 servings **PREP:** 25 minutes **CHILL:** 1 hour
**GRILL:** 15 minutes **STAND:** 10 minutes

- **¼ cup snipped fresh parsley**
- **2 tablespoons snipped fresh basil**
- **1 tablespoon snipped fresh oregano**
- **2 teaspoons olive oil**
- **1 to 2 teaspoons cracked black pepper**
- **½ teaspoon salt**
- **2 beef top loin steaks, cut 1½ inches thick**
- **2 medium red or yellow sweet peppers, cut into ½-inch rings and seeds removed**
- **1 tablespoon olive oil**
- **Salt**
- **Ground black pepper**

**1** For rub, in a small bowl combine parsley, basil, oregano, the 2 teaspoons oil, cracked black pepper, and the ½ teaspoon salt. Trim fat from meat. Sprinkle half of the mixture evenly on both sides of meat; rub in with your fingers. Set aside remaining herb mixture. Cover and chill steaks for 1 hour. Meanwhile, brush pepper rings with the 1 tablespoon oil. Lightly sprinkle with salt and ground black pepper.

**2** For a charcoal grill, place meat on the rack of an uncovered grill directly over medium coals. Grill until meat reaches desired doneness, turning once halfway through grilling. (Allow 15 to 19 minutes for medium rare [145°] or 18 to 23 minutes for medium [160°]). Grill sweet pepper rings next to the meat during the last 8 to 10 minutes of grilling or until peppers are tender, turning once halfway through grilling. (For a gas grill, preheat grill. Reduce heat to medium. Place meat on grill rack over heat. Cover and grill meat and sweet pepper rings as above.) Remove meat from grill and sprinkle with the remaining herb mixture. Cover and let stand for 10 minutes.

**3** To serve, slice meat across the grain. Serve with sweet pepper rings.

**PER SERVING:** 246 cal., 10 g total fat (3 g sat. fat), 64 mg chol., 379 mg sodium, 3 g carbo., 1 g fiber, 34 g pro.

Sesame Orange Beef

The best way to section an orange is to cut a slice off of each end, then cut the peel off down the side of the orange, from top to bottom. To remove the sections without the membrane, slip a thin knife on either side of each section to release.

## Sesame Orange Beef

**MAKES:** 4 servings **START TO FINISH:** 35 minutes

- **12 ounces boneless beef sirloin steak**
- **8 ounces green beans, halved crosswise**
- **2 teaspoons sesame seeds**
- **½ cup orange juice**
- **2 tablespoons reduced-sodium soy sauce**
- **1 tablespoon toasted sesame oil**
- **1 teaspoon cornstarch**
- **½ teaspoon finely shredded orange peel**
- **Nonstick cooking spray**
- **½ cup bias-sliced green onions (4)**
- **1 tablespoon grated fresh ginger**
- **2 cloves garlic, minced**
- **1 teaspoon vegetable oil**
- **2 cups hot cooked brown rice**
- **2 oranges, peeled and sectioned or thinly sliced crosswise**

**1** If desired, partially freeze meat for easier slicing. Trim fat from meat. Thinly slice meat across the grain into bite-size pieces. Set aside. In a covered medium saucepan cook green beans in a small amount of boiling water for 6 to 8 minutes or until crisp-tender. Drain; set aside.

**2** Meanwhile, in a dry small skillet cook sesame seeds over medium heat for 1 to 2 minutes or until toasted, stirring frequently. Set aside.

**3** For sauce, in a small bowl combine orange juice, soy sauce, sesame oil, cornstarch, and orange peel; set aside.

**4** Coat a large nonstick skillet with cooking spray. Preheat over medium-high heat. Add green onions, ginger, and garlic to hot skillet; stir-fry for 1 minute. Add the cooked green beans; stir-fry for 2 minutes. Remove vegetables from skillet.

**5** Carefully add oil to the hot skillet. Add meat; stir-fry about 3 minutes or until desired doneness. Remove from skillet.

**6** Stir sauce; add to skillet. Cook and stir until thickened and bubbly; cook and stir for 2 minutes more. Return meat and vegetables to skillet. Heat through, stirring to coat all ingredients with sauce. Serve over hot cooked brown rice. Top with orange sections and sprinkle with toasted sesame seeds.

**PER SERVING:** 348 cal., 10 g total fat (2 g sat. fat), 52 mg chol., 341 mg sodium, 41 g carbo., 6 g fiber, 24 g pro.

## Salsa Swiss Steak

**MAKES:** 6 servings **PREP:** 15 minutes
**COOK:** 9 to 10 hours (low) or 4½ to 5 hours (high)

- 2 pounds boneless beef round steak, cut ¾ inch thick
- 1 large green sweet pepper, seeded and cut into bite-size strips
- 1 medium onion, sliced
- 1 10.75-ounce can condensed cream of mushroom soup
- 1 cup salsa
- 2 tablespoons all-purpose flour
- 1 teaspoon dry mustard
- 3 cups hot cooked rice

**1** Trim fat from meat. Cut meat into 6 serving-size pieces. Place meat, sweet pepper, and onion in a 3½- or 4-quart slow cooker.
**2** In a medium bowl combine mushroom soup, salsa, flour, and dry mustard. Pour over meat and vegetables in cooker.
**3** Cover and cook on low-heat setting for 9 to 10 hours or on high-heat setting for 4½ to 5 hours. Serve with hot cooked rice.

**PER SERVING:** 410 cal., 12 g total fat (4 g sat. fat), 66 mg chol., 533 mg sodium, 32 g carbo., 2 g fiber, 41 g pro.

Steaks with Tomato Salsa

## Steaks with Tomato Salsa (30)

**MAKES:** 4 servings **START TO FINISH:** 25 minutes

- **¾ teaspoon kosher salt or ½ teaspoon regular salt**
- **½ teaspoon ground cumin**
- **½ teaspoon chili powder**
- **½ teaspoon dried oregano, crushed**
- **½ teaspoon packed brown sugar**
- **2 8-ounce boneless beef ribeye steaks, cut ½ to ¾ inch thick**
- **Nonstick cooking spray**
- **½ cup chopped onion (1 medium)**
- **2 cloves garlic, minced**
- **2 tablespoons olive oil**
- **2 cups red and/or yellow cherry or pear tomatoes, halved**
- **1 canned chipotle chile pepper in adobo sauce, drained and finely chopped (see note, page 182)**
- **2 tablespoons lime juice**
- **¼ cup snipped fresh cilantro**

**1** In a small bowl stir together ½ teaspoon of the kosher salt or ¼ teaspoon of the regular salt, the cumin, chili powder, dried oregano, and brown sugar. Sprinkle over all sides of steaks; rub in with your fingers.

**2** Lightly coat a grill pan with cooking spray. Preheat pan over medium-high heat. Add steaks. Reduce heat to medium. Cook for 8 to 10 minutes or until desired doneness, turning occasionally.

**3** For salsa, in large skillet cook and stir onion and garlic in hot oil over medium heat until tender. Stir in tomatoes, chile pepper, lime juice, and the remaining ¼ teaspoon salt. Cook and stir for 1 minute. Transfer to a bowl; stir in cilantro. Cut each steak in half; serve with salsa.

**Note:** For a charcoal grill, grill steaks on the rack of an uncovered grill directly over medium coals until desired doneness. Allow 8 to 10 minutes for medium-rare doneness (145°) or 10 to 12 minutes for medium doneness (160°). (For a gas grill, preheat grill. Reduce heat to medium. Place steaks on grill rack over heat. Cover and grill as above.)

**PER SERVING:** 267 cal., 14 g total fat (4 g sat. fat), 54 mg chol., 451 mg sodium, 8 g carbo., 2 g fiber, 26 g pro.

## Grilled Beef Fillets with Portobello Relish

**MAKES:** 4 servings **PREP:** 15 minutes **GRILL:** 15 minutes

- 4 beef tenderloin steaks, cut 1 inch thick (about 1¼ pounds total)
- Kosher salt
- Cracked black pepper
- 1 medium yellow onion, cut into ½-inch slices
- 8 ounces portobello mushrooms, stems removed
- 4 roma tomatoes, halved lengthwise
- 3 tablespoons snipped fresh basil
- 2 tablespoons minced garlic (6 cloves)
- 2 tablespoons olive oil
- 1 teaspoon kosher salt
- 1 teaspoon cracked black pepper

**1** Trim fat from steaks. Season steaks with salt and pepper. For a charcoal grill, grill steaks, onion slices, mushrooms, and tomatoes on the rack of an uncovered grill directly over medium coals until steaks are desired doneness and vegetables are tender, turning once halfway through grilling. For steaks, allow 10 to 12 minutes for medium-rare doneness (145°) or 12 to 15 minutes for medium doneness (160°). For vegetables, allow 15 minutes for onion and 10 minutes for mushrooms and tomatoes. (For a gas grill, preheat grill. Reduce heat to medium. Place steaks and vegetables on grill rack over heat. Cover and grill as above.)
**2** Meanwhile, in a medium bowl stir together basil, garlic, oil, the 1 teaspoon kosher salt, and the 1 teaspoon cracked black pepper; set aside.
**3** For relish, cut grilled onion, mushrooms, and tomatoes into 1-inch pieces. Add vegetables to basil mixture; toss to coat. To serve, spoon warm relish over steaks.

**PER SERVING:** 329 cal., 18 g total fat (5 g sat. fat), 87 mg chol., 617 mg sodium, 9 g carbo., 2 g fiber, 33 g pro.

## Southwestern Shredded Beef Sandwiches

**MAKES:** 16 sandwiches **PREP:** 25 minutes
**COOK:** 10 to 12 hours (low) or 5 to 6 hours (high)

- 1 3- to 3½-pound boneless beef chuck pot roast
- 1 tablespoon ground cumin
- 1 tablespoon chili powder
- ¼ teaspoon salt
- ⅛ teaspoon ground black pepper
- 1 cup coarsely chopped onion (1 large)
- 1 14.5-ounce can stewed tomatoes, undrained
- 1 7-ounce can chopped green chile peppers or two 4-ounce cans chopped green chile peppers
- 2 tablespoons chopped pickled jalapeño chile peppers (optional) (see note, page 182)
- ¼ cup snipped fresh cilantro
- 2 cups shredded reduced-fat cheddar or Monterey Jack cheese (8 ounces)
- 16 onion or kaiser rolls, split and toasted
- Lettuce leaves (optional)

**1** Trim fat from roast. In a small bowl combine cumin, chili powder, salt, and black pepper. Sprinkle evenly over roast; rub in with your fingers. If necessary, cut roast to fit into a 4- or 4½-quart slow cooker. Place roast in slow cooker. Add onion, undrained tomatoes, green chile peppers, and, if desired, jalapeño chile peppers.
**2** Cover and cook on low-heat setting for 10 to 12 hours or on high-heat setting for 5 to 6 hours. Transfer roast to a cutting board, reserving juices in slow cooker. Using two forks, pull meat apart into thin shreds. Return meat to slow cooker; heat through. Stir in cilantro.
**3** To serve, sprinkle cheese over bottoms of rolls. Using a slotted spoon, place about ½ cup of the meat mixture on top of the cheese on each roll. If desired, add a lettuce leaf to each. Replace roll tops.

**PER SANDWICH:** 338 cal., 9 g total fat (3 g sat. fat), 60 mg chol., 591 mg sodium, 34 g carbo., 2 g fiber, 28 g pro.

Southwestern Shredded Beef Sandwiches

Asian Flank Steak

Steamed sugar
snap peas

Grilled
potato wedges

Asian Flank Steak
[below]

Double Pumpkin Bars
[page 289]

## Asian Flank Steak

**MAKES:** 6 servings **PREP:** 15 minutes **MARINATE:** 2 to 24 hours
**GRILL:** 17 minutes

- **1 1½-pound beef flank steak**
- **¼ cup lower-sodium beef broth**
- **3 tablespoons hoisin sauce**
- **2 tablespoons reduced-sodium soy sauce**
- **2 tablespoons thinly sliced green onion (1)**
- **1 tablespoon dry sherry (optional)**
- **2 cloves garlic, minced**
- **½ teaspoon grated fresh ginger**

**1** Trim fat from steak. Score both sides of steak in a diamond pattern by making shallow diagonal cuts at 1-inch intervals. Place meat in a resealable plastic bag set in a shallow dish. For marinade, in a small bowl combine broth, hoisin sauce, soy sauce, green onion, sherry (if using), garlic, and ginger. Pour over meat. Seal bag; turn to coat meat. Marinate in the refrigerator for 2 to 24 hours, turning bag occasionally.

**2** Drain meat, discarding marinade. For a charcoal grill, grill meat on the rack of an uncovered grill directly over medium coals for 17 to 21 minutes or until medium doneness (160°), turning once halfway through grilling. (For a gas grill, preheat grill. Reduce heat to medium. Place meat on grill rack over heat. Cover and grill as above.) To serve, thinly slice meat across the grain.

**PER SERVING:** 205 cal., 9 g total fat (4 g sat. fat), 46 mg chol., 419 mg sodium, 5 g carbo., 0 g fiber, 26 g pro.

## Horseradish Flank Steak

**MAKES:** 4 servings **PREP:** 20 minutes
**MARINATE:** 6 to 24 hours **GRILL:** 12 minutes

- **1 1-pound beef flank steak**
- **3 tablespoons Dijon-style mustard**
- **3 tablespoons lemon juice**
- **4½ teaspoons reduced-sodium Worcestershire sauce**
- **⅓ cup fat-free sour cream or fat-free mayonnaise dressing or salad dressing**
- **2 tablespoons finely chopped green onion (1)**
- **1 to 2 teaspoons prepared horseradish**

**1** Trim fat from steak. Score both sides of steak in a diamond pattern by making shallow diagonal cuts at 1-inch intervals. Place meat in a resealable plastic bag set in a shallow dish.

**2** For marinade, in a small bowl combine 2 tablespoons of the mustard, the lemon juice, and Worcestershire sauce. Pour over meat. Seal bag; turn to coat meat. Marinate in the refrigerator for 6 to 24 hours, turning bag occasionally.

**3** For dipping sauce, in a small bowl combine the remaining 1 tablespoon mustard, the sour cream or mayonnaise, green onion, and horseradish. Cover and refrigerate. Remove from refrigerator 30 minutes before serving time.

**4** Drain the steak, discarding the marinade. For a charcoal grill, grill steak on the rack of an uncovered grill directly over medium coals for 12 to 14 minutes or until medium doneness (160°), turning once halfway through grilling. (For a gas grill, preheat grill. Reduce heat to medium. Place steak on grill rack over heat. Cover and grill as above.)

**5** To serve, thinly slice meat across the grain. Serve with dipping sauce.

**PER SERVING:** 208 cal., 9 g total fat (3 g sat. fat), 53 mg chol., 398 mg sodium, 6 g carbo., 0 g fiber, 24 g pro.

## Herb-Pepper Sirloin Steak (30)

**MAKES:** 4 servings **PREP:** 10 minutes **BROIL:** 15 minutes

- 1 pound boneless beef top sirloin steak, cut 1 inch thick
- 1 tablespoon vegetable oil
- 1 tablespoon snipped fresh basil or 1 teaspoon dried basil, crushed
- 2 teaspoons snipped fresh rosemary or ½ teaspoon dried rosemary, crushed
- ½ teaspoon garlic salt
- ¼ teaspoon coarse ground black pepper
- ⅛ teaspoon ground cardamom (optional)

**1** Preheat broiler. Trim fat from steak. In a small bowl combine oil, basil, rosemary, garlic salt, pepper, and, if desired, cardamom. Spread oil mixture evenly over both sides of steak.
**2** Place steak on the unheated rack of a broiler pan. Broil 3 to 4 inches from the heat until desired doneness, turning once halfway through broiling. Allow 15 to 17 minutes for medium-rare doneness (145°) or 20 to 22 minutes for medium doneness (160°). Cut steak into 4 serving-size pieces.

**PER SERVING:** 171 cal., 7 g total fat (2 g sat. fat), 53 mg chol., 180 mg sodium, 0 g carbo., 0 g fiber, 24 g pro.

## Beef and Noodles

**MAKES:** 4 servings **PREP:** 30 minutes **COOK:** 1 hour 40 minutes

- 1 pound boneless beef round steak or chuck roast
- ¼ cup all-purpose flour
- 1 tablespoon vegetable oil
- ½ cup chopped onion (1 medium)
- 2 cloves garlic, minced
- 3 cups beef broth
- 1 teaspoon dried marjoram or basil, crushed
- ¼ teaspoon ground black pepper
- 8 ounces frozen noodles
- 2 tablespoons snipped fresh parsley

**1** Trim fat from meat. Cut meat into ¾-inch cubes. Pour flour into a large resealable plastic bag. Add meat to bag. Seal bag; shake to coat meat with the flour. In a large saucepan brown half of the meat in hot oil. Remove from saucepan. Brown the remaining meat with the onion and garlic, adding more oil if necessary. Drain off fat. Return all meat to the saucepan.
**2** Stir in broth, marjoram, and pepper. Bring to boiling; reduce heat. Simmer, covered, for 1¼ to 1½ hours or until meat is tender.
**3** Stir noodles into broth mixture. Bring to boiling; reduce heat. Cook, uncovered, for 25 to 30 minutes or until noodles are tender. To serve, sprinkle with parsley.

**PER SERVING:** 351 cal., 12 g total fat (3 g sat. fat), 94 mg chol., 677 mg sodium, 29 g carbo., 1 g fiber, 31 g pro.

## Broiled Sirloin with Simmered Vegetables

**MAKES:** 4 servings **START TO FINISH:** 1 hour

- 4 slices bacon
- 4 small onions, peeled and cut into 1-inch slices
- 8 small carrots, halved lengthwise
- 4 small red potatoes, cut up
- ½ cup beef broth
- ¼ cup beer or beef broth
- 1 tablespoon packed brown sugar
- 1 teaspoon dried thyme, crushed
- 1¼ pounds boneless beef top sirloin steak, cut 1½ to 2 inches thick
- ¼ teaspoon salt
- ¼ teaspoon ground black pepper
- Snipped fresh thyme (optional)

**1** In a 12-inch skillet cook bacon over medium heat until crisp. Remove from skillet; drain bacon on paper towels. Drain all but about 1 tablespoon of the drippings from the skillet.
**2** In the skillet cook onions in reserved dripping about 6 minutes or until brown, turning to brown evenly. Remove onions; set aside. Add carrots to skillet; cook about 5 minutes or until light brown, turning occasionally. Remove skillet from heat. Carefully add potatoes, broth, beer, brown sugar, and half of the dried thyme. Return onions to skillet. Return skillet to heat. Bring to boiling; reduce heat. Simmer, covered, for 30 to 35 minutes or until vegetables are tender.
**3** Preheat broiler. Season beef with remaining dried thyme, the salt, and pepper. Place meat on the unheated rack of broiler pan. Broil 4 to 5 inches from heat until desired doneness, turning once halfway through broiling. Allow 25 to 27 minutes for medium-rare (145°) or 30 to 32 minutes for medium (160°) doneness. Cut into 4 pieces.
**4** Using a slotted spoon, remove vegetables from skillet. Boil cooking liquid in skillet for 1 to 2 minutes or until slightly thickened. Divide steak, vegetables, and bacon among 4 plates. Spoon juices over. Sprinkle with fresh thyme.

**PER SERVING:** 396 cal., 12 g total fat (4 g sat. fat), 94 mg chol., 451 mg sodium, 33 g carbo., 5 g fiber, 36 g pro.

Broiled Sirloin with
Simmered Vegetables

Deviled Steak Strips

Hot cooked
rice or linguine

Honey-Balsamic
Beef Stir-Fry
[right]

Date-Ginger
Cake
[page 309]

## Deviled Steak Strips

**MAKES:** 2 or 3 servings **PREP:** 15 minutes
**COOK:** 6 to 8 hours (low) or 3 to 4 hours (high)

- **12 ounces boneless beef round steak**
- **1 8-ounce can tomato sauce**
- **½ cup chopped onion (1 medium)**
- **1 4-ounce can (drained weight) sliced mushrooms, drained**
- **¼ cup water**
- **1 tablespoon horseradish mustard**
- **1 tablespoon quick-cooking tapioca***
- **1 teaspoon instant beef bouillon granules**
- **⅛ teaspoon ground black pepper**
- **1 to 1½ cups hot mashed potatoes**
- **Sour cream (optional)**
- **Fresh snipped chives (optional)**

**1** If desired, partially freeze meat for easier slicing. Trim fat from meat. Thinly slice meat across the grain into bite-size strips. In a 1½-quart slow cooker combine tomato sauce, onion, mushrooms, the water, horseradish mustard, tapioca, bouillon granules, and pepper. Stir meat strips into onion mixture.

**2** Cover. If cooker has heat-setting choices, cook on low-heat setting for 6 to 8 hours or on high-heat setting for 3 to 4 hours. If cooker does not have heat-setting choices, cook for 5 to 6 hours. Serve over mashed potatoes. If desired, top with sour cream and chives.

***Note:** For a smoother sauce, grind the tapioca in a clean coffee grinder or blender.

**PER SERVING:** 407 cal., 9 g total fat (3 g sat. fat), 83 mg chol., 1,627 mg sodium, 36 g carbo., 5 g fiber, 43 g pro.

## Honey-Balsamic Beef Stir-Fry

**MAKES:** 4 servings **START TO FINISH:** 35 minutes

- **12 ounces beef sirloin or top round steak**
- **¾ cup beef broth**
- **3 tablespoons reduced-sodium soy sauce**
- **2 tablespoons balsamic vinegar**
- **2 tablespoons honey**
- **2 tablespoons cornstarch**
- **¼ teaspoon crushed red pepper**
- **2 tablespoons vegetable oil**
- **1 tablespoon finely chopped fresh ginger**
- **2 medium red sweet peppers, seeded and cut into bite-size strips**
- **1 medium red onion, cut into thin wedges**
- **4 cups thin strips bok choy or baby bok choy**
- **2 cups hot cooked rice or linguine**

**1** If desired, partially freeze meat for easier slicing. Trim fat from meat. Thinly slice meat across the grain into bite-size strips.

**2** For sauce, in a small bowl whisk together beef broth, soy sauce, vinegar, honey, cornstarch, and crushed red pepper. Set aside.

**3** In a very large skillet heat 1 tablespoon of the oil over medium-high heat. Add ginger; stir-fry for 15 seconds. Add sweet pepper and onion; stir-fry for 5 minutes. Add bok choy; stir-fry for 2 to 3 minutes more or until vegetables are crisp-tender. Remove vegetables from the skillet.

**4** Add the remaining 1 tablespoon oil to skillet; add meat to skillet. Stir-fry for 2 to 3 minutes or until meat is brown. Push the meat from the center of the skillet. Stir sauce until well mixed. Add the sauce to the center of the skillet. Cook and stir until thickened and bubbly. Return the cooked vegetables to the skillet. Stir all ingredients together to coat with sauce. Cook and stir for 1 minute more. Serve meat mixture over rice.

**Fast Honey-Balsamic Beef Stir-Fry:** Prepare as directed, except replace beef steak with one 12-ounce package beef stir-fry strips and replace sweet peppers, onion, and bok choy with one 16-ounce package frozen pepper (yellow, green, and red) and onion stir-fry vegetables. Cook and stir only 4 to 6 minutes or until crisp-tender. Remove vegetables from skillet, draining any excess liquid. Continue as directed in Step 4.

**PER SERVING:** 424 cal., 15 g total fat (4 g sat. fat), 42 mg chol., 713 mg sodium, 51 g carbo., 3 g fiber, 21 g pro.

## Lime Salsa Chops

**MAKES:** 6 servings **PREP:** 30 minutes **MARINATE:** 2 to 4 hours **GRILL:** 7 minutes

- 6 boneless pork top loin chops, cut ¾ inch thick
- ¼ cup finely chopped red onion
- ¼ cup lime juice
- 2 fresh serrano or jalapeño chile peppers, seeded and finely chopped (see note, page 182)
- 1 tablespoon toasted sesame oil
- 1 teaspoon cumin seeds, crushed
- 4 roma tomatoes, chopped
- 1 small cucumber, seeded and chopped
- ¼ cup sliced green onions (2)
- 2 tablespoons snipped fresh cilantro
- 1 tablespoon honey
- 3 tablespoons jalapeño pepper jelly

**1** Trim fat from chops. Place chops in a resealable plastic bag set in a shallow dish. For marinade, in a small bowl combine onion, lime juice, finely chopped chile peppers, sesame oil, and cumin seeds. Set aside 2 tablespoons of the marinade for salsa. Pour the remaining marinade over chops. Seal bag; turn to coat chops. Marinate in the refrigerator for 2 to 4 hours, turning bag occasionally.

**2** For salsa, in a medium bowl combine the 2 tablespoons reserved marinade, the tomatoes, cucumber, green onions, cilantro, and honey. Cover and refrigerate until ready to serve.

**3** Drain chops, reserving marinade. Transfer the marinade to a small saucepan. Add the jalapeño jelly to marinade; cook and stir until mixture boils. Set aside.

**4** For a charcoal grill, grill chops on the rack of an uncovered grill directly over medium coals for 7 to 9 minutes or until juices run clear (160°), turning once and brushing occasionally with jelly mixture during the last 5 minutes of grilling. (For a gas grill, preheat grill. Reduce heat to medium. Place chops on grill rack over heat. Cover and grill as above.) Serve the chops with salsa.

**Broiler method:** To broil, preheat broiler. Place chops on the unheated rack of a broiler pan. Broil 3 to 4 inches from

Lime Salsa Chops

the heat for 9 to 11 minutes or until juices run clear (160°), turning once and brushing occasionally with jelly mixture during the last 5 minutes of broiling.

**PER SERVING:** 211 cal., 10 g total fat (3 g sat. fat), 51 mg chol., 46 mg sodium, 14 g carbo., 1 g fiber, 17 g pro.

## Peppercorn Steaks

**MAKES:** 4 servings **START TO FINISH:** 35 minutes

- **2 6-ounce boneless beef ribeye steaks or beef top sirloin steaks, cut 1 inch thick**
- **1 tablespoon multicolor peppercorns, crushed**
- **½ teaspoon salt**
- **2 tablespoons butter or margarine, softened**
- **2 teaspoons mild-flavor molasses**
- **¼ teaspoon finely shredded lemon peel**
- **1 teaspoon lemon juice**
- **2 cups sugar snap peas**
- **½ cup carrot cut into thin bite-size strips**
- **Lemon peel strips (optional)**

**1** Preheat broiler. Trim fat from steaks. Sprinkle crushed peppercorns and salt evenly onto both sides of each steak; press in with your fingers.

**2** Place steaks on the unheated rack of a broiler pan. Broil 3 to 4 inches from the heat until desired doneness, turning once halfway through broiling time. For ribeye steaks, allow 12 to 14 minutes for medium-rare doneness (145°) or 15 to 18 minutes for medium doneness (160°). For sirloin steaks, allow 15 to 17 minutes for medium-rare doneness (145°) or 20 to 22 minutes for medium doneness (160°).

**3** Meanwhile, in a small bowl combine softened butter, molasses, finely shredded lemon peel, and lemon juice (mixture will appear curdled). Set aside.

**4** Remove strings and tips from peas. In a covered medium saucepan cook peas and carrot in a small amount of boiling salted water for 2 to 4 minutes or until crisp-tender. Drain well. Stir in 1 tablespoon of the molasses mixture.

**5** To serve, dot remaining molasses mixture evenly over steaks. Slice steaks and toss with vegetable mixture. If desired, garnish with lemon peel strips.

**PER SERVING:** 247 cal., 12 g total fat (6 g sat. fat), 66 mg chol., 418 mg sodium, 13 g carbo., 3 g fiber, 20 g pro.

Peppercorn Steaks

Peppercorn blends contain four types of dried pepper—black, white, green, and pink. Pink peppercorns aren't actually peppercorns though; but the dried berry of a type of rose. They have a mild, fruity flavor.

# Menu

Hearts of romaine with balsamic vinaigrette

Mashed potatoes

Swiss Steak [right]

Swiss Steak

# or a beef-and-veggie kabob.

Steak and Potato Kabobs

## Steak and Potato Kabobs

**MAKES:** 4 servings **PREP:** 30 minutes **MARINATE:** 4 to 6 hours
**GRILL:** 12 minutes

- **1 pound boneless beef sirloin steak, cut 1 inch thick**
- **¼ cup bottled red wine vinaigrette salad dressing**
- **2 tablespoons snipped fresh thyme or 2 teaspoons dried thyme, crushed**
- **2 tablespoons Worcestershire sauce**
- **¼ teaspoon garlic powder**
- **12 ounces tiny new potatoes, halved or quartered**
- **2 small green and/or yellow sweet peppers, seeded and cut into 1-inch squares**
- **1 medium red onion, cut into wedges**

**1** Trim fat from meat. Cut meat into 1-inch cubes. Place meat cubes in a resealable plastic bag set in a shallow dish. For marinade, in a small bowl combine salad dressing, thyme, Worcestershire sauce, and garlic powder. Pour marinade over meat. Seal bag; turn to coat meat. Marinate in the refrigerator for 4 to 6 hours, turning bag occasionally.
**2** Place twelve 10-inch wooden skewers in a shallow dish; add enough water to cover. Soak for 1 hour; drain. In a covered large saucepan cook potatoes in enough lightly salted boiling water to cover for 7 minutes; drain and cool.
**3** Drain steak, reserving marinade. On skewers, alternately thread meat, sweet pepper, onion, and potatoes.
**4** For a charcoal grill, grill skewers on the rack of an uncovered grill directly over medium coals until meat is desired doneness, turning once and brushing occasionally with reserved marinade up to the last 5 minutes of grilling. Allow 12 to 14 minutes for medium doneness (160°). Discard any remaining marinade. (For a gas grill, preheat grill. Reduce heat to medium. Place skewers on grill rack over heat. Cover and grill as above.)

**PER SERVING:** 289 cal., 10 g total fat (2 g sat. fat), 69 mg chol., 401 mg sodium, 22 g carbo., 3 g fiber, 26 g pro.

## Beef and Sweet Onion Sandwiches (30)

**MAKES:** 6 sandwiches **START TO FINISH:** 30 minutes

- **1 to 1½ pounds boneless beef sirloin or top round steak, cut 1 inch thick**
- **½ teaspoon coarse ground black pepper**
- **1 tablespoon vegetable oil**
- **½ of a large sweet onion (such as Vidalia or Walla Walla), sliced**
- **3 tablespoons Dijon-style mustard**
- **1 16-ounce loaf Italian flatbread (focaccia) or twelve 1-inch slices sourdough or marbled rye bread**
- **2 cups fresh spinach leaves or fresh basil leaves**
- **1 cup roasted red sweet peppers, drained and cut into ½-inch strips (about ½ of a 12-ounce jar)**

**1** Trim fat from steak. Sprinkle coarsely ground black pepper over both sides of the steak; press in with your fingers. In a large skillet cook steak in hot oil over medium heat for 15 to 20 minutes or until desired doneness (145° for medium-rare doneness to 160° for medium doneness), turning once halfway through cooking. Remove from skillet; keep warm.
**2** Add onion to drippings in skillet. Cook for 5 to 10 minutes or until onion is nearly tender, stirring occasionally. Stir in mustard; remove from heat.
**3** Meanwhile, if using focaccia bread, cut into 6 wedges; split each wedge in half horizontally. If using bread, toast bread if desired. To serve, cut steak into bite-size strips. Top bottom halves of the focaccia bread with spinach, steak strips, roasted pepper strips, onion mixture, and top halves of the focaccia bread.

**PER SANDWICH:** 335 cal., 8 g total fat (3 g sat. fat), 46 mg chol., 227 mg sodium, 41 g carbo., 4 g fiber, 26 g pro.

## Beef Roast with Tomato-Wine Gravy

**MAKES:** 6 servings **PREP:** 30 minutes
**COOK:** 10 to 12 hours (low) or 5 to 6 hours (high)

- **1 2- to 2½-pound beef chuck pot roast**
- **Nonstick cooking spray**
- **2 medium turnips, peeled and cut into 1-inch pieces (2 cups)**
- **3 medium carrots, cut into ½-inch pieces**
- **1 15-ounce can tomato sauce**
- **¼ cup dry red wine or reduced-sodium beef broth**
- **3 tablespoons quick-cooking tapioca**
- **¼ teaspoon salt**
- **⅛ teaspoon ground allspice**
- **⅛ teaspoon ground black pepper**
- **1 pound winter squash, peeled, seeded, and cut into thin wedges or 1½- to 2-inch pieces (2 cups)**

**1** Trim fat from roast. Coat a large nonstick skillet with cooking spray. Preheat skillet over medium heat. Brown roast on all sides in hot skillet.
**2** Meanwhile, in a 3½- or 4-quart slow cooker stir together turnip, carrot, tomato sauce, red wine or beef broth, tapioca, salt, allspice, and pepper. Place roast on top of vegetables. Place squash on top of roast. Cover and cook on low-heat setting for 10 to 12 hours or on high-heat setting for 5 to 6 hours.
**3** Transfer roast and vegetables to serving platter. Skim fat from tomato sauce mixture in slow cooker. Pass tomato sauce mixture with roast.

**PER SERVING:** 270 cal., 6 g total fat (2 g sat. fat), 89 mg chol., 576 mg sodium, 18 g carbo., 3 g fiber, 34 g pro.

## Mediterranean-Style Pot Roast

**MAKES:** 6 servings **PREP:** 20 minutes
**COOK:** 8 to 10 hours (low) or 4 to 5 hours (high)

- **1 2- to 3-pound boneless beef chuck pot roast**
- **1 tablespoon vegetable oil**
- **1 medium onion, sliced**
- **1 14.5-ounce can diced tomatoes with basil, oregano, and garlic, undrained**
- **¼ cup sliced pitted ripe olives**
- **1 tablespoon Worcestershire sauce**
- **2 teaspoons dried herbes de Provence, crushed**
- **1 teaspoon coarse ground black pepper**
- **½ cup crumbled feta cheese (2 ounces)**

**1** Trim fat from meat. If necessary, cut meat to fit into a 3½- or 4-quart slow cooker. In a large skillet brown meat on all sides in hot oil. Drain off fat. Set aside.
**2** Place onion in cooker. Add meat. In a medium bowl stir together undrained tomatoes, olives, Worcestershire sauce, herbes de Provence, and pepper. Pour over mixture in cooker.
**3** Cover and cook on low-heat setting for 8 to 10 hours or on high-heat setting for 4 to 5 hours.
**4** Remove meat from cooker; cut into 6 serving-size pieces and arrange on serving platter. Using a slotted spoon, transfer vegetables to platter, reserving juices. Spoon juices over meat and vegetables. Sprinkle with feta cheese.

**PER SERVING:** 274 cal., 10 g total fat (4 g sat. fat), 98 mg chol., 641 mg sodium, 9 g carbo., 1 g fiber, 35 g pro.

## Dilled Pot Roast

**MAKES:** 8 servings **PREP:** 20 minutes
**COOK:** 10 to 12 hours (low) or 5 to 6 hours (high)

- **1 2½- to 3-pound boneless beef chuck pot roast**
- **1 tablespoon vegetable oil**
- **½ cup water**
- **1 tablespoon snipped fresh dill or 1 teaspoon dried dill**
- **½ teaspoon ground black pepper**
- **¼ teaspoon salt**
- **½ cup plain low-fat yogurt**
- **2 tablespoons all-purpose flour**
- **4 cups hot cooked noodles**

**1** If necessary, cut roast to fit into a 3½- or 4-quart slow cooker. In a large skillet brown roast on all sides in hot oil. Transfer roast to slow cooker; add the water to cooker. Sprinkle roast with 2 teaspoons of the fresh dill or ¾ teaspoon of the dried dill, the pepper, and salt.

**2** Cover and cook on low-heat setting for 10 to 12 hours or on high-heat setting for 5 to 6 hours. Transfer roast to a serving platter, reserving juices; cover roast and keep warm. Pour cooking juices into a glass measuring cup; skim off fat. Measure 1 cup of the reserved juices.

**3** For sauce, in a small saucepan stir together yogurt and flour until combined. Stir in the 1 cup reserved cooking juices and the remaining 1 teaspoon fresh dill or ¼ teaspoon dried dill. Cook and stir over low to medium heat until thickened and bubbly. Cook and stir for 1 minute more. Serve sauce with meat and noodles.

**PER SERVING:** 313 cal., 8 g total fat (2 g sat. fat), 111 mg chol., 185 mg sodium, 22 g carbo., 1 g fiber, 35 g pro.

## Southwestern Tri-Tip Roast

**MAKES:** 6 to 8 servings **PREP:** 15 minutes **CHILL:** 6 to 24 hours **ROAST:** 30 minutes **STAND:** 15 minutes **OVEN:** 425°

- 1 tablespoon dried chipotle chile peppers, seeded and finely chopped (about 2 teaspoons) (see note, page 182)
- 1 tablespoon snipped fresh oregano or 1 teaspoon dried oregano, crushed
- 1 tablespoon olive oil
- 1 teaspoon ground cumin
- 2 cloves garlic, minced
- ½ teaspoon salt
- 1 1½- to 2-pound boneless beef tri-tip roast (bottom sirloin)

**1** For rub, in a small bowl combine chile peppers, oregano, oil, cumin, garlic, and salt. Spread onto roast, rubbing in with glove-covered hands. Cover and chill in the refrigerator for 6 to 24 hours.

**2** Preheat oven to 425°. Place meat on a rack in a shallow roasting pan. Insert an oven-going meat thermometer into center of roast. Roast until desired doneness. Allow 30 to 35 minutes for medium-rare doneness (135°) or 40 to 45 minutes for medium doneness (150°). Cover with foil and let stand for 15 minutes. The temperature of the meat after standing should be 145° for medium-rare or 160° for medium doneness.

**PER SERVING:** 156 cal., 7 g total fat (2 g sat. fat), 45 mg chol., 248 mg sodium, 1 g carbo., 0 g fiber, 21 g pro.

Southwestern Tri-Tip Roast

## Oven-Barbecued Beef Brisket

**MAKES:** 10 to 12 servings **PREP:** 15 minutes **BAKE:** 3 hours **OVEN:** 325°

- 1 3- to 3½-pound fresh beef brisket
- ¾ cup water
- ½ cup chopped onion (1 medium)
- 3 tablespoons Worcestershire sauce
- 2 tablespoons cider vinegar or white wine vinegar
- 1 tablespoon chili powder
- 2 cloves garlic, minced
- 1 teaspoon instant beef bouillon granules
- ⅛ teaspoon cayenne pepper
- 1½ cups barbecue sauce

**1** Preheat oven to 325°. Trim fat from meat. Place meat in a 13×9×2-inch baking pan. In a small bowl stir together the water, onion, Worcestershire sauce, vinegar, chili powder, garlic, bouillon granules, and cayenne pepper. Pour over meat. Cover with foil.

**2** Bake about 3 hours or until tender, turning once. Remove meat; discard juices. Thinly slice meat across the grain. Place on a serving platter. Serve with barbecue sauce.

**PER SERVING:** 244 cal., 7 g total fat (2 g sat. fat), 78 mg chol., 735 mg sodium, 13 g carbo., 0 g fiber, 29 g pro.

## Gyro Burgers

**MAKES:** 4 servings **PREP:** 20 minutes **GRILL:** 14 minutes

- 1 egg, beaten
- ¼ cup fine dry bread crumbs
- 2 tablespoons plain low-fat yogurt
- 1 clove garlic, minced
- ¼ teaspoon salt
- ¼ teaspoon ground cumin
- ⅛ teaspoon ground black pepper
- 1 pound lean ground lamb or ground beef
- 4 large pita bread rounds
- ½ of a medium cucumber, thinly sliced
- ¼ cup plain low-fat yogurt
- ½ cup chopped tomato (1 medium)

**1** In a medium bowl combine egg, bread crumbs, the 2 tablespoons yogurt, the garlic, salt, cumin, and pepper. Add meat; mix well. Shape meat mixture into four

"Scaloppine" is an Italian termw that refers to a thin scallop of meat. Pounding the meat thin tenderizes it and makes it cook quickly. The same technique can be applied to beef, pork, chicken, and turkey. Be sure to always pound from the center out to the edges to make it even.

¾-inch-thick oblong patties. If meat mixture is sticky, use wet hands to shape.

**2** For a charcoal grill, grill patties on the rack of an uncovered grill directly over medium heat for 14 to 18 minutes or until internal temperature of each patty registers 160° on an instant-read thermometer, turning once halfway through grilling. (For a gas grill, preheat grill. Reduce heat to medium. Place patties on grill rack over heat. Cover and grill as above.)

**3** Serve in pitas lined with cucumber slices and topped with yogurt and tomato.

**PER SERVING:** 556 cal., 29 g total fat (12 g sat. fat), 137 mg chol., 625 mg sodium, 43 g carbo., 2 g fiber, 29 g pro.

## Veal Scaloppine

**MAKES:** 4 servings **START TO FINISH:** 35 minutes

- **12 ounces boneless veal leg round steak or veal leg sirloin steak, cut ¼ inch thick**
- **¼ teaspoon salt**
- **¼ teaspoon ground black pepper**
- **½ cup chopped onion (1 medium)**
- **¼ cup water**
- **2 cloves garlic, minced**
- **1 14.5-ounce can no-salt-added diced tomatoes, undrained**
- **3 tablespoons dry white wine or reduced-sodium chicken broth**
- **1 tablespoon snipped fresh oregano or 1 teaspoon dried oregano, crushed**
- **1 tablespoon capers, rinsed and drained (optional)**
- **Nonstick cooking spray**
- **2 cups hot cooked whole wheat pasta**

**1** Trim fat from meat; cut meat into 8 pieces. Place each piece of meat between 2 pieces of plastic wrap. Working from center to edges, pound with flat side of a meat mallet to about an ⅛-inch thickness. Remove plastic wrap. Sprinkle meat with salt and half of the pepper. Set aside.

**2** For sauce, in a medium saucepan combine onion, the water, and garlic. Cook, covered, until onion is tender. Stir in undrained tomatoes, wine, oregano, capers (if using), and the remaining pepper. Bring to boiling; reduce heat. Simmer, uncovered, about 15 minutes or until desired consistency. Keep warm.

**3** Meanwhile, lightly coat a large skillet with cooking spray. Preheat over medium-high heat. Cook veal, half at a time, in hot skillet for 2 to 4 minutes or until desired doneness, turning once halfway through cooking.

**4** Serve sauce over veal with hot cooked pasta.

**PER SERVING:** 219 cal., 2 g total fat (1 g sat. fat), 66 mg chol., 244 mg sodium, 26 g carbo., 4 g fiber, 23 g pro.

Mustard-Rosemary Grilled Lamb

## Mustard-Rosemary Grilled Lamb

**MAKES:** 4 servings **PREP:** 20 minutes **CHILL:** 2 to 3 hours
**GRILL:** 12 minutes

- 8 lamb rib or loin chops, cut 1 inch thick (about 2 pounds)
- ¼ cup stoneground mustard
- ¼ cup thinly sliced green onion (2)
- 2 tablespoons dry white wine
- 1 tablespoon balsamic vinegar or rice vinegar
- 3 cloves garlic, minced
- 1 teaspoon snipped fresh rosemary
- 1 teaspoon honey
- ½ teaspoon salt
- ½ teaspoon freshly ground black pepper

**1** Trim fat from chops; set chops aside. In a small bowl stir together mustard, green onions, wine, vinegar, garlic, rosemary, honey, salt, and pepper. Spread mixture evenly over all sides of chops. Place chops on a large plate; cover loosely with plastic wrap. Chill in the refrigerator for 2 to 3 hours.

**2** For a charcoal grill, grill chops on the rack of an uncovered grill directly over medium coals until desired doneness, turning once halfway through grilling. Allow 12 to 14 minutes for medium-rare doneness (145°) or 15 to 17 minutes for medium doneness (160°).

**PER SERVING:** 194 cal., 9 g total fat (3 g sat. fat), 64 mg chol., 557 mg sodium, 4 g carbo., 0 g fiber, 21 g pro.

## Mediterranean Lamb Chops (30)

**MAKES:** 6 servings **START TO FINISH:** 30 minutes

- 6 lamb loin chops, cut 1½ inches thick
- 2 teaspoons vegetable oil
- 1 cup red onion cut into thin wedges
- 1 26- to 28-ounce jar garlic and onion pasta sauce
- 1 19-ounce can cannellini beans (white kidney beans), rinsed and drained
- ½ cup pitted kalamata olives, halved
- ½ cup roasted red sweet peppers, cut into strips
- 2 tablespoons balsamic vinegar
- 2 teaspoons snipped fresh rosemary
- Hot cooked orzo pasta or rice

**1** Trim fat from chops. In a 10-inch skillet cook chops in hot oil over medium heat for 11 to 13 minutes or until medium doneness (160°), turning once halfway through cooking. Transfer chops to a large bowl or platter; cover with foil to keep warm.

**2** In the same skillet cook onion in drippings over medium heat until tender. Add pasta sauce, beans, olives, roasted peppers, balsamic vinegar, and rosemary. Cook and stir over medium heat until heated through. Add chops to skillet; cover and heat through for 3 minutes.

**3** Serve lamb chops and sauce over hot cooked orzo or rice.

**Slow cooker method:** Arrange lamb chops on the bottom of a 4- to 5-quart slow cooker. In a medium bowl combine pasta sauce, beans, red onion, olives, roasted peppers, balsamic vinegar, and rosemary. Pour over lamb chops in slow cooker. Cover and cook on low-heat setting for 5 to 6 hours or on high-heat setting for 2½ to 3 hours.

**PER SERVING:** 410 cal., 11 g total fat (3 g sat. fat), 40 mg chol., 798 mg sodium, 58 g carbo., 9 g fiber, 22 g pro.

Greek Lamb Salad
with Yogurt Dressing

## Greek Lamb Salad with Yogurt Dressing (30)

**MAKES:** 4 servings **START TO FINISH:** 30 minutes

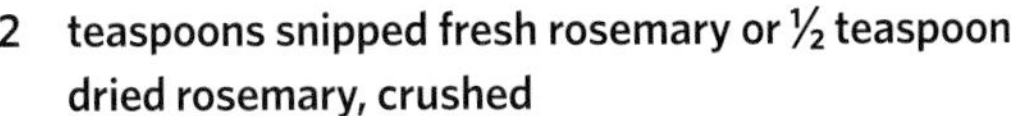
- 2 teaspoons snipped fresh rosemary or ½ teaspoon dried rosemary, crushed
- 1 clove garlic, minced
- 8 ounces boneless lamb leg sirloin chops, cut ½ inch thick
- 8 cups torn fresh spinach or torn mixed salad greens
- 1 15-ounce can garbanzo beans (chickpeas), rinsed and drained
- ¼ cup chopped seeded cucumber
- ½ cup plain low-fat yogurt
- ¼ cup chopped green onions (2)
- 1 clove garlic, minced
- ⅛ to ¼ teaspoon salt
- ⅛ teaspoon ground black pepper
- ¼ cup dried tart cherries or golden raisins

**1** Preheat broiler. In a small bowl combine the rosemary and 1 clove garlic. Sprinkle mixture evenly over all sides of the lamb chops; rub in with your fingers. Place chops on the unheated rack of a broiler pan. Broil 4 to 5 inches from the heat for 12 to 15 minutes, turning once halfway through broiling. Cut lamb chops into thin bite-size slices.

**2** Meanwhile, on a serving platter toss together spinach, garbanzo beans, and cucumber. Arrange lamb slices over spinach mixture.

**3** For dressing, in a small bowl combine yogurt, green onions, 1 clove garlic, salt, and pepper. Drizzle dressing over salad. Sprinkle with cherries.

**PER SERVING:** 243 cal., 6 g total fat (2 g sat. fat), 36 mg chol., 569 mg sodium, 29 g carbo., 8 g fiber, 20 g pro.

## Pork Medallions with Pear-Maple Sauce (30)

**MAKES:** 4 servings **START TO FINISH:** 30 minutes

- 1 12- to 16-ounce pork tenderloin
- 2 teaspoons snipped fresh rosemary or ½ teaspoon dried rosemary, crushed
- 1 teaspoon snipped fresh thyme or ¼ teaspoon dried thyme, crushed
- ¼ teaspoon salt
- ¼ teaspoon ground black pepper
- 1 tablespoon olive oil or vegetable oil
- 2 medium pears, peeled and coarsely chopped
- ¼ cup pure maple syrup or maple-flavor syrup
- 2 tablespoons dried tart red cherries, halved
- 2 tablespoons dry white wine or apple juice

**1** Trim fat from meat. Cut meat into ¼-inch slices. In a medium bowl combine rosemary, thyme, salt, and pepper. Add meat slices; toss to coat. In a large skillet cook meat, half at a time, in hot oil for 2 to 3 minutes or until meat is slightly pink in center, turning once. Remove meat from skillet; set aside.

**2** In the same skillet combine pears, maple syrup, dried cherries, and white wine. Bring to boiling; reduce heat. Boil gently, uncovered, about 3 minutes or just until pears are tender. Return meat to skillet with pears; heat through.

**3** To serve, use a slotted spoon to transfer meat to a warm serving platter. Spoon the pear mixture over meat.

**PER SERVING:** 255 cal., 7 g total fat (2 g sat. fat), 60 mg chol., 179 mg sodium, 29 g carbo., 3 g fiber, 19 g pro.

# Menu

Poached pears

Sliced roasted beets

Pork Chops with Raspberry-Dressed Spinach
[below]

Frozen vanilla yogurt

## Pork Chops with Raspberry-Dressed Spinach

**MAKES:** 4 servings **START TO FINISH:** 25 minutes

- 2 boneless pork loin chops, cut ¾ inch thick (about 12 ounces total)
- ¼ teaspoon salt
- ¼ teaspoon ground ginger
- ⅛ teaspoon ground black pepper
- 1 teaspoon vegetable oil
- 2 cloves garlic, minced
- ½ cup sugar snap peas
- ⅓ cup sliced fresh mushrooms
- ⅔ cup bottled reduced-fat raspberry vinaigrette salad dressing
- ½ cup fresh raspberries
- 8 cups torn fresh spinach and/or romaine or purchased torn mixed salad greens

**1** Trim fat from chops. Sprinkle all sides of chops with salt, ginger, and pepper. In a large nonstick skillet cook chops in hot oil over medium heat for 8 to 12 minutes or until juices run clear (160°), turning once halfway through cooking. Remove chops from skillet, reserving drippings. Cover chops; keep warm.
**2** In the same skillet cook and stir garlic in reserved drippings for 30 seconds. Add sugar snap peas and mushrooms to skillet. Pour raspberry vinaigrette dressing over all. Cook, covered, for 2 to 3 minutes or until heated through. Remove from heat. Gently stir in raspberries; set aside and keep warm.
**3** Divide spinach evenly among 4 dinner plates. Thinly slice pork. Arrange pork on spinach. Pour warm raspberry mixture over all.

**PER SERVING:** 248 cal., 12 g total fat (2 g sat. fat), 46 mg chol., 617 mg sodium, 12 g carbo., 7 g fiber, 21 g pro.

Pork Soft Shell Tacos

## Pork Soft Shell Tacos

**MAKES:** 4 servings **START TO FINISH:** 25 minutes

- 8 ounces boneless pork loin
- 2 teaspoons vegetable oil
- ¼ cup light sour cream
- ¼ teaspoon chipotle chili powder, crushed dried chipotle chile pepper, or chili powder
- 4 6-inch flour tortillas, warmed if desired*
- ½ cup shredded lettuce
- ½ cup diced tomato (1 medium)
- ½ cup shredded reduced-fat cheddar cheese (2 ounces)
- Salsa

**1** If desired, partially freeze meat for easier slicing. Trim fat from meat. Thinly slice meat across the grain into bite-size strips. In a large skillet cook meat in hot oil over medium-high heat until brown; set aside.
**2** In a small bowl combine sour cream and chipotle chili powder, chipotle pepper, or chili powder; set aside.
**3** Spoon one-fourth of the meat onto each tortilla just below the center. Top meat with lettuce, tomato, and cheese. Fold top half of each tortilla over filling. Serve with sour cream mixture and salsa.
***Note:** To warm tortillas, preheat oven to 350°. Wrap tortillas in foil. Bake for 10 to 15 minutes or until warmed.

**PER SERVING:** 240 cal., 11 g total fat (4 g sat. fat), 48 mg chol., 263 mg sodium, 14 g carbo., 1 g fiber, 19 g pro.

## Tangy Stir-Fried Pork (30)

**MAKES:** 4 servings **START TO FINISH:** 25 minutes

- 12 ounces pork tenderloin
- 1 teaspoon vegetable oil
- ¼ cup dry white wine or reduced-sodium chicken broth
- ¼ of an orange, thinly sliced and seeds removed
- 2 tablespoons bottled hoisin sauce
- 3 green onions, bias-sliced into ¼-inch pieces
- 1 teaspoon sesame seeds, toasted
- 3 cups hot cooked brown rice

**1** If desired, partially freeze meat for easier slicing. Trim fat from meat. Thinly slice meat across the grain into ¼-inch slices. Set aside.

**2** Pour oil in a wok or large nonstick skillet; heat over medium-high heat. (Add more oil as necessary during cooking.) Add meat; cook and stir about 3 minutes or until cooked through. Remove from wok.

**3** Add wine, orange, and hoisin sauce to wok. Cook and stir for 1 minute.

**4** Return pork to wok. Heat through. Stir in green onions and sesame seeds. Serve over hot cooked rice.

**PER SERVING:** 306 cal., 5 g total fat (1 g sat. fat), 56 mg chol., 184 mg sodium, 39 g carbo., 3 g fiber, 22 g pro.

Tangy Stir-Fried Pork

## Pork Lo Mein

**MAKES:** 6 servings **START TO FINISH:** 50 minutes

- 1¼ to 1½ pounds lean boneless pork or boneless beef top round steak
- 10 ounces dried Chinese egg noodles, spaghetti, or angel hair pasta
- ¼ cup oyster sauce
- ¼ cup reduced-sodium soy sauce
- 2 tablespoons rice wine or dry sherry
- 1 tablespoon vegetable oil
- 1 tablespoon toasted sesame oil
- 2 teaspoons finely chopped fresh ginger
- 1 medium red onion, halved lengthwise and thinly sliced
- 8 ounces fresh mushrooms, sliced
- 2 cups pea pods, halved

**1** If desired, partially freeze meat for easier slicing. Trim fat from meat. Thinly slice meat across the grain into bite-size strips; set aside. Cook noodles or pasta according to package directions until tender; drain. Rinse with cold water; drain well. Set noodles aside. For sauce, in a small bowl stir together oyster sauce, soy sauce, and rice wine. Set aside.

**2** In a large nonstick skillet combine vegetable oil and sesame oil. Heat over medium-high heat. Add ginger; cook and stir for 30 seconds. Add the onion; cook and stir for 2 minutes. Add mushrooms; cook and stir for 2 minutes. Add pea pods; cook and stir for 1 minute. (If necessary, add more oil during cooking.) Remove vegetables from skillet.

**3** Add half of the meat to skillet; cook and stir for 3 to 4 minutes or until no longer pink. Remove from skillet. Repeat with remaining meat. Return all meat to skillet. Add the cooked noodles, vegetables, and sauce. Using 2 spatulas or wooden spoons, lightly toss the mixture about 3 minutes or until heated through. Transfer to a serving platter. Serve immediately.

**PER SERVING:** 408 cal., 11 g total fat (3 g sat. fat), 52 mg chol., 718 mg sodium, 44 g carbo., 3 g fiber, 30 g pro.

How do you get such delicate, thin strips of meat? Partially freeze the meat before slicing.

Pork Lo Mein

Curried Pork and Rice

# Spice your supper with curry.

## Curried Pork and Rice

**MAKES:** 4 servings **PREP:** 25 minutes **BAKE:** 45 minutes
**STAND:** 5 minutes **OVEN:** 350°

- 12 ounces boneless pork loin
- 1 teaspoon vegetable oil
- 2 cups fat-free milk
- 2 tablespoons all-purpose flour
- 1½ teaspoons curry powder
- ¼ teaspoon salt
- ¾ cup instant brown rice
- 1 medium green apple (such as Granny Smith), cored and chopped
- ½ cup coarsely shredded carrot (1 medium)
- 3 green onions, bias-sliced
- 2 tablespoons chopped peanuts
- 2 tablespoons snipped fresh cilantro

**1** Preheat oven to 350°. If desired, partially freeze meat for easier slicing. Trim fat from meat. Thinly slice meat across the grain into bite-size strips. In a large nonstick skillet cook meat in hot oil over medium heat for 3 to 5 minutes or until done. Drain off fat. Set aside.
**2** In a screw-top jar combine ½ cup of the milk, the flour, curry powder, and salt; cover and shake until well mixed. Transfer to a medium saucepan; add the remaining 1½ cups milk. Cook and stir over medium heat until thickened and bubbly. Stir in cooked meat, uncooked rice, apple, carrot, and green onions. Transfer to a 1½-quart casserole. Place casserole on a baking sheet.
**3** Bake, covered, about 45 minutes or until rice is tender and most of the liquid is absorbed. Let stand, covered, on a wire rack for 5 minutes. Sprinkle with peanuts and cilantro before serving.

**PER SERVING:** 275 cal., 7 g total fat (2 g sat. fat), 56 mg chol., 289 mg sodium, 27 g carbo., 3 g fiber, 25 g pro.

## Lime Jerked Pork Tenderloins

**MAKES:** 12 servings **PREP:** 20 minutes **MARINATE:** 1 to 2 hours
**GRILL:** 30 minutes **STAND:** 10 minutes

- 3 tablespoons finely shredded lime peel
- ¾ cup lime juice
- ¼ cup packed brown sugar
- 3 tablespoons Jamaican jerk seasoning
- 3 tablespoons canola oil
- 4 cloves garlic, minced
- ½ to ¾ teaspoon cayenne pepper
- 3 1¼-pound pork tenderloins

**1** For marinade, in a small bowl combine lime peel, lime juice, brown sugar, jerk seasoning, oil, garlic, and cayenne pepper. Place pork in a 3-quart rectangular baking dish or a large resealable plastic bag set in a shallow dish. Pour marinade over pork. Cover dish, if using, or seal bag. Marinate in the refrigerator for 1 to 2 hours, turning pork or bag occasionally. Drain pork, discarding marinade.
**2** For a charcoal grill, arrange hot coals around a drip pan. Test for medium-hot heat above pan. Place meat on grill rack over the drip pan. Cover and grill for 30 to 35 minutes or until internal temperature of each tenderloin registers 155° on an instant-read thermometer. (For a gas grill, preheat grill. Reduce heat to medium-high. Adjust for indirect cooking. Place meat on rack in a roasting pan; place on grill rack over unlit side. Grill as above.) Let stand for 10 minutes. The temperature of the meat after standing should be 160°.

**PER SERVING:** 170 cal., 4 g total fat (1 g sat. fat), 92 mg chol., 136 mg sodium, 2 g carbo., 0 g fiber, 30 g pro.

Lime Jerked Pork Tenderloins

Stuffed Pork Loin

Pinwheeling the roast for this spiraled Stuffed Pork Loin involves rotating the roast as you cut it lengthwise. It's not difficult to do, but if you are intimidated by the prospect, you can ask the butcher to do it. Watch how he does it so you'll know the next time!

## Stuffed Pork Loin

**MAKES:** 12 servings **PREP:** 40 minutes
**ROAST:** 1 hour 40 minutes **STAND:** 15 minutes **OVEN:** 325°

- 3 ounces fresh spinach, coarsely chopped
- 1 tablespoon olive oil
- ¾ cup cooked wild rice
- ½ cup chopped dried tart cherries
- ⅓ cup chopped pecans
- ¾ teaspoon salt
- ¾ teaspoon dried sage, crushed
- ¼ teaspoon ground black pepper
- 1 3½-pound boneless pork center loin roast
- ½ teaspoon salt
- ½ teaspoon ground black pepper
- ¼ teaspoon dried sage, ground
- ⅛ teaspoon dried thyme, ground
- ½ cup apricot jam
- 3 tablespoons water

**1** In a large skillet cook spinach in hot oil until wilted. In a medium bowl combine cooked spinach, cooked wild rice, dried cherries, pecans, the ¾ teaspoon salt, the ¾ teaspoon sage, and the ¼ teaspoon pepper; set aside.

**2** Preheat oven to 325°. Trim excess fat from meat. To pinwheel the pork loin, start cutting lengthwise ½ inch under the fat cap on the roast. As you cut the roast, gently rotate the roast at the same time. This will allow the roast to unroll as you cut it. When the roast is completely cut, it should be a rectangular piece of meat between ½ and 1 inch thick.

**3** Sprinkle the cut surface of the meat rectangle with the ½ teaspoon salt, the ½ teaspoon pepper, the ¼ teaspoon sage, and the thyme. Spread the spinach mixture on the cut side of the meat. Roll up the meat tightly to resemble the initial roast. Tie securely with clean 100-percent-cotton kitchen string.

**4** Place the meat on a rack in a roasting pan; insert an oven-going meat thermometer into the thickest part of the meat. Roast for 1½ to 1¾ hours or until meat thermometer registers 140°.

**5** Meanwhile, in a small saucepan combine apricot jam and the water. Cook and stir until jam melts.

**6** Remove meat from oven and brush on about half of the jam mixture. Return to oven. Roast for 10 to 15 minutes more or until meat thermometer registers 150°. Remove from oven; brush with the remaining jam mixture. Cover and let stand for 15 minutes in a warm place before carving. The temperature of the meat after standing should be 160°.

**PER SERVING:** 330 cal., 12 g total fat (3 g sat. fat), 73 mg chol., 315 mg sodium, 23 g carbo., 2 g fiber, 31 g pro.

Pork Tenderloin with Pears and Barley

## Pork Tenderloin with Pears and Barley

**MAKES:** 4 to 6 servings **PREP:** 25 minutes **ROAST:** 25 minutes
**STAND:** 15 minutes **OVEN:** 425°

- **1 1-pound pork tenderloin**
- **2 tablespoons snipped fresh sage**
- **2 cloves garlic, minced**
- **¼ teaspoon salt**
- **¼ teaspoon ground black pepper**
- **6 ounces red boiling onions, peeled and halved (about 6)**
- **2 medium red and/or yellow sweet peppers, seeded and cut into bite-size pieces**
- **¼ cup balsamic vinegar**
- **1 29-ounce can pear halves in light syrup**
- **1 cup quick-cooking barley**
- **2 teaspoons snipped fresh sage**
- **½ teaspoon salt**

**1** Preheat oven to 425°. Starting on a long side, split pork tenderloin in half lengthwise, cutting almost to the opposite side. In a small bowl combine the 2 tablespoons sage, the garlic, the ¼ teaspoon salt, and the black pepper. Sprinkle mixture onto cut surfaces of pork; pat in with your fingers. Fold cut sides together; place meat in a 13×9×2-inch baking pan. Arrange onions and sweet peppers around pork.

**2** Drizzle vinegar over pork and vegetables. Roast for 15 minutes. Meanwhile, drain pears, reserving syrup. Halve each pear half; add pears to roasting pan with vegetables. Stir gently to coat with vinegar. Roast for 10 to 20 minutes more or until internal temperature of tenderloin registers 155° on an instant-read thermometer. Cover and let stand for 15 minutes. The temperature of the meat after standing should be 160°.

**3** Meanwhile, add enough water to the reserved pear syrup to measure 2 cups total liquid. In a medium saucepan combine syrup mixture, barley, the 2 teaspoons sage, and the ½ teaspoon salt. Bring to boiling; reduce heat. Simmer, covered, for 10 to 12 minutes or until barley is tender and most of the liquid is absorbed. Spoon barley onto a serving platter. Slice meat; arrange on top of barley. Using a slotted spoon, transfer vegetables and pears to platter. Serve with pan juices.

**PER SERVING:** 434 cal., 4 g total fat (1 g sat. fat), 73 mg chol., 499 mg sodium, 71 g carbo., 9 g fiber, 29 g pro.

# Pork lends itself beautifully

Roast Pork Salad with Ginger-Pineapple Dressing

## Roast Pork Salad with Ginger-Pineapple Dressing

**MAKES:** 4 servings **PREP:** 25 minutes **ROAST:** 25 minutes
**STAND:** 5 minutes **OVEN:** 425°

- 1 12-ounce pork tenderloin
- ⅛ teaspoon salt
- ⅛ teaspoon ground black pepper
- 2 tablespoons honey mustard
- 6 cups torn romaine and/or fresh spinach
- 2 cups fresh or canned pineapple chunks* and/or sliced fresh nectarines or peaches
- Cracked black pepper (optional)
- 1 recipe Ginger-Pineapple Dressing

**1** Preheat oven to 425°. Trim fat from meat; sprinkle with salt and ground black pepper. Place meat on a rack in a shallow roasting pan. Roast for 20 minutes.

**2** Spoon honey mustard onto pork. Roast for 5 to 15 minutes or until internal temperature of tenderloin registers 160° on an instant-read thermometer. Cover and let stand for 5 minutes.

**3** To serve, thinly slice pork. In 4 salad bowls or plates arrange greens, pork, and fruit. If desired, sprinkle salads with cracked black pepper. Stir Ginger-Pineapple Dressing; drizzle over salads.

**Ginger-Pineapple Dressing:** In a small bowl combine ¼ cup low-fat mayonnaise dressing, ¼ cup unsweetened pineapple juice or orange juice, 1 tablespoon honey mustard, and 1 teaspoon grated fresh ginger. Cover; chill until serving time or up to 24 hours.

***Note:** If you use fresh pineapple, cut it up over a bowl and save the juice for the dressing.

**PER SERVING:** 240 cal., 8 g total fat (2 g sat. fat), 60 mg chol., 219 mg sodium, 22 g carbo., 3 g fiber, 19 g pro.

## Pork Chops with Chili-Apricot Glaze (30)

**MAKES:** 4 servings **PREP:** 10 minutes **BROIL:** 9 minutes

- ¼ cup apricot jam or preserves
- ¼ cup chili sauce
- 1 tablespoon sweet-hot mustard or brown mustard
- 1 tablespoon water
- 4 boneless pork loin chops, cut 1 inch thick

**1** Preheat broiler. For the glaze, cut up any large pieces of fruit in jam. In a small saucepan combine jam, chili sauce, mustard, and the water. Cook and stir over medium-low heat until heated through. Remove from heat.

**2** Trim fat from chops. Place chops on the unheated rack of a broiler pan. Broil 3 to 4 inches from heat for 9 to 11 minutes or until juices run clear (160°), turning once halfway through broiling and brushing generously with glaze during the last 2 to 3 minutes of broiling. Spoon any remaining glaze over chops before serving.

**PER SERVING:** 307 cal., 8 g total fat (3 g sat. fat), 106 mg chol., 331 mg sodium, 17 g carbo., 1 g fiber, 38 g pro.

# Menu

Barley Waldorf Salad
[page 270]

Shredded Pork Sandwiches
[below]

Double Chocolate Brownies
[page 286]

Shredded Pork Sandwiches

Pork shoulder (also called Boston butt) is a great choice for feeding a crowd. It's one of the most economical cuts of meat because it tends to be tough. Slow, moist cooking makes it meltingly tender.

## Shredded Pork Sandwiches

**MAKES:** 16 sandwiches **PREP:** 20 minutes
**COOK:** 8 to 10 hours (low) or 4 to 5 hours (high)

- **1½ teaspoons garlic powder**
- **1½ teaspoons onion powder**
- **1½ teaspoons ground black pepper**
- **1 teaspoon celery salt**
- **1 3-pound boneless pork shoulder roast**
- **2 large onions, cut into thin wedges**
- **½ cup water**
- **2 cups packaged shredded broccoli (broccoli slaw mix)**
- **1 cup light mayonnaise or salad dressing**
- **16 whole grain hamburger buns**

**1** In a small bowl stir together garlic powder, onion powder, pepper, and celery salt. Trim fat from roast. Sprinkle pepper mixture evenly over roast; rub in with your fingers. If necessary, cut meat to fit into a 3½- or 4-quart slow cooker.
**2** Place onion in the bottom of the slow cooker. Add roast. Pour the water over roast.
**3** Cover and cook on low-heat setting for 8 to 10 hours or on high-heat setting for 4 to 5 hours. Remove roast and onions from cooker to a cutting board; discard cooking liquid. Using 2 forks, pull meat and onions apart into shreds. Return meat and onions to slow cooker to keep warm.
**4** In a small bowl combine shredded broccoli and ¼ cup of the mayonnaise. Spread bottoms of the buns with the remaining ¾ cup mayonnaise. Place meat mixture on bottoms of buns. Top with broccoli mixture; replace tops of buns.

**PER SANDWICH:** 270 cal., 10 g total fat (3 g sat. fat), 55 mg chol., 500 mg sodium, 24 g carbo., 2 g fiber, 22 g pro.

## Chipotle Baby Back Ribs

**MAKES:** 8 servings **PREP:** 20 minutes **BROIL:** 10 minutes
**COOK:** 6 to 7 hours (low) or 3 to 3½ hours (high) + 15 minutes

- **3 pounds pork loin back ribs or meaty pork spareribs**
- **¾ cup no-salt-added tomato sauce**
- **½ cup barbecue sauce**
- **2 canned chipotle chile peppers in adobo sauce, seeded and finely chopped***
- **2 tablespoons cornstarch**
- **2 tablespoons cold water**
- **Shredded cabbage with carrot (coleslaw mix) and/or thinly sliced fresh jalapeño chile peppers* (optional)**

**1** Preheat broiler. Cut ribs into 2-rib portions. Place ribs on the unheated rack of a broiler pan. Broil 6 inches from the heat about 10 minutes or until brown, turning once.** Transfer ribs to a 4- to 5-quart slow cooker.

**2** In a medium bowl combine tomato sauce, barbecue sauce, and chipotle chile peppers. Pour over ribs in cooker.

**3** Cover and cook on low-heat setting for 6 to 7 hours or on high-heat setting for 3 to 3½ hours.

**4** Transfer ribs to a serving platter, reserving cooking liquid. Cover ribs to keep warm. Skim the fat from the cooking liquid.

**5** If using low-heat setting, turn to high-heat setting. In a small bowl combine cornstarch and the cold water. Stir into liquid in cooker. Cover and cook about 15 minutes more or until thickened. Serve ribs with sauce. If desired, serve ribs over coleslaw mix and/or thinly sliced jalapeño peppers.

***Note:** Chile peppers contain oils that can burn your skin and eyes. When working with chile peppers, wear plastic or rubber gloves. If your bare hands do touch the peppers, wash your hands and nails well with soap and warm water.

****Note:** Broiling will make the ribs less fatty. But you may omit this step, if desired.

**PER SERVING:** 286 cal., 8 g total fat (3 g sat. fat), 91 mg chol., 526 mg sodium, 10 g carbo., 1 g fiber, 40 g pro.

Plum and Rosemary Pork Roast

4 Transfer meat to a cutting board; cover with foil and let stand for 15 minutes. The temperature of the meat after standing should be 160°.
5 Meanwhile, using a slotted spoon, transfer plums to a serving platter. For sauce, place Dutch oven over medium-high heat on the rangetop. Reduce heat; boil gently, uncovered, about 10 minutes or until sauce is reduced to about ¾ cup.
6 To serve, thinly slice meat. Arrange meat slices on platter with plums. Serve with sauce. If desired, garnish with fresh rosemary sprigs.

**PER SERVING:** 367 cal., 10 g total fat (3 g sat. fat), 83 mg chol., 249 mg sodium, 19 g carbo., 2 g fiber, 34 g pro.

## Plum and Rosemary Pork Roast

**MAKES:** 6 servings **PREP:** 35 minutes **ROAST:** 40 minutes **STAND:** 15 minutes **OVEN:** 300°

- **1 2-pound boneless pork top loin roast (single loin)**
- **Kosher salt**
- **Freshly ground black pepper**
- **1 tablespoon olive oil**
- **½ cup chopped onion (1 medium)**
- **½ cup chopped carrot (1 medium)**
- **2 tablespoons snipped fresh rosemary**
- **2 cloves garlic, minced**
- **1½ cups port wine**
- **¼ cup reduced-sodium chicken broth**
- **6 fresh plums, pitted and quartered**
- **Fresh rosemary sprigs (optional)**

1 Preheat oven to 300°. Sprinkle meat with kosher salt and pepper. In a 4- to 5-quart oven-going Dutch oven heat oil over medium heat. Add meat; cook for 5 to 8 minutes or until brown, turning to brown evenly on all sides. Remove meat from Dutch oven; set aside.
2 Add onion and carrot to Dutch oven. Cook about 5 minutes or until onion is golden brown, stirring frequently. Stir in the snipped rosemary and the garlic; cook and stir for 1 minute more. Add port wine and broth. Return meat to the Dutch oven. Heat just until boiling.
3 Roast, covered, for 20 minutes. Add plums to Dutch oven. Roast, covered, for 20 to 25 minutes more or until internal temperature of meat registers 150° on an instant-read thermometer.

## Ham and Potato Skillet

**MAKES:** 4 servings **START TO FINISH:** 35 minutes

- **1 pound small potatoes**
- **8 ounces fresh green beans, cut into 1-inch pieces, or one 9-ounce package frozen cut green beans**
- **1 cup water**
- **1 cup plain low-fat yogurt**
- **2 tablespoons all-purpose flour**
- **2 teaspoons yellow mustard**
- **¼ teaspoon dried dill**
- **⅛ teaspoon ground black pepper**
- **1½ cups cubed cooked ham (8 ounces)**

1 Slice potatoes; halve any large slices. In a covered large skillet cook potatoes and fresh green beans (if using) in the water about 15 minutes or until potatoes and beans are tender. (If using frozen beans, add to potatoes for the last 5 minutes of cooking.) Drain well.
2 Meanwhile, in a small saucepan stir together yogurt, flour, mustard, dill, and pepper. Cook and stir until thickened and bubbly. Pour over vegetables in skillet. Stir in ham. Heat through.

**PER SERVING:** 181 cal., 4 g total fat (2 g sat. fat), 31 mg chol., 708 mg sodium, 20 g carbo., 1 g fiber, 16 g pro.

Scalloped Potatoes and Ham

## Scalloped Potatoes and Ham

**MAKES:** 6 servings **PREP:** 40 minutes **BAKE:** 30 minutes
**STAND:** 10 minutes **OVEN:** 350°

- **½ cup chopped onion (1 medium)**
- **1½ cups fat-free milk**
- **3 tablespoons all-purpose flour**
- **⅛ teaspoon ground black pepper**
- **1 teaspoon snipped fresh rosemary or ½ teaspoon dried rosemary, crushed**
- **1 medium round red potato, cut into ¼-inch slices**
- **1 medium sweet potato, peeled and cut into ¼-inch slices**
- **1 medium turnip, peeled and cut into ¼-inch slices**
- **¼ cup water**
- **8 ounces low-fat, reduced-sodium cooked boneless ham, cut into thin strips**
- **Paprika**

**1** Preheat oven to 350°. For sauce, in a medium saucepan cook onion in a small amount of boiling water over medium heat for 3 to 5 minutes or until tender. Drain; return onion to saucepan. In a screw-top jar combine milk, flour, and pepper; cover and shake until well mixed. Add milk mixture to saucepan. Cook and stir over medium heat until thickened and bubbly. Stir in rosemary.

**2** Meanwhile, in a 2-quart microwave-safe baking dish combine potatoes, turnip, and the ¼ cup water. Cover with vented plastic wrap. Microwave on 100 percent power (high) about 8 minutes or just until vegetables are tender. Carefully drain in a colander.

**3** In the same 2-quart baking dish layer half of the ham, half of the potato mixture, and half of the sauce. Repeat layers. Sprinkle with paprika. Bake, uncovered, about 30 minutes or until heated through. Let stand for 10 minutes before serving.

**PER SERVING:** 120 cal., 2 g total fat (1 g sat. fat), 17 mg chol., 466 mg sodium, 17 g carbo., 2 g fiber, 10 g pro.

Simple Stromboli

## Simple Stromboli ✪

**MAKES:** 8 servings **PREP:** 20 minutes **BAKE:** 25 minutes
**OVEN:** 375°

- **1 16-ounce loaf frozen wheat or white bread dough, thawed**
- **8 ounces lean cooked ham, thinly sliced**
- **¼ cup coarsely chopped pitted ripe olives**
- **¼ cup coarsely chopped pimiento-stuffed green olives**
- **¼ cup shredded mozzarella cheese (1 ounce)**
- **⅛ teaspoon crushed red pepper**
- **1 tablespoon reduced-fat milk**
- **1 tablespoon shredded Parmesan cheese (optional)**

**1** Preheat oven to 375°. Line a 15×10×1-inch baking pan with foil; grease foil. Set aside. On a lightly floured surface, roll bread dough to a 15×8-inch rectangle. (If dough is difficult to roll out, cover and let rest for a few minutes.) Arrange ham slices on dough rectangle, leaving about ½ inch around the edges. Top ham with olives, mozzarella cheese, and crushed red pepper. Brush dough edges with water.

**2** Starting with a long end, roll up in a spiral, pinching edge to seal. Pinch ends and tuck under. Place, seam side down, on prepared baking pan. Brush surface with milk. Using a sharp knife, make shallow diagonal cuts at 2-inch intervals along the top to allow steam to escape. If desired, sprinkle with Parmesan cheese.

**3** Bake for 25 to 30 minutes or until brown. If necessary to prevent overbrowning, cover loosely with foil after 20 minutes of baking.

**PER SERVING:** 206 cal., 5 g total fat (1 g sat. fat), 16 mg chol., 878 mg sodium, 28 g carbo., 2 g fiber, 14 g pro.

page 195
page 206

# Make-'em-Main

# Meatless Dishes

# Fill up and feel good about

## Garlic Asparagus and Pasta with Lemon Cream (30)

**MAKES:** 6 servings **START TO FINISH:** 25 minutes

- **8 ounces dried mafalda or rotini pasta**
- **2 cups 2-inch pieces fresh asparagus**
- **8 baby sunburst squash and/or pattypan squash halved (4 to 6 ounces), or 1 medium zucchini or yellow summer squash, cut into 8 pieces**
- **2 cloves garlic, minced**
- **1 tablespoon butter or margarine**
- **1 12-ounce can evaporated fat-free milk**
- **1 tablespoon all-purpose flour**
- **¼ teaspoon salt**
- **¼ cup finely shredded Parmesan cheese**
- **1 to 2 teaspoons finely shredded lemon peel**
- **Finely shredded Parmesan cheese (optional)**

**1** Cook pasta according to package directions. Drain. Return pasta mixture to pot. Cover and keep warm.
**2** Meanwhile, in a large skillet cook asparagus, squash, and garlic in hot butter over medium heat for 2 to 4 minutes or until vegetables are crisp-tender, stirring frequently. Remove with a slotted spoon and add to warm pasta.
**3** For sauce, in a medium bowl whisk together evaporated milk, flour, and salt until very well combined and no lumps of flour remain. Add milk mixture to hot skillet. Cook and stir over medium heat until mixture is thickened and bubbly. Cook and stir for 1 minute more. Reduce heat to low. Stir in the ¼ cup Parmesan cheese and the lemon peel; heat through.
**4** Serve sauce over pasta and vegetables; toss lightly to coat. If desired, serve with additional Parmesan cheese. Serve immediately.

**PER SERVING:** 233 cal., 4 g total fat (2 g sat. fat), 10 mg chol., 235 mg sodium, 38 g carbo., 2 g fiber, 12 g pro.

## Herbed Pasta Primavera (30)

**MAKES:** 4 servings **START TO FINISH:** 30 minutes

- **1¾ cups dried multigrain or whole wheat penne pasta (8 ounces)**
- **8 ounces packaged peeled baby carrots, halved lengthwise (1¾ cups)**
- **1 tablespoon olive oil**
- **8 ounces fresh green beans, trimmed and cut into 2-inch pieces (1½ cups)**
- **½ cup sliced green onions (4) or ½ cup chopped onion (1 medium)**
- **¾ cup chicken broth**
- **2 cloves garlic, minced**
- **1 medium zucchini and/or yellow summer squash, halved lengthwise and cut into ¼-inch slices (2 cups)**
- **2 tablespoons snipped fresh basil or 1 teaspoon dried basil, crushed**
- **¼ teaspoon salt**
- **¼ cup sliced almonds, toasted**
- **Grated or finely shredded Parmesan cheese (optional)**
- **Cracked black pepper**

**1** Cook pasta according to package directions. Drain. Return pasta mixture to pot. Cover and keep warm.
**2** Meanwhile, in a large skillet cook and stir carrots in hot oil for 5 minutes. Add green beans and green onions. Stir in broth and garlic; reduce heat. Simmer, uncovered, for 3 minutes, stirring occasionally. Stir in zucchini. Simmer, uncovered, for 4 to 5 minutes more or until vegetables are crisp-tender, stirring occasionally.
**3** Toss vegetable mixture, basil, and salt with warm pasta. Sprinkle with almonds, Parmesan cheese (if using), and pepper. Serve immediately.

**PER SERVING:** 284 cal., 9 g total fat (1 g sat. fat), 0 mg chol., 375 mg sodium, 42 g carbo., 7 g fiber, 12 g pro.

To toast sliced almonds, spread them in a single layer on a rimmed baking sheet and toast in a 350° oven until golden brown, about 5 to 6 minutes. Stir once or twice for even toasting—and watch carefully, they burn very quickly.

a veggie-packed pasta dish.

Herbed Pasta Primavera

Creamy Springtime Fettuccine

# Menu

Crusty baguette slices

Creamy Springtime Fettuccine
[below]

Fruit and Chip Cookies
[page 285]

## Creamy Springtime Fettuccine (30)

**MAKES:** 4 servings **START TO FINISH:** 25 minutes

- **8 ounces dried fettuccine or linguine**
- **8 ounces fresh asparagus spears, trimmed and cut into 1½-inch pieces**
- **3 cups sliced fresh mushrooms (8 ounces)**
- **⅓ cup leek (1 medium) or ⅓ cup chopped onion (1 small)**
- **3 cloves garlic, minced**
- **1 tablespoon olive oil**
- **⅓ cup vegetable broth**
- **¼ cup half-and-half or light cream**
- **¼ teaspoon salt**
- **⅛ teaspoon ground black pepper**
- **1 cup chopped roma tomatoes (3 medium)**
- **1 tablespoon shredded fresh basil leaves**
- **1 tablespoon snipped fresh oregano**
- **2 tablespoons pine nuts, toasted**
- **Finely shredded Parmesan cheese (optional)**

**1** Cook pasta according to package directions, adding asparagus the last 2 minutes of cooking time. Drain. Return pasta mixture to pot. Cover and keep warm.
**2** Meanwhile, for sauce, in a large skillet cook mushrooms, leek, and garlic in hot oil over medium-high heat for 4 to 5 minutes or until most of the liquid is evaporated. Stir in broth, half-and-half, salt, and pepper. Bring to boiling; reduce heat. Simmer, uncovered, for 4 to 5 minutes or until mixture is slightly thickened. Stir in tomatoes, basil, and oregano; heat through.
**3** Serve sauce over warm pasta mixture; toss lightly to coat. Sprinkle with pine nuts and, if desired, Parmesan cheese. Serve immediately.

**PER SERVING:** 332 cal., 10 g total fat (2 g sat. fat), 6 mg chol., 182 mg sodium, 51 g carbo., 3 g fiber, 13 g pro.

## Fettuccine-Vegetable Toss 

**MAKES:** 4 servings **START TO FINISH:** 25 minutes

- **1 9-ounce package refrigerated spinach or plain fettuccine**
- **1 tablespoon olive oil**
- **2 tablespoons chopped green onion (1)**
- **2 cups chopped red and/or yellow tomatoes (4 medium)**
- **½ cup finely chopped carrot (1 medium)**
- **¼ cup oil-packed dried tomatoes, drained and snipped**
- **½ cup crumbled garlic-and-herb feta cheese, peppercorn feta cheese, or plain feta cheese (2 ounces)**

**1** Cook pasta according to package directions. Drain. Return pasta mixture to pot. Cover and keep warm.
**2** Meanwhile, in a large skillet heat oil over medium heat. Add green onion. Cook and stir for 30 seconds. Stir in fresh tomatoes, carrot, and dried tomato pieces. Cook, covered, for 5 minutes, stirring once.
**3** Serve tomato mixture over warm pasta. Sprinkle with feta cheese; toss lightly to mix. Serve immediately.

**PER SERVING:** 311 cal., 11 g total fat (4 g sat. fat), 73 mg chol., 250 mg sodium, 44 g carbo., 2 g fiber, 13 g pro.

## Weeknight Pasta Toss 30

**MAKES:** 6 servings **START TO FINISH:** 25 minutes

- 8 ounces dried linguine, fettuccine, or malfalda pasta
- 3 cups fresh asparagus pieces, broccoli florets, or cauliflower florets
- 4 cloves garlic, minced
- ½ teaspoon crushed red pepper
- ¼ cup olive oil
- ¼ cup finely shredded Pecorino Romano cheese or Parmesan cheese (1 ounce)
- 2 tablespoons snipped fresh Italian (flat-leaf) parsley
- ¼ teaspoon ground black pepper
- Salt

**1** Cook pasta according to package directions. Drain. Return to pot. Cover and keep warm.

**2** Meanwhile, place a steamer basket in a saucepan. Add water to just below the bottom of the basket. Bring water to boiling. Add vegetables to the steamer basket. Cover and reduce heat. Steam until the vegetables are crisp-tender. For asparagus, allow 3 to 5 minutes; for cauliflower or broccoli, allow 8 to 10 minutes. Add steamed vegetables to warm pasta.

**3** In a small saucepan cook garlic and crushed red pepper in hot oil over medium heat for 30 seconds to 1 minute or until fragrant.

**4** Add garlic mixture and steamed vegetables to warm pasta; toss lightly to coat. Add cheese, parsley, and black pepper; toss lightly to mix. Season to taste with salt. Serve immediately.

**PER SERVING:** 116 cal., 10 g total fat (2 g sat. fat), 3 mg chol., 102 mg sodium, 5 g carbo., 2 g fiber, 3 g pro.

Menu

Egg drop soup

Vegetable and Tofu Stir-Fry [below]

Spiced Apricot Bars [page 290]

Hot tea

Ratatouille over Polenta

## Vegetable and Tofu Stir-Fry (30)

**MAKES:** 4 servings **START TO FINISH:** 30 minutes

- 1½ cups uncooked instant brown rice
- ½ cup vegetable broth
- ¼ cup dry sherry
- 1 tablespoon cornstarch
- 1 tablespoon reduced-sodium soy sauce
- 1 teaspoon grated fresh ginger
- ½ teaspoon crushed red pepper (optional)
- Nonstick olive oil cooking spray
- 1 cup thinly bias-sliced carrot
- 3 cloves garlic, minced
- 3 cups fresh broccoli florets
- 6 ounces firm tofu (fresh bean curd), drained and cut into ½- to 1-inch cubes
- 1 cup fresh or frozen shelled green sweet soybeans (edamame), thawed if necessary (optional)

**1** Prepare the rice according to package directions. Cover and keep warm.
**2** For sauce, in a small bowl combine broth, dry sherry, cornstarch, soy sauce, ginger, and, if desired, crushed red pepper. Set sauce aside.
**3** Coat an unheated wok or large skillet with cooking spray. Preheat over medium-high heat. Add carrot and garlic to hot wok. Cook and stir for 2 minutes. Add broccoli. Cook and stir for 3 to 4 minutes more or until vegetables are crisp-tender. Push vegetables from center of wok.
**4** Stir sauce; add to center of wok. Cook and stir until thickened and bubbly. Add tofu, and, if desired, edamame; gently stir to coat all ingredients with sauce. Cook and stir gently for 1 minute more. Serve vegetable mixture over hot cooked rice.

**PER SERVING:** 214 cal., 3 g total fat (0 g sat. fat), 0 mg chol., 315 mg sodium, 38 g carbo., 5 g fiber, 9 g pro.

## Ratatouille over Polenta

**MAKES:** 4 to 6 servings **START TO FINISH:** 35 minutes

- 1 16-ounce tube refrigerated cooked polenta
- 1 small green sweet pepper, seeded and cut into thin strips
- 1 small onion, thinly sliced
- 1 clove garlic, minced
- 1 tablespoon cooking oil
- ½ small eggplant, cut into ½-inch pieces
- 1 large yellow summer squash or zucchini, sliced
- 1 large tomato, cut into wedges
- 1 cup small pattypan squash, quartered
- 1 tablespoon snipped fresh basil
- ⅛ teaspoon salt
- ⅛ teaspoon ground black pepper
- 3 tablespoons snipped fresh parsley
- Finely shredded Parmesan cheese (optional)

**1** Cut polenta into 8 to 12 slices. Prepare polenta according to package directions. Cover and keep warm.
**2** For ratatouille, in a large saucepan cook and stir the sweet pepper, onion, and garlic in hot oil over medium heat for 5 minutes. Add eggplant. Cook and stir for 5 minutes. Stir in summer squash, tomato, pattypan squash, basil, salt, and black pepper. Cook, covered, for 5 to 7 minutes more or until vegetables are tender, stirring occasionally. Stir in parsley.
**3** To serve, place 2 slices of polenta on each of 4 to 6 dinner plates. Spoon warm ratatouille over each serving. If desired, sprinkle with Parmesan cheese.

**PER SERVING:** 260 cal., 8 g total fat (1 g sat. fat), 9 mg chol., 576 mg sodium, 38 g carbo., 5 g fiber, 10 g pro.

Vegetable Fried Rice

Always use cold rice (leftover rice works well) to make fried rice. Chilling gives the grains time to firm up and excess moisture to evaporate so the grains separate when stir fried. If you try to use hot rice, you'll get fried mush.

## Vegetable Fried Rice

**MAKES:** 8 servings **PREP:** 25 minutes **CHILL:** 1 hour

- 2 cups water
- 1 cup uncooked long grain rice
- 1 tablespoon toasted sesame oil
- 2 teaspoons minced garlic
- 2 teaspoons minced fresh ginger
- 3 cups assorted cut-up fresh vegetables (such as sweet peppers, red onion, sliced fresh mushrooms, broccoli flowerets, and/or matchstick carrots)
- 1½ cups coarsely chopped bok choy
- ¼ cup reduced-sodium soy sauce
- ¼ cup snipped fresh cilantro or thinly sliced green onions (2)

**1** In a medium saucepan combine the water and rice. Bring to boiling. Simmer, covered, about 15 minutes. Cover and chill in the refrigerator for at least 1 hour.
**2** In an extra-large nonstick skillet heat oil over medium heat. Add garlic and ginger. Cook and stir for 30 seconds. Add assorted vegetables and bok choy. Cook and stir for 3 to 4 minutes or until vegetables are crisp-tender.
**3** Add chilled rice and soy sauce to vegetable mixture. Cook and stir for 3 minutes more. Sprinkle with cilantro. Serve immediately.

**PER SERVING:** 113 cal., 2 g total fat (0 g sat. fat), 0 mg chol., 269 mg sodium, 21 g carbo., 1 g fiber, 3 g pro.

## Garden Veggie Burgers 

**MAKES:** 4 servings **PREP:** 10 minutes **GRILL:** 15 minutes

- 2 medium red onions
- 4 refrigerated or frozen meatless burger patties
- ¼ cup bottled vinaigrette salad dressing, at room temperature
- 4 cups fresh spinach leaves
- 1 clove garlic, minced
- 1 tablespoon olive oil
- ½ cup crumbled feta cheese (2 ounces)
- 4 hamburger buns, split

**1** For onion topping, cut onions into ½-inch slices. For a charcoal grill, grill onion slices on the rack of an uncovered grill directly over medium coals for 15 to 20 minutes or until tender, turning once halfway through grilling. Grill burger patties directly over the coals alongside the onions for 8 to 10 minutes or until heated through, turning once halfway through grilling. (For a gas grill, preheat grill. Reduce heat to medium. Cover and grill as above.) Brush grilled onions with the salad dressing.
**2** Meanwhile, for spinach topping, in a large skillet cook and stir the spinach and garlic in hot olive oil over medium-high heat for 30 seconds or until spinach is just wilted. Remove skillet from heat. Stir in feta cheese.
**3** To serve, place onion slices on bottoms of buns. Top with burger patties, spinach mixture, and bun tops.

**PER SERVING:** 350 cal., 14 g total fat (4 g sat. fat), 17 mg chol., 920 mg sodium, 37 g carbo., 7 g fiber, 21 g pro.

## Meatless Tacos 

**MAKES:** 8 tacos **START TO FINISH:** 30 minutes

- ½ cup water
- ¼ cup dry brown lentils, rinsed and drained
- ¼ cup chopped onion
- 8 taco shells
- 1 8-ounce can tomato sauce
- ½ of a 1.125- or 1.25-ounce envelope (5 teaspoons) taco seasoning mix
- 8 ounces firm or extra-firm tub-style tofu (fresh bean curd), drained and finely chopped
- 1½ cups shredded lettuce
- ½ cup chopped tomato (1 medium)
- ½ cup shredded cheddar cheese (2 ounces)
- ½ cup salsa (optional)

**1** In a medium saucepan combine the water, lentils, and onion. Bring to boiling; reduce heat. Simmer, covered, for 25 to 30 minutes or until lentils are tender and liquid is absorbed.

**2** Meanwhile, heat taco shells according to package directions.

**3** Stir tomato sauce and taco seasoning mix into lentils. Bring to boiling; reduce heat. Simmer, uncovered, for 5 minutes. Stir in tofu; heat through. Spoon tofu mixture into taco shells. Top with lettuce, tomato, and cheese. If desired, serve with salsa.

**PER TACO:** 148 cal., 7 g total fat (2 g sat. fat), 7 mg chol., 460 mg sodium, 16 g carbo., 3 g fiber, 7 g pro.

**Vegetable Tacos:** Prepare as directed, except stir 1 cup frozen whole kernel corn and ¾ cup shredded carrot into the tomato sauce mixture. Increase number of taco shells to 12.

**PER TACO:** 133 cal., 6 g total fat (2 g sat. fat), 5 mg chol., 326 mg sodium, 17 g carbo., 3 g fiber, 6 g pro.

Meatless Tacos

# Hearty grains and great flavors

Peppers Stuffed with Cranberry Bulgur

## Peppers Stuffed with Cranberry Bulgur (30)

**MAKES:** 4 servings **START TO FINISH:** 30 minutes

- 1 14-ounce can vegetable or chicken broth
- ½ cup shredded carrot (1 medium)
- ¼ cup chopped onion
- ¾ cup bulgur
- ⅓ cup dried cranberries, cherries, or raisins
- 2 large or 4 small sweet green, yellow, and/or red peppers
- ¾ cup shredded Muenster, brick, or mozzarella cheese (3 ounces)
- ½ cup water
- 2 tablespoons sliced almonds or chopped pecans, toasted

**1** In a large skillet combine the broth, carrot, and onion. Bring to boiling; reduce heat. Simmer, covered, for 5 minutes. Stir in bulgur and cranberries. Remove from heat. Cover and let stand for 5 minutes. Drain off excess liquid, if necessary.
**2** Meanwhile, halve the sweet peppers lengthwise, removing the seeds and membranes. Stir shredded cheese into bulgur mixture; spoon into sweet pepper halves.
**3** Place sweet pepper halves in skillet; add the water. Bring to boiling; reduce heat. Simmer, covered, for 5 to 10 minutes or until sweet peppers are crisp-tender and bulgur mixture is heated through. Sprinkle with nuts.

**PER SERVING:** 260 cal., 9 g total fat (4 g sat. fat), 20 mg chol., 552 mg sodium, 37 g carbo., 8 g fiber, 10 g pro.

mean no one will miss the meat.

## Eggplant Parmesan

**MAKES:** 8 servings **PREP:** 15 minutes **BAKE:** 50 minutes
**STAND:** 10 minutes **OVEN:** 375°

- Nonstick olive oil cooking spray
- 2 medium eggplants (2 pounds total)
- 2 tablespoons olive oil
- 1 tablespoon minced garlic (6 cloves)
- 3 tablespoons snipped fresh thyme, oregano, or marjoram
- 3 cups purchased marinara sauce
- 3 tablespoons snipped fresh basil
- 1½ cups shredded part-skim mozzarella cheese (6 ounces)
- ½ cup grated Parmesan cheese

**1** Preheat oven to 375°. Coat 2 large baking sheets with cooking spray; set aside. Trim ends from eggplant; discard. Cut eggplant crosswise into ½-inch slices. Arrange eggplant slices in a single layer on prepared baking sheets. In a small bowl combine olive oil, garlic, and thyme. Drizzle over eggplant slices. Bake for 20 to 25 minutes or just until tender eggplant is softened.
**2** Meanwhile, coat a 2-quart rectangular baking dish with cooking spray. In a medium bowl combine marinara sauce and basil. In a small bowl combine mozzarella cheese and Parmesan cheese. Spread ½ cup of the sauce in prepared baking dish. Top with one-third of the eggplant slices, overlapping if necessary. Top with one-third of the remaining sauce and one-third of the cheese mixture. Repeat layers twice, starting with eggplant and ending with cheese.
**3** Bake, covered, for 30 to 35 minutes or until heated through. Uncover; let stand for 10 minutes before serving.

**PER SERVING:** 196 cal., 11 g total fat (4 g sat. fat), 18 mg chol., 644 mg sodium, 17 g carbo., 6 g fiber, 10 g pro.

## Open-Face Garden Sandwich (30)

**MAKES:** 4 servings **PREP:** 15 minutes **ROAST:** 10 minutes
**BROIL:** 3 minutes **OVEN:** 450°

- 1 small zucchini, thinly sliced
- 1 small yellow summer squash, thinly sliced
- 1 medium onion, sliced
- ⅓ cup sliced fresh mushrooms
- ½ of a medium red sweet pepper, cut into thin bite-size strips
- Nonstick olive oil cooking spray
- Salt
- Ground black pepper
- 4 pita bread rounds
- 4 teaspoons bottled reduced-calorie Italian salad dressing
- ¾ cup shredded Swiss cheese (3 ounces)

**1** Preheat oven to 450°. Place vegetables in a single layer on a large baking sheet; coat vegetables with cooking spray. Roast about 10 minutes or until tender. Season with salt and black pepper.
**2** Preheat broiler. Arrange vegetables on pita bread; drizzle with dressing. Top with cheese. Place sandwiches on the unheated rack of a broiler pan. Broil 4 to 5 inches from the heat about 3 minutes or until cheese melts.

**PER SERVING:** 269 cal., 7 g total fat (4 g sat. fat), 20 mg chol., 453 mg sodium, 38 g carbo., 1 g fiber, 12 g pro.

Open-Face Garden Sandwich

## Risotto with Beans and Vegetables (30)

**MAKES:** 4 servings **START TO FINISH:** 30 minutes

- **3 cups vegetable broth**
- **2 cups sliced fresh mushrooms**
- **½ cup chopped onion (1 medium)**
- **2 cloves garlic, minced**
- **2 tablespoons olive oil**
- **1 cup uncooked Arborio rice**
- **1 cup finely chopped zucchini (1 small)**
- **1 cup finely chopped carrots (2 medium)**
- **1 15-ounce can cannellini beans (white kidney beans) or pinto beans, rinsed and drained**
- **½ cup finely shredded Parmesan cheese**
- **2 tablespoons snipped fresh Italian (flat-leaf) parsley**
- **Finely shredded Parmesan cheese (optional)**

**1** In a medium saucepan bring broth to boiling; reduce heat. Simmer until needed. Meanwhile, in a large saucepan cook mushrooms, onion, and garlic in hot oil over medium heat about 5 minutes or until onion is tender. Add uncooked rice. Cook and stir about 5 minutes more or until rice is golden brown.

**2** Slowly add 1 cup of the broth to rice mixture, stirring constantly. Continue to cook and stir until liquid is absorbed. Add another ½ cup of the broth, the zucchini, and carrots to rice mixture, stirring constantly. Continue to cook and stir until liquid is absorbed. Add another 1 cup broth, ½ cup at a time, stirring constantly until broth is absorbed. (This should take about 20 minutes.)

**3** Stir the remaining ½ cup broth into rice mixture. Cook and stir until rice is slightly creamy and just tender. Stir in drained beans and the ½ cup Parmesan cheese; heat through. Sprinkle with parsley and, if desired, additional Parmesan cheese.

**PER SERVING:** 340 cal., 11 g total fat (3 g sat. fat), 9 mg chol., 1,074 mg sodium, 53 g carbo., 7 g fiber, 15 g pro.

## Zesty Vegetable Enchiladas

**MAKES:** 4 servings **PREP:** 30 minutes **BAKE:** 15 minutes
**OVEN:** 350°

- 1⅓ cups water
- ½ cup dry brown lentils, rinsed and drained
- Nonstick cooking spray
- 8 8-inch flour tortillas
- 1 cup thinly sliced carrots (2 medium)
- 2 small zucchini or yellow summer squash, quartered lengthwise and sliced (2 cups)
- 1 teaspoon ground cumin
- 1 8-ounce can tomato sauce
- 1 cup shredded reduced-fat Monterey Jack cheese (4 ounces)
- Dash bottled hot pepper sauce (optional)
- 1 14.5-ounce can Mexican-style stewed tomatoes, undrained and cut up
- Fresh cilantro sprigs (optional)

**1** In a medium saucepan combine the water and lentils. Bring to boiling; reduce heat. Simmer, covered, for 25 to 30 minutes or until lentils are tender; drain.
**2** Preheat oven to 350°. Coat a 2-quart rectangular baking dish with cooking spray; set aside. Stack tortillas and wrap tightly in foil. Bake about 10 minutes or until warm.
**3** Lightly coat an unheated large skillet with cooking spray. Preheat over medium heat. Add carrots. Cook and stir for 2 minutes. Add zucchini and cumin. Cook and stir for 2 to 3 minutes or until vegetables are crisp-tender. Remove from heat. Stir in drained lentils, tomato sauce, ¾ cup of the cheese, and, if desired, hot pepper sauce.
**4** Divide lentil mixture among warm tortillas; roll up tortillas. Arrange tortillas, seam sides down, in the prepared baking dish. Sprinkle with the remaining ¼ cup cheese. Spoon undrained tomatoes over tortillas.
**5** Bake, uncovered, for 15 to 20 minutes or until heated through. If desired, garnish with cilantro.

**PER SERVING:** 450 cal., 15 g total fat (4 g sat. fat), 20 mg chol., 929 mg sodium, 57 g carbo., 11 g fiber, 22 g pro.

## Crustless Cheese Quiche

**MAKES:** 6 servings **PREP:** 15 minutes **BAKE:** 40 minutes
**COOL:** 10 minutes **OVEN:** 350°

- Nonstick cooking spray
- 4 eggs
- ⅓ cup whole wheat pastry flour or whole wheat flour
- ¼ teaspoon ground black pepper
- ⅛ teaspoon salt
- 1½ cups low-fat cottage cheese (12 ounces), drained
- 1 10-ounce package frozen chopped broccoli, cooked according to package directions and drained
- 1 cup shredded reduced-fat cheddar cheese (4 ounces)
- ¾ cup crumbled reduced-fat feta cheese (3 ounces)

**1** Preheat oven to 350°. Lightly coat a 9-inch pie pan or pie plate with cooking spray; set aside.
**2** In a medium bowl lightly beat eggs with a rotary beater or wire whisk. Beat in flour, pepper, and salt. Stir in drained cottage cheese, cooked broccoli, cheddar cheese, and feta cheese. Spoon into prepared pie pan.
**3** Bake for 40 to 45 minutes or until a knife inserted near center comes out clean. Cool on a wire rack for 10 minutes before serving.

**PER SERVING:** 207 cal., 10 g total fat (5 g sat. fat), 162 mg chol., 731 mg sodium, 9 g carbo., 2 g fiber, 21 g pro.

The only flour in this crustless quiche is used to thicken and give body to the three-cheese filling. Going crustless saves about 190 calories and 12 grams of fat per serving. The filling is bulked up with broccoli and low-fat cottage cheese. A little bit of reduced-fat feta cheese—already a lower-fat cheese—gives it great tangy flavor.

page 238
page 221

Satisfying

# Soup & Stews

Harvest Vegetable Soup

Garden-Fresh Gazpacho
[below]

Buttermilk Corn Muffins
[page 275]

Sunshine Cake
[page 311]

## Garden-Fresh Gazpacho

**MAKES:** 4 servings **PREP:** 25 minutes **CHILL:** 2 to 24 hours

- 3 cups chopped tomatoes (6 medium)
- 1¼ cups peeled, seeded, and chopped cucumber (1 small)
- ¾ cup chopped green sweet pepper (1 medium)
- ¼ cup finely chopped red onion
- 2 tablespoons snipped fresh cilantro
- 1 fresh jalapeño chile pepper, seeded and finely chopped (see note, page 182)
- 2 cloves garlic, minced
- 1 cup tomato juice
- ¾ cup beef broth
- ¼ cup dry red wine or tomato juice
- 1 tablespoon red wine vinegar
- Salt
- Ground black pepper
- Chopped avocado, sour cream, and/or croutons (optional)

**1** In an extra-large bowl stir together tomatoes, cucumber, sweet pepper, red onion, cilantro, jalapeño pepper, and garlic. Stir in tomato juice, broth, wine, and vinegar. Sprinkle with salt and pepper to taste. Cover and chill for 2 to 24 hours.

**2** If desired, top each serving with avocado, sour cream, and/or croutons.

**PER SERVING:** 29 cal., 0 g total fat, 0 mg chol., 309 mg sodium, 6 g carbo., 1 g fiber, 3 g pro.

## Harvest Vegetable Soup

**MAKES:** 8 to 10 servings **PREP:** 20 minutes **COOK:** 30 minutes

- 5 cups water
- 3 vegetable or beef bouillon cubes
- 2 medium Yukon gold potatoes, peeled and cut into 1-inch pieces
- 1 cup chopped roma tomato or one 14.5-ounce can diced tomatoes, undrained
- 1 cup chopped celery (2 stalks)
- ½ cup chopped green sweet pepper (1 small)
- ⅓ cup chopped onion (1 small)
- 2 cups shredded cabbage
- 1 15-ounce can red kidney beans, rinsed and drained
- 4 ounces fresh green beans, trimmed and cut in half (about 1 cup)
- 1 cup chopped zucchini (1 small)
- ¼ cup ketchup
- 8 to 10 fresh oregano sprigs, tied in a bunch with kitchen string
- ¼ teaspoon ground black pepper
- Dash bottled hot pepper sauce
- Salt
- Ground black pepper

**1** In a Dutch oven combine the water and bouillon cubes; bring to boiling. Stir in potatoes, tomato, celery, sweet pepper, and onion. Return to boiling; reduce heat. Simmer, uncovered, for 15 minutes.

**2** Stir in cabbage, drained kidney beans, green beans, zucchini, ketchup, oregano, the ¼ teaspoon black pepper, and hot pepper sauce. Return to boiling; reduce heat. Simmer, uncovered, about 15 minutes more or until vegetables are tender. Remove and discard oregano. Season to taste with salt and additional black pepper.

**PER SERVING:** 93 cal., 0 g total fat, 0 mg chol., 702 mg sodium, 19 g carbo., 6 g fiber, 4 g pro.

Vegetable-Pasta Soup

In a soup that contains pasta, the pasta is always the last thing to be cooked before serving. If it sits in the soup too long, it gets mushy. Not only does pasta contribute a toothsome bite to soup, but some of the starch in the pasta seeps into the soup while cooking, helping to thicken it and give it some some body.

## Vegetable-Pasta Soup

**MAKES:** 6 servings **START TO FINISH:** 35 minutes

- 6 cloves garlic, minced
- 2 teaspoons olive oil
- 1½ cups coarsely shredded carrots (3 medium)
- 1 cup chopped onion (1 large)
- 1 cup thinly sliced celery (2 stalks)
- 1 32-ounce container reduced-sodium chicken broth
- 4 cups water
- 1½ cups dried ditalini pasta
- ¼ cup shaved Parmesan cheese (1 ounce)
- 2 tablespoons snipped fresh parsley

**1** In a 5- to 6-quart Dutch oven cook and stir garlic in hot oil over medium heat for 15 seconds. Add carrots, onion, and celery; cook for 5 to 7 minutes or until tender, stirring occasionally.

**2** Add broth and the water. Bring to boiling. Stir in pasta. Return to boiling; reduce heat. Boil gently, uncovered, for 7 to 8 minutes or until pasta is tender. Top each serving with cheese and parsley.

**PER SERVING:** 172 cal., 4 g total fat (0 g sat. fat), 2 mg chol., 454 mg sodium, 28 g carbo., 2 g fiber, 8 g pro.

## Avocado Soup

**MAKES:** 6 appetizer servings **PREP:** 20 minutes
**CHILL:** 1 to 24 hours

- 2 medium ripe avocados, seeded, peeled, and cut up
- ½ cup chopped peeled cucumber
- ⅓ cup chopped onion (1 small)
- ¼ cup shredded carrot
- 1 clove garlic, minced
- 2 14-ounce cans reduced-sodium chicken broth
- Several dashes bottled hot pepper sauce
- 1½ teaspoons paprika
- ⅓ cup bottled salsa (optional)

**1** In a blender or food processor combine avocados, cucumber, onion, carrot, and garlic. Add 1 can of the broth. Cover and blend or process until nearly smooth.

**2** Add the remaining can of broth and pepper sauce. Cover and blend or process until smooth. Pour mixture into a bowl. Cover surface with plastic wrap and chill for 1 to 24 hours.

**3** To serve, ladle soup into chilled soup bowls. Sprinkle with paprika. If desired, top with salsa.

**PER SERVING:** 92 cal., 7 g total fat (1 g sat. fat), 0 mg chol., 322 mg sodium, 6 g carbo., 4 g fiber, 3 g pro.

Avocado Soup

# A big, warming bowl of

## Creamy Carrot and Pasta Soup (30)

**MAKES:** 4 servings **START TO FINISH:** 30 minutes

- 2 14-ounce cans vegetable broth or chicken broth
- 2 cups sliced carrots (4 medium)
- 1 cup chopped peeled potato (1 large)
- 1 cup chopped onion (1 large)
- 1 tablespoon grated fresh ginger
- ½ teaspoon Jamaican jerk seasoning
- 8 ounces dried radiatore or rotini pasta
- 1½ cups milk
- Fresh chives (optional)

**1** In a large saucepan combine broth, carrots, potato, onion, ginger, and jerk seasoning. Bring to boiling; reduce heat. Simmer, covered, for 15 to 20 minutes or until vegetables are very tender. Cool slightly.
**2** Meanwhile, cook pasta according to package directions; drain.
**3** Place one-fourth of the vegetable mixture in a food processor. Cover and process until smooth. Transfer vegetable mixture to a bowl. Repeat three more times. Return all of the vegetable mixture to saucepan. Stir in cooked pasta and milk; heat through. If desired, top each serving with chives.

**PER SERVING:** 351 cal., 4 g total fat (2 sat. fat), 7 mg chol., 937 mg sodium, 67 g carbo., 3 g fiber, 14 g pro.

Creamy Carrot and Pasta Soup

## Black Bean Soup

**MAKES:** 6 to 8 servings **PREP:** 25 minutes **COOK:** 12 to 14 hours (low) or 6 to 7 hours (high) **STAND:** 1 hour

- 1 pound dried black beans
- 10 cups water
- 1 14-ounce can vegetable broth or reduced-sodium chicken broth
- 1 cup coarsely chopped onion (1 large)
- 1 cup coarsely chopped celery (2 stalks)
- 1 tablespoon chili powder
- 2 teaspoons dried oregano, crushed
- 2 teaspoons ground cumin
- 2 teaspoons ground coriander
- 4 cloves garlic, minced
- ½ teaspoon ground black pepper
- 1 teaspoon salt*
- 1 cup light sour cream

**1** Rinse beans. In a large saucepan combine beans and 6 cups of the water. Bring to boiling; reduce heat. Simmer, uncovered, for 10 minutes. Remove from heat. Cover and let stand for 1 hour. Drain and rinse beans.
**2** In a 4- to 5-quart slow cooker combine beans, the remaining 4 cups water, broth, onion, celery, chili powder, oregano, cumin, coriander, garlic, and pepper.
**3** Cover and cook on low-heat setting for 12 to 14 hours or on high-heat setting for 6 to 7 hours.
**4** Stir in salt. Mash beans slightly just before serving. Serve with sour cream.
***Note:** Adding salt before cooking the beans can slow the cooking. That's why it's best to add salt after cooking.

**PER SERVING:** 330 cal., 5 g total fat (2 g sat. fat), 11 mg chol., 601 mg sodium, 54 g carbo., 13 g fiber, 19 g pro.

## Ratatouille Soup with Beans

**MAKES:** 6 servings **PREP:** 20 minutes **COOK:** 8 to 10 hours (low) or 4 to 5 hours (high)

- ½ cup coarsely chopped onion (1 medium)
- 2 medium zucchini, halved lengthwise and sliced ¼ inch thick
- 1 15- or 19-ounce can cannellini beans (white kidney beans) or Great Northern beans, rinsed and drained
- 2 cups peeled and cubed eggplant
- ¾ cup coarsely chopped red sweet pepper (1 medium)
- ¾ cup coarsely chopped green sweet pepper (1 medium)

- 1 14.5-ounce can diced tomatoes with basil, garlic, and oregano, undrained
- 1 14-ounce can reduced-sodium chicken broth
- 1 cup hot-style vegetable juice or vegetable juice
- 1 2.25-ounce can sliced pitted ripe olives, drained
- 6 tablespoons finely shredded Parmesan cheese

**1** Place onion in a 3½- or 4-quart slow cooker. Add zucchini, drained beans, eggplant, and sweet peppers. Pour undrained tomatoes, broth, and vegetable juice over mixture in cooker.
**2** Cover and cook on low-heat setting for 8 to 10 hours or on high-heat setting for 4 to 5 hours. Before serving, stir in olives. Top each serving with cheese.

**PER SERVING:** 148 cal., 3 g total fat (1 g sat. fat), 6 mg chol., 945 mg sodium, 25 g carbo., 6 g fiber, 10 g pro.

## Cheddar Cheese Soup ✪

**MAKES:** 12 appetizer servings **PREP:** 30 minutes
**COOK:** 40 minutes

- 1 tablespoon olive oil
- 1 cup coarsely chopped onion (1 large)
- ½ cup sliced celery (1 stalk)
- 4 cloves garlic, sliced
- 3 14-ounce cans reduced-sodium chicken broth
- 2 12-ounce cans evaporated fat-free milk
- ½ cup instant flour or all-purpose flour
- 2 cups reduced-fat shredded cheddar cheese (8 ounces)
- ¼ teaspoon ground white pepper (optional)
- ½ cup reduced-fat shredded cheddar cheese (2 ounces) (optional)

**1** In a Dutch oven heat oil over medium heat. Add onion, celery, and garlic; cook and stir until tender. Add broth; bring to boiling. Reduce heat; simmer, covered, for 25 minutes.
**2** Strain vegetable mixture through a sieve into a bowl; discard vegetables. Add the strained liquid to Dutch oven. In a bowl stir together evaporated milk and flour; stir into liquid. Cook and stir until thickened. Reduce heat to low.
**3** Gradually add the 2 cups cheese, stirring until cheese is melted. If desired, stir in pepper. If desired, sprinkle each serving with additional shredded cheese.

**PER SERVING:** 147 cal., 5 g total fat (3 g sat. fat), 16 mg chol., 464 mg sodium, 13 g carbo., 0 g fiber, 11 g pro.

Cheddar Cheese Soup

When you're trying to eat healthfully, you can still indulge in creamy, cheesy soups. In almost any soup recipe that calls for half-and-half or whipping cream, you can substitute the same amount of evaporated fat-free milk. You get almost the same effect for a fraction of the fat and calories.

## Pumpkin-Sage Soup

**MAKES:** 8 servings **PREP:** 15 minutes
**COOK:** 6 to 8 hours (low) or 3 to 4 hours (high)

- **3 14-ounce cans reduced-sodium chicken broth**
- **1 15-ounce can pumpkin**
- **⅔ cup sliced leeks (2 medium)**
- **2 teaspoons ground sage**
- **⅛ teaspoon salt**
- **⅛ teaspoon ground black pepper**
- **1 cup fat-free half-and-half**
- **Finely shredded Parmesan cheese (optional)**

**1** In a 3½- or 4-quart slow cooker combine broth, pumpkin, leek, sage, salt, and pepper.
**2** Cover and cook on low-heat setting for 6 to 8 hours or on high-heat setting for 3 to 4 hours. Stir in half-and-half. If desired, sprinkle each serving with cheese.

**PER SERVING:** 53 cal., 0 g total fat, 0 mg chol., 388 mg sodium, 9 g carbo., 2 g fiber, 3 g pro.

## Minestra

**MAKES:** 6 servings **PREP:** 15 minutes **COOK:** 25 minutes

- **1 19-ounce can cannellini beans (white kidney beans), rinsed and drained**
- **2 cups peeled and cubed potatoes (2 medium)**
- **1 14.5-ounce can Italian-style stewed tomatoes, undrained and cut up**
- **1 14-ounce can lower-sodium beef broth or vegetable broth**
- **8 ounces cooked Italian sausage links, cut into ½-inch slices**
- **4 cloves garlic, minced**
- **¼ teaspoon crushed red pepper**
- **2 cups chopped escarole or Swiss chard leaves**
- **⅓ cup shredded Parmesan or Asiago cheese**

**1** In a 4-quart Dutch oven combine drained cannellini beans, potatoes, undrained tomatoes, broth, sausage, garlic, and crushed red pepper. Bring to boiling; reduce heat. Simmer, covered, for 25 to 30 minutes or until potatoes are tender.
**2** Before serving, stir in escarole. Sprinkle each serving with cheese.

**PER SERVING:** 256 cal., 12 g total fat (4 g sat. fat), 25 mg chol., 942 mg sodium, 26 g carbo., 6 g fiber, 16 g pro.

**Quick Chicken Soup:** Prepare as directed, except substitute two 6-ounce packages refrigerated cooked Italian-style chicken breast strips for the sausage, one 9-ounce package frozen cut green beans for the potatoes, and reduced-sodium chicken broth for the beef broth. Reduce cooking time to about 15 minutes or until green beans are tender. Before serving, stir in 2 cups torn fresh spinach leaves in place of the escarole. Sprinkle each serving with cheese.

**PER SERVING:** 187 cal., 3 g total fat (1 g sat. fat), 40 mg chol., 1,037 mg sodium, 21 g carb., 6 g dietary fiber, 22 g pro.

## Acorn Squash Bisque

**MAKES:** 8 appetizer servings **PREP:** 30 minutes
**BAKE:** 50 minutes **COOL:** 10 minutes **COOK:** 20 minutes
**OVEN:** 325°

- **2 medium acorn squash, halved and seeded (about 2½ pounds total)**
- **1 tablespoon olive oil**
- **½ cup chopped onion (1 medium)**
- **1 14-ounce can reduced-sodium chicken broth**
- **¼ cup water**
- **2 tablespoons packed brown sugar**
- **¼ teaspoon salt**
- **¼ teaspoon ground cinnamon**
- **⅛ to ¼ teaspoon ground white pepper or black pepper**
- **¼ cup half-and-half or light cream**
- **Pumpkin seeds (pepitas) (optional)**
- **Ground cinnamon (optional)**

**1** Preheat oven to 325°. Place squash halves, cut sides down, in a 3-quart rectangular baking dish. Bake for 50 to 60 minutes or until tender. Let squash stand about 10 minutes or until cool enough to handle. Using a spoon, remove squash pulp from shells. Discard shells.
**2** In a saucepan heat oil over medium heat. Add onion; cook in hot oil until tender. Add squash pulp, broth, and the water. Cook over medium-high heat until mixture just reaches boiling, stirring frequently. Stir in brown sugar, salt, ¼ teaspoon cinnamon, and the white pepper. Cool slightly.
**3** Place half of the squash mixture in a blender or food processor. Cover and blend or process until smooth. Transfer pureed squash to a medium bowl. Repeat with the remaining squash mixture. Return all squash mixture to saucepan. Stir in half-and-half; heat through. If desired, garnish with pumpkin seeds and additional cinnamon.

**PER SERVING:** 89 cal., 3 g total fat (1 g sat. fat), 3 mg chol., 206 mg sodium, 16 g carbo., 2 g fiber, 2 g pro.

Acorn Squash Bisque

## Menu

Pepper-Corn Chowder
[right]

Grilled or roasted chicken breast

Salad of baby spinach, dried blueberries, toasted sliced almonds, and vinaigrette

Pepper-Corn Chowder

## Pepper-Corn Chowder

**MAKES:** 8 servings **PREP:** 30 minutes **COOK:** 25 minutes

- **10** ears of corn or 5 cups frozen whole kernel corn
- Nonstick cooking spray
- **1** cup chopped onion (1 large)
- **⅓** cup chopped leek (1 medium)
- **2** 14-ounce cans reduced-sodium chicken broth or vegetable broth
- **¾** cup chopped red sweet pepper (1 medium)
- **⅛** teaspoon ground black pepper
- **⅛** teaspoon cayenne pepper

**1** If using fresh corn, remove husks and silks from ears of corn. Using a sharp knife, cut corn kernels off cobs; set aside.
**2** Coat a 4- to 5-quart Dutch oven with cooking spray; heat Dutch oven over medium heat. Add onion and leek; cook about 5 minutes or until tender, stirring occasionally.
**3** Stir in fresh or frozen corn. Cook about 5 minutes or until corn is softened, stirring occasionally. Add 1 can of the broth. Bring to boiling; reduce heat. Simmer, covered, about 25 minutes or until corn is very tender. Cool slightly.
**4** Transfer half of the corn mixture at a time to a blender or food processor. Cover and blend or process until smooth. Return all of the pureed corn mixture to Dutch oven. Stir in the remaining can of broth, sweet pepper, black pepper, and cayenne pepper; heat through.

**PER SERVING:** 126 cal., 1 g total fat (0 g sat. fat), 0 mg chol., 245 mg sodium, 29 g carbo., 4 g fiber, 5 g pro.

## Hot-and-Sour Soup with Shrimp

**MAKES:** 4 servings **START TO FINISH:** 35 minutes

- **12** ounces fresh or frozen peeled and deveined shrimp
- **4** ounces fresh shiitake mushrooms (stemmed) or button mushrooms, sliced
- **1** tablespoon vegetable oil
- **2** 14-ounce cans chicken broth
- **14** cup rice vinegar or white vinegar
- **2** tablespoons soy sauce
- **1** teaspoon sugar
- **1** teaspoon grated fresh ginger or ¼ teaspoon ground ginger
- **½** teaspoon ground black pepper
- **1** tablespoon cornstarch
- **1** tablespoon cold water
- **½** cup frozen peas
- **½** cup shredded carrot (1 medium)
- **2** tablespoons thinly sliced green onion (1)
- **1** egg, lightly beaten

**1** Thaw shrimp, if frozen. Rinse shrimp; pat dry with paper towels. Set aside.
**2** In a large saucepan cook and stir mushrooms in hot oil over medium-high heat until tender. Add broth, vinegar, soy sauce, sugar, ginger, and pepper. Bring to boiling; reduce heat. Simmer, covered, for 2 minutes. Stir in shrimp. Return to boiling; reduce heat. Simmer, covered, for 1 minute more.
**3** In a small bowl combine cornstarch and the water; stir into broth mixture. Cook and stir until slightly thickened and bubbly. Cook and stir for 2 minutes more. Stir in frozen peas, carrot, and green onion. Pour egg into soup in a steady stream, stirring a few times to create shreds.

**Hot-and-Sour Soup with Tofu:** Prepare as directed, except substitute one 12-ounce package firm, silken-style tofu (fresh bean curd), cut into bite-size pieces, for the shrimp.

**PER SERVING:** 154 cal., 6 g total fat (1 g sat. fat), 55 mg chol., 1,377 mg sodium, 14 g carbo., 2 g fiber, 10 g pro.

Most soups, stews, and chilies are good for stashing in the freezer for a hot meal on a cold day. If you plan to freeze soup, remember that hot foods bound for the freezer need to cool quickly. To do this, divide the soup into portions that are 2 to 3 inches deep and stir them while cooling. Arrange the containers in a single layer in the freezer until frozen; this allows air to circulate around the containers so the soup freezes faster.

## Cajun Fish Soup (30)

**MAKES:** 6 servings **START TO FINISH:** 30 minutes

- 12 ounces fresh or frozen fish fillets or peeled and deveined medium shrimp
- 1 14-ounce can vegetable broth or chicken broth
- 1 medium yellow summer squash or zucchini, halved lengthwise and sliced (about 1¼ cups)
- 1 cup sliced fresh mushrooms
- ½ cup finely chopped onion (1 medium)
- 2 cloves garlic, minced
- 1 teaspoon dried Cajun seasoning, crushed
- 1 teaspoon dried oregano, crushed
- 2 14.5-ounce cans stewed tomatoes, undrained and cut up
- ½ teaspoon finely shredded lemon peel

**1** Thaw fish or shrimp, if frozen. Rinse fish or shrimp; pat dry with paper towels. If using fish, cut into 1-inch pieces.
**2** In a large saucepan or Dutch oven combine broth, squash, mushrooms, onion, garlic, Cajun seasoning, and oregano. Bring to boiling; reduce heat. Simmer, covered, for 5 to 7 minutes or until vegetables are tender.
**3** Stir in fish or shrimp and undrained tomatoes. Bring just to boiling; reduce heat. Simmer, covered, for 2 to 3 minutes or until fish flakes easily when tested with a fork or shrimp are opaque. Remove from heat. Stir in lemon peel.

**Tex-Mex Fish Soup:** Prepare as directed, except substitute one 10-ounce package frozen corn, thawed, for the squash and 2 teaspoons dried Mexican seasoning, crushed, for the Cajun seasoning; omit oregano and lemon peel. If desired, garnish with Mexican-style sour cream dip and fresh cilantro sprigs.

**PER SERVING:** 106 cal., 0 g total fat, 24 mg chol., 563 mg sodium, 14 g carbo., 2 g fiber, 12 g pro.

## Cioppino

**MAKES:** 6 servings **PREP:** 55 minutes **COOK:** 25 minutes

- 2½ pounds fresh or frozen firm white fish (such as halibut or cod) and/or fresh or frozen peeled and deveined medium shrimp
- ¾ teaspoon chili powder
- 2 tablespoons olive oil
- 1 cup chopped onion (1 large)
- 1 cup frozen whole kernel corn
- 6 cloves garlic, minced
- 1 15- or 19-ounce can cannellini beans (white kidney beans), rinsed and drained
- 1 14.5-ounce can diced tomatoes, undrained
- 1 14-ounce can chicken broth
- 1 8-ounce bottle clam juice
- 1 4-ounce can diced green chile peppers, undrained
- ⅓ cup snipped fresh cilantro

**1** Thaw fish and/or shrimp, if frozen. Rinse fish and/or shrimp; pat dry with paper towels. If using, cut fish into 1-inch pieces. In a large shallow bowl sprinkle fish and/or shrimp with chili powder; toss gently to coat.
**2** In a 4-quart Dutch oven heat 1 tablespoon of the oil over medium-high heat. Add half of the fish and/or shrimp; cook about 4 minutes or just until fish flakes easily when tested with a fork and/or shrimp are opaque, gently turning with a spatula occasionally. Using a slotted spoon, transfer fish and/or shrimp to a medium bowl. Repeat with the remaining fish and/or shrimp. (Add additional oil as necessary during cooking.) Cover and chill fish and/or shrimp.
**3** In the same Dutch oven heat the remaining 1 tablespoon oil over medium heat. Add onion, corn, and garlic; cook for 3 minutes, stirring occasionally. Stir in drained beans, undrained tomatoes, broth, clam juice, and undrained green chile peppers. Bring to boiling; reduce heat. Simmer, covered, for 20 minutes. Stir in fish and/or shrimp; heat through. Sprinkle each serving with cilantro.

**PER SERVING:** 350 cal., 9 g total fat (1 g sat. fat), 61 mg chol., 944 mg sodium, 23 g carbo., 6 g fiber, 48 g pro.

Cioppino

Creamy Seafood Soup with Basil

## Creamy Seafood Soup with Basil

**MAKES:** 8 appetizer servings **PREP:** 30 minutes
**COOK:** 25 minutes

- **2 pounds live mussels in shells or 12 ounces fresh small shrimp in shells**
- **12 quarts (48 cups) cold water**
- **1 cup salt**
- **1 14-ounce can reduced-sodium chicken broth**
- **1½ cups water**
- **1 tablespoon olive oil**
- **1 cup finely chopped leeks (3 medium)***
- **2 cloves garlic, minced**
- **¼ teaspoon saffron threads or ⅛ teaspoon ground turmeric**
- **¼ teaspoon ground black pepper**
- **1 cup fat-free half-and-half**
- **1 tablespoon finely shredded fresh basil**

**1** If using mussels, scrub live mussels under cold running water. Using your fingers, pull out the beards that are visible between the shells. In an extra-large bowl combine 4 quarts (16 cups) of the cold water and 1/3 cup of the salt. Add mussels; soak for 15 minutes. Drain in a colander. Rinse mussels, discarding water. Repeat two more times with the remaining 8 quarts water and the 2/3 cup salt. Rinse well. (If using shrimp, rinse shrimp. Pat dry with paper towels.)

**2** In a Dutch oven combine broth and the 1½ cups water; bring to boiling. Add mussels; reduce heat. Simmer, covered, for 5 to 7 minutes or until shells open and mussels are cooked through. Discard any mussels that do not open. (If using shrimp, simmer for 2 to 3 minutes or until shells are pink and shrimp are opaque.)

**3** Using a slotted spoon, remove mussels or shrimp; set aside until cool enough to handle. Strain cooking liquid through a cheesecloth-lined sieve into a large bowl; set aside. Remove meat from mussel shells and set aside, discarding shells. (Or peel and devein shrimp, discarding shells.)

**4** In a large saucepan heat oil over medium heat. Add leeks and garlic; cook and stir for 3 to 5 minutes or until tender. Stir in the reserved cooking liquid, saffron, and pepper. Bring to boiling; reduce heat. Boil gently, uncovered, about 15 minutes or until reduced to 3 cups. Stir in half-and-half; heat through.

**5** Before serving, stir mussels or shrimp into soup. Sprinkle with basil.

***Note:** To clean leeks, remove root ends and remove any heavy dark green portions. Slice lengthwise and submerge in a bowl of cool clean water. Gently open layers and rinse thoroughly to remove any grit or sand. Repeat as needed.

**PER SERVING:** 79 cal., 4 g total fat (1 g sat. fat), 16 mg chol., 456 mg sodium, 7 g carbo., 0 g fiber, 3 g pro.

## Spicy Seafood Stew

**MAKES:** 4 servings **PREP:** 30 minutes **COOK:** 25 minutes

- 8 ounces fresh or frozen skinless fish fillets or steaks (such as halibut, orange roughy, or sea bass)
- 6 ounces fresh or frozen peeled and deveined shrimp
- ⅔ cup chopped onion
- ½ cup finely chopped carrot (1 medium)
- ½ cup chopped red or green sweet pepper (1 small)
- 2 cloves garlic, minced
- 2 teaspoons olive oil
- 1 14.5-ounce can no-salt-added diced tomatoes, undrained
- 1 8-ounce can no-salt-added tomato sauce
- 1 cup reduced-sodium chicken broth
- ¼ cup dry red wine or reduced-sodium chicken broth
- 2 bay leaves
- 1 tablespoon snipped fresh thyme or 1 teaspoon dried thyme, crushed
- ½ teaspoon Cajun seasoning
- ¼ teaspoon ground cumin
- ¼ teaspoon crushed red pepper (optional)

**1** Thaw fish and shrimp, if frozen. Rinse fish and shrimp; pat dry with paper towels. Cut fish into 1-inch pieces. Cover and chill fish and shrimp until needed (up to 2 hours).
**2** In a large saucepan cook and stir onion, carrot, sweet pepper, and garlic in hot oil over medium heat until tender. Stir in undrained tomatoes, tomato sauce, broth, wine, bay leaves, dried thyme (if using), Cajun seasoning, cumin, and, if desired, crushed red pepper. Bring to boiling; reduce heat. Simmer, covered, for 20 minutes.
**3** Gently stir in fish, shrimp, and, if using, fresh thyme. Simmer, covered, about 5 minutes more or until fish flakes easily when tested with a fork and shrimp are opaque. Remove and discard bay leaves.

**PER SERVING:** 213 cal., 5 g total fat (1 g sat. fat), 83 mg chol., 284 mg sodium, 16 g carbo., 3 g fiber, 24 g pro.

Spicy Seafood Stew

Chicken-and-Shrimp Tortilla Soup [below]

Baby arugula salad blend with sliced avocados, sliced red onions, and dressing

Ciabatta rolls

## Chicken-and-Shrimp Tortilla Soup 30

**MAKES:** 6 servings **START TO FINISH:** 30 minutes

- 6 ounces fresh or frozen peeled and deveined medium shrimp
- 1 tablespoon vegetable oil
- 1 cup chopped onion (1 large)
- 1 teaspoon cumin seeds
- 4½ cups reduced-sodium chicken broth
- 1 14.5-ounce can Mexican-style stewed tomatoes, undrained
- 3 tablespoons snipped fresh cilantro
- 2 tablespoons lime juice
- 1⅔ cups shredded cooked chicken breast (8 ounces)
- 1 recipe Crisp Tortilla Shreds
- Lime wedges (optional)

**1** Thaw shrimp, if frozen. Rinse shrimp; pat dry with paper towels.
**2** In a large saucepan heat oil over medium heat. Add onion and cumin seeds; cook and stir about 5 minutes or until onion is tender. Carefully add broth, undrained tomatoes, cilantro, and lime juice. Bring to boiling; reduce heat. Simmer, covered, for 8 minutes. Stir in shrimp and chicken. Simmer, uncovered, about 3 minutes more or until shrimp are opaque, stirring occasionally.
**3** Top each serving with Crisp Tortilla Shreds. If desired, serve with lime wedges.

**Crisp Tortilla Shreds:** Preheat oven to 350°. Brush four 6-inch corn tortillas with 1 tablespoon vegetable oil. In a small bowl combine ½ teaspoon salt and ⅛ teaspoon ground black pepper; sprinkle on tortillas. Cut tortillas into thin strips. Arrange in a single layer on a baking sheet. Bake about 8 minutes or until crisp. Cool on pan on a wire rack.

**PER SERVING:** 240 cal., 7 g total fat (1 g sat. fat), 76 mg chol., 1,356 mg sodium, 21 g carbo., 1 g fiber, 23 g pro.

Chicken-and-Shrimp
Tortilla Soup

## Chicken Tortilla Soup ✪

**MAKES:** 6 servings **START TO FINISH:** 35 minutes

- 1 2- to 2¼-pound purchased roasted chicken
- 2 14-ounce cans chicken broth with roasted garlic
- 1 15-ounce can chopped tomatoes and green chile peppers, undrained
- 1 11-ounce can whole kernel corn with sweet peppers, drained
- 1 small fresh jalapeño chile pepper, seeded and finely chopped (see note, page 182)
- 1 teaspoon ground cumin
- 2 tablespoons snipped fresh cilantro
- 1 tablespoon lime juice
- Tortilla chips with lime or regular tortilla chips, broken

**1** Remove and discard skin and bones from chicken. Using 2 forks, shred enough chicken to measure 2 cups; set aside. Reserve any remaining chicken for another use.

**2** In a large saucepan combine broth, undrained tomatoes, drained corn, jalapeño pepper, and cumin. Bring to boiling; reduce heat. Simmer, covered, for 10 minutes. Stir in chicken, cilantro, and lime juice; heat through. Top each serving with tortilla chips.

**PER SERVING:** 183 cal., 5 g total fat (1 g sat. fat), 43 mg chol., 1,080 mg sodium, 18 g carbo., 2 g fiber, 16 g pro.

## Chicken and Rice Soup ✪

**MAKES:** 6 servings **PREP:** 15 minutes **COOK:** 35 minutes

- 5 cups water
- 12 ounces skinless, boneless chicken breast halves
- ⅓ cup chopped onion (1 small)
- 1 bay leaf
- ½ teaspoon salt
- ½ teaspoon ground cumin
- ½ teaspoon dried oregano, crushed
- 1 clove garlic, minced
- ¼ teaspoon ground black pepper
- 1 14.5-ounce can diced tomatoes, undrained
- 1 14-ounce can lower-sodium beef broth
- 1 cup frozen whole kernel corn
- ¾ cup chopped green sweet pepper (1 medium)
- ⅔ cup uncooked long grain rice
- ⅓ cup snipped fresh cilantro
- 2 teaspoons chili powder

**1** In a Dutch oven combine the water, chicken, onion, bay leaf, salt, cumin, oregano, garlic, and black pepper. Bring to boiling; reduce heat. Simmer, uncovered, for 10 to 12 minutes or until chicken is no longer pink (170°). Using tongs, remove chicken from Dutch oven. Using 2 forks, shred chicken into bite-size pieces.

**2** Stir undrained tomatoes, broth, corn, sweet pepper, uncooked rice, cilantro, and chili powder into Dutch oven. Bring to boiling; reduce heat. Simmer, covered, about 25 minutes or until rice is tender. Stir in shredded chicken; heat through. Remove and discard bay leaf.

**PER SERVING:** 197 cal., 2 g total fat (0 g sat. fat), 33 mg chol., 477 mg sodium, 28 g carbo., 2 g fiber, 17 g pro.

## Ginger-Chicken Noodle Soup

**MAKES:** 5 servings **PREP:** 20 minutes **COOK:** 28 minutes

- 1 pound skinless, boneless chicken thighs, cut into 1-inch pieces
- 1 tablespoon vegetable oil
- 3 14-ounce cans reduced-sodium chicken broth
- 2 medium carrots, cut into thin bite-size strips
- 1 cup water
- 2 tablespoons rice vinegar
- 1 tablespoon reduced-sodium soy sauce
- 2 to 3 teaspoons grated fresh ginger or ½ to ¾ teaspoon ground ginger
- ¼ teaspoon ground black pepper
- 2 ounces dried rice vermicelli noodles or medium noodles
- 1 6-ounce package frozen pea pods, thawed and halved diagonally
- Reduced-sodium soy sauce (optional)

**1** In a Dutch oven cook half of the chicken at a time in hot oil over medium-high heat until brown. Drain off fat. Return all of the chicken to Dutch oven.

**2** Add broth, carrots, the water, vinegar, the 1 tablespoon soy sauce, ginger, and pepper. Bring to boiling; reduce heat. Simmer, covered, for 20 minutes.

**3** Stir in noodles. Return to boiling; reduce heat. Simmer, uncovered, for 8 to 10 minutes or until noodles are tender, adding pea pods during the last 1 to 2 minutes of cooking. If desired, serve with additional soy sauce.

**PER SERVING:** 221 cal., 6 g total fat (1 g sat. fat), 72 mg chol., 805 mg sodium, 16 g carbo., 2 g fiber, 23 g pro.

A bowl of noodles, meat, and vegetables in a flavorful broth is comfort food, Asian style.

Ginger-Chicken Noodle Soup

Caraway Chicken
and Vegetable Stew

Beef Goulash Soup

## Beef Goulash Soup

**MAKES:** 4 servings **PREP:** 30 minutes **COOK:** 20 minutes

- 6 ounces boneless beef top sirloin steak
- 1 teaspoon olive oil
- ½ cup chopped onion (1 medium)
- 2 cups water
- 1 14.5-ounce can no-salt-added diced tomatoes, undrained
- 1 14-ounce can beef broth
- ½ cup thinly sliced carrot (1 medium)
- 1 teaspoon unsweetened cocoa powder
- 1 clove garlic, minced
- 1 cup thinly sliced cabbage
- 1 ounce dried wide noodles (about ½ cup)
- 2 teaspoons paprika
- ¼ cup light sour cream
- Snipped fresh parsley (optional)
- Paprika (optional)

**1** Trim fat from meat. Cut meat into ½-inch pieces. In a large saucepan cook and stir meat in hot oil over medium-high heat about 6 minutes or until meat is brown. Add onion; cook and stir about 3 minutes more or until tender.

**2** Stir in the water, undrained tomatoes, broth, carrot, cocoa powder, and garlic. Bring to boiling; reduce heat. Simmer, uncovered, about 15 minutes or until meat is tender.

**3** Stir in cabbage, uncooked noodles, and the 2 teaspoons paprika. Simmer, uncovered, for 5 to 7 minutes more or until noodles are tender but still firm.

**4** Serve with sour cream. If desired, sprinkle with parsley and additional paprika.

**PER SERVING:** 188 cal., 7 g total fat (3 g sat. fat), 36 mg chol., 397 mg sodium, 16 g carbo., 3 g fiber, 14 g pro.

## Menu

Tuscan Bean Soup with Spinach [right]

Salad of mesclun, toasted pepitas, and Italian vinaigrette

Baguette slices

Assorted olives

## Beef and Noodle Soup

**MAKES:** 8 servings **PREP:** 15 minutes
**COOK:** 8 to 10 hours (low) or 4 to 5 hours (high) + 30 minutes

- 1 pound beef stew meat, cut into ½-inch pieces
- 1 16-ounce package frozen mixed vegetables
- 5 cups water
- 1 14.5-ounce can diced tomatoes, undrained
- 1 8-ounce can tomato sauce
- 2 bay leaves
- 2 tablespoons instant beef bouillon granules
- 1½ teaspoons dried basil, crushed
- ½ teaspoon dried marjoram, crushed
- ¼ teaspoon ground black pepper
- 2 cups dried medium noodles

**1** In a 4½- to 6-quart slow cooker combine meat, frozen vegetables, the water, undrained tomatoes, tomato sauce, bay leaves, bouillon granules, basil, marjoram, and pepper.
**2** Cover and cook on low-heat setting for 8 to 10 hours or on high-heat setting for 4 to 5 hours.
**3** If using low-heat setting, turn to high-heat setting. Stir in uncooked noodles. Cover and cook for 30 minutes more. Remove and discard bay leaves.

**PER SERVING:** 179 cal., 4 g total fat (1 g sat. fat), 36 mg chol., 1,106 mg sodium, 19 g carbo., 4 g fiber, 17 g pro.

## Tuscan Bean Soup with Spinach

**MAKES:** 8 to 10 servings **PREP:** 30 minutes **STAND:** 1 hour
**COOK:** 2 hours

- 8 ounces dried cannellini beans (white kidney beans)
- 6 cups water
- 1 pound beef shank cross cuts (1 to 1½ inches thick)
- ¼ teaspoon salt
- ¼ teaspoon ground black pepper
- 1 tablespoon olive oil
- 1½ cups chopped onions (3 medium)
- 1½ cups chopped carrots (3 medium)
- 1 cup fennel wedges or chopped celery
- 4 cloves garlic, minced
- 6 cups water
- 12 ounces meaty smoked pork hocks
- 1 bay leaf
- 1 tablespoon instant beef bouillon granules
- 2 teaspoons snipped fresh thyme or ½ teaspoon dried thyme, crushed
- 2 teaspoons snipped fresh rosemary or ½ teaspoon dried rosemary, crushed
- ½ teaspoon salt
- 1 14.5-ounce can diced tomatoes, undrained
- 4 cups torn fresh spinach leaves

**1** Rinse beans. In a 4½- to 6-quart Dutch oven combine beans and 6 cups water. Bring to boiling; reduce heat. Simmer, uncovered, for 2 minutes. Remove from heat. Cover and let stand for 1 hour. Drain and rinse beans; set aside.
**2** Sprinkle beef with the ¼ teaspoon salt and pepper. In the same Dutch oven cook beef in hot oil over medium-high heat about 5 minutes or until brown, turning once. Remove beef, reserving drippings in Dutch oven.
**3** Add onions, carrots, fennel, and garlic to the reserved drippings. Cook, covered, over medium heat about 10 minutes or until vegetables are tender, stirring occasionally. Return beans and beef to Dutch oven.
**4** Stir in 6 cups water, pork, bay leaf, bouillon granules, dried thyme and dried rosemary (if using), and ½ teaspoon salt. Bring to boiling; reduce heat. Simmer, covered, for 1½ hours. Stir in undrained tomatoes. Simmer, covered, about 30 minutes or until beans, beef, and pork are tender.
**5** Remove beef and pork; cool slightly. Remove meat from bones; discard bones. Cut meat into bite-size pieces; return to vegetable mixture. Remove and discard bay leaf. Skim off fat. Stir in spinach and, if using, fresh thyme and fresh rosemary; heat through.

**PER SERVING:** 231 cal., 6 g total fat (2 g sat. fat), 21 mg chol., 803 mg sodium, 27 g carbo., 11 g fiber, 17 g pro.

Tuscan Bean Soup with Spinach

Teriyaki Beef Soup

## Teriyaki Beef Soup

**MAKES:** 5 (1⅓-cup) servings **START TO FINISH:** 30 minutes

- 8 ounces boneless beef top sirloin steak
- 1 large shallot, cut into thin rings
- 2 teaspoons olive oil
- 2 14-ounce cans lower-sodium beef broth
- 1 cup water
- ½ cup apple juice or apple cider
- 2 medium carrots, cut into thin bite-size strips (1 cup)
- ⅓ cup instant brown rice or quick-cooking barley
- 2 tablespoons light teriyaki sauce
- 1 tablespoon grated fresh ginger
- 3 cloves garlic, minced
- ¼ teaspoon crushed red pepper
- 2 cups coarsely chopped broccoli

**1** If desired, partially freeze steak for easier slicing. Trim fat from steak. Cut steak into thin bite-size strips. In a large saucepan cook and stir steak and shallot in hot oil over medium-high heat for 2 to 3 minutes or until beef is brown. Remove beef mixture with a slotted spoon; set aside.

**2** In the same saucepan combine the broth, water, apple juice, carrots, uncooked brown rice or barley, teriyaki sauce, ginger, garlic, and crushed red pepper. Bring to boiling; reduce heat. Simmer, covered, for 10 minutes.

**3** Stir in broccoli and the beef mixture. Bring to boiling; reduce heat. Simmer, covered, for 3 to 5 minutes or until rice and vegetables are tender.

**PER SERVING:** 162 cal., 4 g total fat (1 g sat. fat), 28 mg chol., 481 mg sodium, 18 g carbo., 2 g fiber, 13 g pro.

# Soup always hits the spot.

## Mediterranean Stew with Olives and Oranges

**MAKES:** 6 servings **PREP:** 20 minutes
**BAKE:** 2 hours **OVEN:** 350°

- 1½ pounds boneless beef round
- 1 tablespoon vegetable oil
- ½ cup chopped onion (1 medium)
- 3 cloves garlic, minced
- 1 14.5-ounce can diced tomatoes, undrained
- 1 cup chicken broth or beef broth
- ½ cup bottled roasted red sweet peppers, drained and coarsely chopped
- ¼ cup quartered pitted kalamata olives or ripe olives
- 2 teaspoons finely shredded orange peel
- 1½ teaspoons dried Italian seasoning, crushed
- 2 medium yellow summer squash, halved lengthwise and sliced
- 3 oranges, peeled and sectioned
- Ground black pepper
- 3 cups hot cooked couscous or orzo pasta

**1** Preheat oven to 350°. Trim fat from meat. Cut meat into ¾-inch pieces. In a 4-quart Dutch oven cook half of the meat at a time in hot oil over medium-high heat until brown. Drain off fat. Return all of the meat to Dutch oven.
**2** Add onion and garlic; cook and stir for 1 minute. Stir in undrained tomatoes, broth, roasted sweet peppers, olives, orange peel, and Italian seasoning. Bake, covered, for 1½ hours.
**3** Stir in squash. Bake, covered, about 30 minutes more or until meat is tender. Before serving, stir in orange sections and season to taste with black pepper. Serve with hot cooked couscous.
**Rangetop method:** Prepare as directed, except in Step 2, simmer the mixture, covered, for 1¼ hours and in Step 3 simmer, covered, about 15 minutes more.

**PER SERVING:** 342 cal., 9 g total fat (2 g sat. fat), 72 mg chol., 304 mg sodium, 32 g carbo., 6 g fiber, 33 g pro.

## Hearty Bavarian Soup

**MAKES:** 6 to 8 servings **PREP:** 25 minutes **COOK:** 1¼ hours

- 1 pound boneless beef top round
- ½ cup chopped onion (1 medium)
- 2 tablespoons vegetable oil
- 2 tablespoons all-purpose flour
- 1 tablespoon Hungarian paprika
- 2 cloves garlic, minced
- 3 14-ounce cans chicken broth
- 1 14.5-ounce can diced tomatoes, undrained
- 1½ cups sliced carrots (3 medium)
- 2 tablespoons tomato paste
- 1 bay leaf
- ½ teaspoon dried marjoram, crushed
- ½ teaspoon caraway seeds, crushed
- ½ teaspoon ground black pepper
- 2 cups peeled and cubed potatoes (2 medium)
- Light sour cream (optional)

**1** Trim fat from meat. Cut meat into ½-inch pieces. In a 4- to 5-quart Dutch oven cook meat and onion in hot oil over medium-high heat about 5 minutes or until meat is brown and onion is tender.
**2** Add flour, paprika, and garlic; cook and stir for 3 minutes. Stir in broth, undrained tomatoes, carrots, tomato paste, bay leaf, marjoram, caraway seeds, and pepper. Bring to boiling; reduce heat. Simmer, covered, for 50 minutes, stirring occasionally.
**3** Stir in potatoes. Simmer, covered, for 25 to 30 minutes more or until meat and potatoes are tender. Remove and discard bay leaf. If desired, top each serving with sour cream.

**PER SERVING:** 244 cal., 9 g total fat (2 g sat. fat), 42 mg chol., 996 mg sodium, 19 g carbo., 3 g fiber, 21 g pro.

page 254
page 277

Simply

Sides

Customize the flavor of your homemade applesauce with the apples you use to make it. Pick a tart cooking apple such as Granny Smith or McIntosh if you like your applesauce on the tart side. Choose a sweeter cooking apple, such as Golden Delicious, if you like it sweet. Or use a blend of apples for a truly one-of-a-kind applesauce.

## Lemon Spice Applesauce

**MAKES:** 16 servings **PREP:** 45 minutes **COOK:** 40 minutes

- 15 cups peeled and sliced cooking apples (about 5 pounds)
- 2½ cups water
- 1 to 1½ cups packed brown sugar
- 3 tablespoons finely shredded lemon peel
- ¾ cup lemon juice
- 1½ teaspoons apple pie spice or 2 teaspoons ground cinnamon
- 1 tablespoon vanilla

**1** In a heavy 6-quart Dutch oven combine apples, the water, brown sugar, lemon peel, lemon juice, and apple pie spice. Bring to boiling; reduce heat. Simmer, covered, about 40 minutes or until apples are very soft, stirring occasionally. Remove from heat. Stir in vanilla.
**2** Mash mixture with a potato masher or the back of a large wooden spoon. Serve warm or cover and chill before serving.
**Note:** To freeze, place the Dutch oven with applesauce in a sink filled with ice water; stir mixture to cool. Ladle into pint wide-top freezer containers, leaving a ½-inch headspace. Seal and label; freeze for up to 6 months.

**PER SERVING:** 127 cal., 0 g total fat, 0 mg chol.,7 mg sodium, 33 g carbo., 3 g fiber, 0 g pro.

## Five-Cup Fruit Salad

**MAKES:** 6 servings **PREP:** 10 minutes **CHILL:** 2 to 24 hours

- 1 8-ounce can pineapple chunks (juice pack), undrained
- 1 cup coconut
- 1 cup tiny marshmallows
- 1 11-ounce can mandarin orange sections, drained
- 1 8-ounce carton sour cream
- 2 tablespoons chopped pecans

**1** Drain pineapple, reserving 1 tablespoon of the juice. In a medium bowl combine the reserved juice, pineapple chunks, coconut, marshmallows, drained mandarin orange sections, and sour cream. Cover and chill for 2 to 24 hours. Before serving, sprinkle with pecans.

**PER SERVING:** 279 cal., 16 g total fat (12 g sat. fat), 17 mg chol., 94 mg sodium, 33 g carbo., 2 g fiber, 3 g pro.

## Honey-Lime Fruit Salad 

**MAKES:** 6 servings **START TO FINISH:** 20 minutes

- 1 6-ounce carton plain low-fat yogurt
- ½ teaspoon finely shredded lime peel or lemon peel
- 3 tablespoons lime juice or lemon juice
- 2 to 3 tablespoons honey
- 2 cups sliced Granny Smith or Golden Delicious apples (2 medium)
- Leaf lettuce
- ½ of a small honeydew melon, peeled, halved crosswise, and sliced
- 1 cup halved seedless red or green grapes
- ½ cup pistachio nuts or slivered almonds (optional)

**1** For dressing, in a small bowl combine yogurt, lime peel, 2 tablespoons of the lime juice, and the honey. In a medium bowl combine apples and the remaining 1 tablespoon lime juice; toss gently to coat.
**2** Line 6 salad plates with lettuce. Arrange apple slices, honeydew slices, and grapes on top of lettuce. Drizzle with desired amount of dressing. (Cover and chill any remaining dressing for up to 5 days.) If desired, sprinkle with pistachios.

**PER SERVING:** 119 cal., 1 g total fat (0 g sat. fat), 2 mg chol., 36 mg sodium, 27 g carbo., 2 g fiber, 3 g pro.

## Apple Spinach Salad with Thyme-Dijon Vinaigrette 30

**MAKES:** 4 servings **START TO FINISH:** 25 minutes

- **4** cups fresh baby spinach
- **1** cup sliced Granny Smith apple (1 medium)
- **¼** cup thin red onion wedges
- **2** tablespoons snipped dried tart cherries
- **¼** cup Thyme-Dijon Vinaigrette
- **½** cup crumbled feta cheese or blue cheese (2 ounces) (optional)

**1** In a large bowl combine spinach, apple, red onion, and dried cherries. Drizzle with Thyme-Dijon Vinaigrette; toss gently to coat. If desired, top each serving with cheese.

**Thyme-Dijon Vinaigrette:** In a screw-top jar combine ¼ cup olive oil; ¼ cup white or regular balsamic vinegar; 2 teaspoons snipped fresh thyme or ½ teaspoon dried thyme, crushed; 1 teaspoon Dijon-style mustard; and ¼ teaspoon salt. Cover and shake well. Chill until ready to serve. Shake before using. Makes ⅔ cup.

**PER SERVING:** 93 cal., 6 g total fat (1 g sat. fat), 0 mg chol., 96 mg sodium, 11 g carbo., 2 g fiber, 1 g pro.

Avocado and Grapefruit Salad

Sweet Mustard Halibut
[page 72]

Avocado and Grapefruit Salad
[below]

Orzo-Broccoli Pilaf
[page 270]

Iced green tea

## Avocado and Grapefruit Salad

**MAKES:** 6 servings **START TO FINISH:** 20 minutes

- **8 cups torn mixed salad greens or fresh baby spinach**
- **2 grapefruit, peeled and sectioned**
- **1 avocado, seeded, peeled, and sliced**
- **2 tablespoons raspberry vinegar**
- **2 tablespoons avocado oil or olive oil**
- **1 tablespoon water**
- **1 teaspoon sugar**
- **⅛ teaspoon salt**

**1** On a large serving platter or 6 salad plates, arrange salad greens, grapefruit sections, and avocado slices.
**2** For dressing, in a bowl whisk together vinegar, oil, the water, sugar, and salt. Drizzle dressing over greens mixture.

**PER SERVING:** 134 cal., 9 g total fat (1 g sat. fat), 0 mg chol., 60 mg sodium, 14 g carbo., 4 g fiber, 2 g pro.

## Berry-Best Salad

**MAKES:** 4 servings **START TO FINISH:** 15 minutes

- **¼ cup orange juice**
- **1 tablespoon vegetable oil**
- **2 teaspoons honey mustard or Dijon-style mustard**
- **1 teaspoon sugar**
- **¼ teaspoon salt**
- **4 cups torn lettuce**
- **1½ cups fresh blueberries, raspberries, and/or quartered strawberries**
- **2 tablespoons bite-size cheese crackers or 1 tablespoon sunflower kernels**

**1** For dressing, in a screw-top jar combine orange juice, oil, mustard, sugar, and salt. Cover and shake well. Place lettuce in a medium bowl. Drizzle with dressing; toss gently to coat.
**2** Divide lettuce among 4 salad plates. Top with berries and sprinkle with crackers.

**PER SERVING:** 86 cal., 4 g total fat (1 g sat. fat), 0 mg chol., 208 mg sodium, 13 g carbo., 3 g fiber, 1 g pro.

Berry-Best Salad

## Blue Cheese-Stuffed Endive

**MAKES:** 18 servings **START TO FINISH:** 40 minutes

- **1** 8-ounce package fat-free cream cheese
- **½** cup crumbled Roquefort cheese or blue cheese (2 ounces)
- **¼** cup finely chopped green onion (2) or chives
- **2** slices bacon, crisp-cooked, drained, and crumbled
- **2** tablespoons hazelnuts (filberts), toasted* and finely chopped
- **36** Belgian endive leaves (about 3 heads)

**1** In a medium bowl combine cream cheese, Roquefort cheese, green onions, crumbled bacon, and hazelnuts. If desired, cover and chill for up to 4 hours.

**2** To serve, spoon 2 teaspoons of the cheese mixture into the cup of each Belgian endive leaf.

***Note:** To toast hazelnuts, preheat oven to 350°. Spread hazelnuts in a single layer in a shallow baking pan. Bake about 10 minutes or until light golden brown, watching carefully and stirring once or twice so the nuts don't burn. Cool slightly. Place the nuts on a clean kitchen towel; fold towel over top and rub vigorously to remove the skins.

**PER SERVING:** 35 cal., 2 g total fat (1 g sat. fat), 6 mg chol., 71 mg sodium, 1 g carbo., 0 g fiber, 3 g pro.

## Chilled Asparagus Salad

**MAKES:** 6 servings **START TO FINISH:** 20 minutes

- ½ cup light mayonnaise or salad dressing
- ½ teaspoon finely shredded orange peel
- ⅓ cup orange juice
- ¼ cup plain fat-free yogurt
- ⅛ teaspoon lemon-pepper seasoning
- 1 pound fresh asparagus spears
- 6 cups torn butterhead (Boston or Bibb) lettuce
- 1 11-ounce can mandarin orange sections, drained
- 1 small red onion, cut into thin wedges

**1** For dressing, in a small bowl combine mayonnaise, orange peel, orange juice, yogurt, and lemon-pepper seasoning. Cover and chill for up to 6 hours or until ready to serve.
**2** Snap off and discard woody bases from asparagus. If desired, scrape off scales. In a covered large saucepan cook asparagus in a small amount of boiling, lightly salted water for 3 to 5 minutes or until crisp-tender; drain. Immediately submerge cooked asparagus in a bowl of ice water to cool quickly. Drain again.
**3** Divide lettuce among 6 salad plates. Arrange asparagus, drained mandarin orange sections, and onion wedges on top of lettuce. Drizzle with dressing.

**PER SERVING:** 119 cal., 7 g total fat (1 g sat. fat), 7 mg chol., 181 mg sodium, 13 g carbo., 2 g fiber, 3 g pro.

Chilled Asparagus Salad

The best time to buy asparagus is spring, when it's in season. For the most tender asparagus, buy the slenderest stalks with heads that are tightly closed. To trim the woody stem, gently bend the spear toward the bottom. The spot where it naturally bends and snaps is the place to break it.

## Penne Salad with Green Beans and Gorgonzola

**MAKES:** 8 servings **START TO FINISH:** 25 minutes

- 6 ounces dried penne or cut ziti pasta
- 8 ounces fresh green beans, trimmed and bias-sliced into 1-inch pieces (about 1½ cups), or one 9-ounce package frozen cut green beans, thawed
- ⅓ cup bottled Italian salad dressing
- 1 tablespoon snipped fresh tarragon or ½ teaspoon dried tarragon, crushed
- ¼ teaspoon ground black pepper
- 1 cup shredded radicchio or red cabbage
- 1 6-ounce package fresh baby spinach
- ½ cup crumbled Gorgonzola or blue cheese (2 ounces) or ¼ cup shaved Parmesan cheese (1 ounce)

**1** Cook pasta according to package directions, adding fresh green beans during the last 5 to 7 minutes of cooking (if using frozen beans, add during the last 3 to 4 minutes); drain. Rinse with cold water; drain again.
**2** In a large bowl combine Italian dressing, tarragon, and pepper. Add cooked pasta mixture and radicchio; toss gently to coat. Line a serving platter with spinach. Spoon pasta mixture on top of spinach. Sprinkle with cheese.

**PER SERVING:** 147 cal., 5 g total fat (2 g sat. fat), 5 mg chol., 280 mg sodium, 20 g carbo., 2 g fiber, 6 g pro.

## Tortellini Tossed Salad

**MAKES:** 8 servings **START TO FINISH:** 20 minutes

- 1 9-ounce package refrigerated cheese tortellini
- 1 16-ounce package torn mixed salad greens
- 1 cup shredded carrots (2 medium)
- ¾ cup red sweet pepper strips (1 medium)
- ¼ cup snipped fresh basil
- 1 2.25-ounce can sliced pitted ripe olives, rinsed and drained
- ¼ cup white wine vinegar or white vinegar
- 2 tablespoons water
- 2 tablespoons olive oil
- 2 teaspoons sugar
- 2 cloves garlic, minced
- ¼ teaspoon ground black pepper
- ½ cup croutons, coarsely crushed

**1** In a large saucepan cook tortellini according to package directions, except omit any oil or salt; drain. Rinse with cold water; drain again.

**2** Meanwhile, in a large bowl combine salad greens, carrots, sweet pepper, basil, and olives. Stir in cooked tortellini.

**3** For dressing, in a screw-top jar combine vinegar, the water, oil, sugar, garlic, and black pepper. Cover and shake well. Pour over tortellini mixture; toss gently to coat. Top each serving with croutons.

**PER SERVING:** 170 cal., 7 g total fat (2 g sat. fat), 12 mg chol., 247 mg sodium, 22 g carbo., 3 g fiber, 6 g pro.

## Ravioli Salad

**MAKES:** 8 servings **PREP:** 30 minutes **CHILL:** 2 to 6 hours

- 1 9-ounce package refrigerated light cheese ravioli
- 3 cups broccoli florets
- 1 cup sliced carrots (2 medium)
- ¼ cup sliced green onions (2)
- ½ cup bottled reduced-calorie Italian salad dressing or balsamic vinaigrette salad dressing
- 1 large tomato, chopped
- 1 cup fresh pea pods, halved crosswise
- Lettuce leaves (optional)

**1** Cook ravioli according to package directions, except omit oil or salt and add broccoli and carrots during the last 3 minutes of cooking; drain. Rinse with cold water; drain.

**2** In a large bowl combine cooked pasta mixture and green onions. Pour dressing over pasta mixture; toss gently to coat. Cover and chill for 2 to 6 hours.

**3** To serve, gently stir tomato and pea pods into pasta mixture. If desired, serve on lettuce-lined salad plates.

**PER SERVING:** 237 cal., 7 g total fat (2 g sat. fat), 40 mg chol., 477 mg sodium, 34 g carbo., 4 g fiber, 11 g pro.

## Italian Pasta Salad

**MAKES:** 6 servings **START TO FINISH:** 25 minutes

- 4 ounces dried whole wheat rotini, penne, or bow tie pasta
- 1 cup fresh sugar snap peas (4 ounces), trimmed
- ½ cup chopped red sweet pepper (1 small)
- ¼ cup shredded fresh basil*
- 2 tablespoons pitted niçoise olives or ripe olives, quartered
- 2 tablespoons red wine vinegar
- 2 tablespoons olive oil
- 1 clove garlic, minced
- ⅛ teaspoon salt
- Dash ground black pepper

**1** Cook pasta according to package directions, adding sugar snap peas during the last 1 minute of cooking; drain. Rinse with cold water; drain again. In a large bowl combine cooked pasta mixture, sweet pepper, basil, and olives.

**2** For dressing, in a screw-top jar combine vinegar, oil, garlic, salt, and black pepper. Cover and shake well. Pour dressing over pasta mixture; toss gently to coat.

***Note:** A quick way to shred (chiffonade) fresh basil is to stack several leaves on top of each other and roll the leaves up like a cigar. Starting at one end, use a sharp knife to cut crosswise into slices.

**PER SERVING:** 118 cal., 5 g total fat (1 g sat. fat), 0 mg chol., 75 mg sodium, 16 g carbo., 2 g fiber, 3 g pro.

Italian Pasta Salad

# Complement grilled chicken

Pepper and Four-Bean Salad

with a colorful, crunchy salad.

## Pepper and Four-Bean Salad

**MAKES:** 14 servings **PREP:** 25 minutes
**MARINATE:** 4 to 24 hours

- 1 pound fresh green and/or wax beans, trimmed and cut into 1½-inch pieces (about 3 cups), or one 16-ounce package frozen cut green beans
- 3 cups green, red, and/or yellow sweet pepper strips (3 medium)
- 1 15-ounce can red kidney beans, rinsed and drained
- 1 15-ounce can garbanzo beans (chickpeas), rinsed and drained
- 1 small red or white onion, thinly sliced and separated into rings
- ½ cup vinegar
- ¼ cup olive oil
- 1 tablespoon sugar
- 2 teaspoons snipped fresh tarragon or thyme or ½ teaspoon dried tarragon or thyme, crushed
- ½ teaspoon ground black pepper
- Lettuce leaves

**1** In a covered large saucepan cook fresh green and/or wax beans in a small amount of boiling water for 5 to 7 minutes or just until tender. (If using frozen beans, cook according to package directions.) Drain. Immediately submerge cooked beans in a bowl of ice water to cool quickly. Drain again.
**2** In a large bowl combine green and/or wax beans, sweet peppers, drained kidney beans, drained garbanzo beans, and onion. For marinade, in a medium bowl whisk together vinegar, oil, sugar, tarragon, and black pepper. Pour marinade over bean mixture; toss gently to coat. Cover and marinate in the refrigerator for 4 to 24 hours, stirring occasionally.
**3** To serve, line a serving bowl with lettuce. Using a slotted spoon, spoon bean mixture into lettuce-lined bowl.

**PER SERVING:** 117 cal., 4 g total fat (1 g sat. fat), 0 mg chol., 146 mg sodium, 17 g carbo., 5 g fiber, 5 g pro.

## Quick-Toss Fruit Slaw (30)

**MAKES:** 10 to 12 servings **START TO FINISH:** 20 minutes

- 4 cups packaged shredded cabbage with carrot (coleslaw mix)
- 1⅓ cups coarsely chopped apple (2 medium)
- 1 cup packaged shredded red cabbage
- ¾ cup mixed dried fruit bits
- ¼ cup chopped pecans, toasted
- 1 6-ounce carton vanilla low-fat yogurt
- ⅛ teaspoon ground nutmeg
- Apple slices (optional)
- Fresh Italian (flat-leaf) parsley sprigs (optional)

**1** In a large bowl toss together coleslaw mix, coarsely chopped apple, red cabbage, dried fruit bits, and pecans.
**2** For dressing, in a small bowl combine yogurt and nutmeg. Pour dressing over cabbage mixture; toss gently to coat. If desired, cover and chill for up to 8 hours. If desired, garnish with apple slices and parsley.

**PER SERVING:** 80 cal., 2 g total fat (0 g sat. fat), 1 mg chol., 26 mg sodium, 15 g carbo., 2 g fiber, 2 g pro.

## Confetti Slaw

**MAKES:** 8 to 10 servings **PREP:** 20 minutes
**CHILL:** 4 to 24 hours

- ⅔ cup mayonnaise or salad dressing
- 4 teaspoons buttermilk ranch dry salad dressing mix
- 1 tablespoon honey
- 4 cups shredded green and/or red cabbage
- 1 cup red and/or green sweet pepper strips
- 1 cup shredded carrots (2 medium)
- ½ cup thinly sliced celery (1 stalk)
- ½ cup dried cranberries or raisins

**1** For dressing, in a small bowl stir together mayonnaise, salad dressing mix, and honey; set aside.
**2** In a large bowl combine cabbage, sweet pepper, carrots, celery, and dried cranberries. Pour dressing over cabbage mixture; toss gently to coat. Cover and chill for 4 to 24 hours.

**PER SERVING:** 186 cal., 15 g total fat (2 g sat. fat), 11 mg chol., 222 mg sodium, 14 g carbo., 2 g fiber, 1 g pro.

## Menu

Grilled turkey burgers

Dilled green beans

Creamy Potato Salad [right]

Angel food cake with fresh peach slices

## Crunchy Trail Mix Salad

**MAKES:** 8 servings **START TO FINISH:** 30 minutes

- **3 cups broccoli florets**
- **1 cup dried tart cherries**
- **¾ cup dry-roasted sunflower kernels**
- **½ cup chopped red onion (1 medium)**
- **⅓ cup light mayonnaise or salad dressing**
- **⅓ cup plain fat-free yogurt**
- **3 tablespoons bottled raspberry vinaigrette salad dressing**
- **5 slices bacon, crisp-cooked, drained, and crumbled**
- **Fat-free milk (optional)**

**1** In a large bowl combine broccoli, dried cherries, sunflower kernels, and red onion.
**2** For dressing, in a small bowl combine mayonnaise, yogurt, and raspberry vinaigrette. Pour dressing over broccoli mixture; toss gently to coat. Sprinkle with crumbled bacon. If desired, cover and chill for up to 24 hours.
**3** Stir before serving. If necessary, stir in a little milk to moisten.

**PER SERVING:** 217 cal., 12 g total fat (2 g sat. fat), 9 mg chol., 279 mg sodium, 23 g carbo., 3 g fiber, 6 g pro.

## Creamy Potato Salad

**MAKES:** 16 servings **PREP:** 30 minutes **COOK:** 20 minutes
**CHILL:** 2 to 24 hours

- **2½ pounds round white and/or red-skinned potatoes (7 to 8 medium)**
- **1 cup light mayonnaise or salad dressing**
- **1 8-ounce carton light sour cream**
- **2 tablespoons fat-free milk**
- **1 teaspoon seasoned pepper**
- **¼ teaspoon salt**
- **3 hard-cooked eggs, peeled and chopped**
- **¾ cup sliced green onions (6)**
- **½ cup cubed reduced-fat cheddar cheese (2 ounces)**
- **Fat-free milk (optional)**
- **1 avocado**
- **2 slices bacon or turkey bacon, crisp-cooked, drained, and crumbled**

**1** In a covered large saucepan cook potatoes in enough boiling water to cover for 20 to 25 minutes or just until tender; drain. Cool slightly. Cut into bite-size pieces.
**2** In an extra-large bowl combine mayonnaise, sour cream, the 2 tablespoons milk, seasoned pepper, and salt. Gently stir in potato pieces, hard-cooked egg, green onions, and cheese. Cover and chill for 2 to 24 hours. Cover and chill bacon separately.
**3** Stir before serving. If necessary, stir in a little milk to moisten. Seed, peel, and chop avocado; stir into potato mixture. Sprinkle with bacon.

**PER SERVING:** 179 cal., 11 g total fat (3 g sat. fat), 54 mg chol., 218 mg sodium, 17 g carbo., 3 g fiber, 5 g pro.

Light mayonnaise and light sour cream make this summertime-favorite salad easy on the waistline.

Creamy Potato Salad

Confetti Potato Salad

3 In an extra-large bowl combine potatoes, green beans, broccoli and/or cauliflower, and carrot. Add salad dressing and pepper; toss gently to coat. Cover and chill for 4 to 24 hours. Before serving, stir in a little milk if necessary to moisten.

**PER SERVING:** 108 cal., 3 g total fat (0 g sat. fat), 5 mg chol., 179 mg sodium, 18 g carbo., 3 g fiber, 3 g pro.

## Marinated Baby Beets

**MAKES:** 8 servings **PREP:** 20 minutes **ROAST:** 40 minutes **MARINATE:** 30 minutes **OVEN:** 425°

- **2 pounds trimmed red and/or yellow baby beets or small beets (about 3½ pounds untrimmed with tops)**
- **2 tablespoons olive oil**
- **¼ teaspoon salt**
- **¼ teaspoon ground black pepper**
- **1 large orange**
- **3 tablespoons white wine vinegar**
- **2 tablespoons thinly sliced shallot (1 medium)**
- **2 teaspoons Dijon-style mustard**

**1** Preheat oven to 425°. If using small beets, cut into 1- to 1½-inch wedges. Place beets in a shallow baking pan. Drizzle with 1 tablespoon of the oil and sprinkle with salt and pepper; stir gently to coat. Cover with foil and roast for 25 minutes. Roast, uncovered, about 15 minutes more or until beets are tender. Cool. If using, peel the small beets (baby beets do not need to be peeled).

**2** Meanwhile, using a knife or citrus tool, remove long shreds of peel from the orange, taking care not to remove the white pith; measure 2 tablespoons peel. Squeeze juice from orange; measure ⅓ cup juice.

**3** In a clear glass serving dish whisk together the remaining 1 tablespoon oil, orange juice, vinegar, shallot, and mustard. Add beets and orange peel; stir gently to coat. Cover and marinate at room temperature for 30 minutes or in the refrigerator for up to 8 hours, stirring occasionally.

**PER SERVING:** 90 cal., 4 g total fat (1 g sat. fat), 0 mg chol., 188 mg sodium, 13 g carbo., 3 g fiber, 2 g pro.

## Confetti Potato Salad

**MAKES:** 8 servings **PREP:** 30 minutes **CHILL:** 4 to 24 hours

- **1½ pounds round red-skinned potatoes (3 to 4 medium)**
- **4 ounces fresh green beans, trimmed and cut into 2-inch pieces (about 1 cup)**
- **2 cups broccoli and/or cauliflower florets**
- **½ cup coarsely shredded carrot (1 medium)**
- **½ cup bottled reduced-calorie ranch salad dressing**
- **¼ teaspoon ground black pepper**
- **Fat-free milk (optional)**

**1** Cut potatoes into ½-inch pieces. In a covered large saucepan cook potatoes in enough boiling water to cover for 5 to 7 minutes or just until tender; drain. Cool slightly.

**2** Meanwhile, in a covered small saucepan cook green beans in a small amount of boiling water for 3 minutes; drain. Rinse with cold water; drain again.

## Broccoli Rabe with Garlic (30)

**MAKES:** 12 servings **START TO FINISH:** 20 minutes

- 3 **pounds broccoli rabe or 7 cups broccoli florets**
- 2 **tablespoons olive oil**
- 6 **cloves garlic, minced**
- ¼ **cup reduced-sodium chicken broth**
- ½ **teaspoon ground black pepper**
- ¼ **teaspoon salt**

**1** If using broccoli rabe, remove large leaves and, if necessary, cut stems to 6- to 8-inch lengths. In a 6- to 8-quart Dutch oven cook broccoli rabe or broccoli florets, half at a time if necessary, in a large amount of boiling water for 3 minutes for broccoli rabe (6 minutes for broccoli florets) or until crisp-tender. Drain in a colander; gently squeeze if necessary to get broccoli really dry.

**2** In the same Dutch oven heat oil over medium heat. Add garlic; cook and stir for 30 seconds. Carefully add drained broccoli rabe or broccoli florets (the oil will spatter if the vegetables are not well drained); cook and stir for 1 minute.

**3** Add broth. Cook, uncovered, until all of the broth is evaporated, stirring frequently. Stir in pepper and salt.

**PER SERVING:** 48 cal., 3 g total fat (0 g sat. fat), 0 mg chol., 98 mg sodium, 4 g carbo., 3 g fiber, 4 g pro.

Broccoli Rabe with Garlic

Peachy Baked Beans

This recipe uses the quick-soak method for soaking the beans, but you can also do it the more leisurely way. Rinse the beans in a colander under cool running water. Transfer beans to a bowl, cover with water, and refrigerate overnight.

## Peachy Baked Beans

**MAKES:** 10 to 12 servings **PREP:** 20 minutes **STAND:** 1 hour **COOK:** 1 hour **BAKE:** 1½ hours **OVEN:** 300°

- 1 pound dry white beans, such as Great Northern, cannellini, or navy beans (about 2⅓ cups)
- 1 to 1½ pounds meaty smoked pork hocks
- 3 medium peaches, pitted and cut into wedges (about 3 cups)
- 1 cup chopped onion (1 large)
- 1 cup peach nectar or apple juice
- ¼ cup packed brown sugar
- 2 tablespoons snipped fresh sage or 2 teaspoons dried sage, crushed
- ½ teaspoon salt
- ½ teaspoon pepper
- 1 or 2 medium peaches, pitted and sliced
- Fresh sage sprig

**1** Rinse beans. In a large Dutch oven or pot combine beans and 8 cups water. Bring to boiling; reduce heat. Simmer for 2 minutes. Remove from heat. Cover and let stand for 1 hour.
**2** Drain and rinse beans. Return beans to Dutch oven. Add pork hocks. Stir in 8 cups fresh water. Bring to boiling; reduce heat. Cover and simmer for 1 to 1½ hours or until beans are tender, stirring occasionally. Remove hocks; set aside. Drain beans. When cool enough to handle, cut meat off bones; coarsely chop meat.
**3** Preheat oven to 300°. In a 2½- to 3-quart casserole combine beans, meat, the 3 cups peach wedges, and onion. Stir in peach nectar, brown sugar, sage, salt, and pepper.
**4** Bake, covered, for 1 hour. Uncover and bake 15 minutes more, stirring occasionally. Before serving, top with remaining peach slices and fresh sage sprig.

**PER SERVING:** 229 cal., 2 g total fat (1 g sat. fat), 6 mg chol., 139 mg sodium, 43 g carbo., 10 g fiber, 12 g pro.

## Marinated Vegetable Salad

**MAKES:** 6 servings **PREP:** 25 minutes **MARINATE:** 30 minutes

- 2 medium red and/or yellow tomatoes or 4 roma tomatoes, cut into wedges
- 1 cup thinly sliced zucchini or yellow summer squash (1 small)
- ¾ cup chopped green sweet pepper (1 medium)
- ½ of a small red onion, thinly sliced
- 2 tablespoons snipped fresh parsley
- 2 tablespoons olive oil
- 2 tablespoons balsamic vinegar or wine vinegar
- 2 tablespoons water
- 1 tablespoon snipped fresh thyme or basil or 1 teaspoon dried thyme or basil, crushed
- 1 clove garlic, minced
- Toasted pine nuts (optional)

**1** In a medium bowl combine tomatoes, zucchini wedges, sweet pepper, red onion, and parsley.
**2** For marinade, in a screw-top jar combine oil, vinegar, the water, thyme, and garlic. Cover and shake well. Pour marinade over vegetable mixture; toss gently to coat.
**3** Cover and marinate at room temperature for 30 to 60 minutes, stirring occasionally. If desired, garnish with pine nuts. Serve with a slotted spoon.
**Note:** To make ahead, prepare as directed through Step 2. Cover and chill for 4 to 24 hours, stirring once or twice. Let stand at room temperature about 30 minutes before serving. Serve as directed.

**PER SERVING:** 64 cal., 5 g total fat (1 g sat. fat), 0 mg chol., 7 mg sodium, 5 g carbo., 1 g fiber, 1 g pro.

Marinated Vegetable Salad

Herb-and-Bean-Stuffed Tomatoes

## Herb-and-Bean-Stuffed Tomatoes

**MAKES:** 4 servings **PREP:** 25 minutes **BAKE:** 20 minutes
**OVEN:** 350°

- 4 large firm red and/or yellow tomatoes
- 1 15-ounce can cannellini beans (white kidney beans), rinsed and drained
- 1½ cups soft bread crumbs (2 slices)
- 2 tablespoons pine nuts, toasted
- 2 tablespoons grated Parmesan cheese
- 1 tablespoon snipped fresh basil or 1 teaspoon dried basil, crushed
- 1 tablespoon olive oil
- 2 cloves garlic, minced
- ⅛ teaspoon salt
- ⅛ teaspoon ground black pepper
- 2 teaspoons snipped fresh thyme or ½ teaspoon dried thyme, crushed
- 2 teaspoons olive oil

**1** Preheat oven to 350°. Cut off ½ inch from the top of each tomato. Finely chop enough of the tops to measure 1 cup; set aside. Scoop pulp out of tomatoes and discard.
**2** In a large bowl stir together the chopped tomatoes, drained beans, ¾ cup of the bread crumbs, the pine nuts, cheese, basil, the 1 tablespoon oil, garlic, salt, and pepper. Spoon bean mixture into tomato shells. Place stuffed tomatoes in a 2-quart square baking dish.
**3** In a small bowl stir together the remaining ¾ cup bread crumbs, thyme, and the 2 teaspoons oil. Sprinkle on top of tomatoes.
**4** Bake about 20 minutes or until crumbs are golden and tomatoes are heated through.

**PER SERVING:** 223 cal., 10 g total fat (2 g sat. fat), 2 mg chol., 399 mg sodium, 31 g carbo., 7 g fiber, 11 g pro.

## Citrus Brussels Sprouts 

**MAKES:** 4 servings **PREP:** 15 minutes **COOK:** 10 minutes

- 2 cups fresh Brussels sprouts or one 10-ounce package frozen Brussels sprouts, thawed
- 3 medium carrots, quartered lengthwise and cut into 1-inch pieces
- ⅓ cup orange juice
- 1 teaspoon cornstarch
- ½ teaspoon sugar
- ¼ teaspoon salt
- ¼ teaspoon ground nutmeg (optional)

**1** If using, halve fresh Brussels sprouts. In a covered large saucepan cook fresh or thawed Brussels sprouts and carrots in a small amount of boiling water for 10 to 12 minutes or until vegetables are crisp-tender. Drain in a colander.
**2** In the same saucepan combine orange juice, cornstarch, sugar, salt, and, if desired, nutmeg. Add Brussels sprouts and carrots. Cook and stir over medium heat until thickened and bubbly. Cook and stir for 2 minutes more.

**PER SERVING:** 61 cal., 1 g total fat (0 g sat. fat), 0 mg chol., 184 mg sodium, 14 g carbo., 4 g fiber, 3 g pro.

## Corn on the Cob Pudding

**MAKES:** 12 servings **PREP:** 30 minutes **BAKE:** 45 minutes
**STAND:** 10 minutes **CHILL:** 2 to 24 hours **OVEN:** 350°

- Nonstick cooking spray
- 3 ears of corn or 1½ cups frozen whole kernel corn, thawed
- 1 cup finely chopped onion (1 large)
- 1 tablespoon olive oil
- 12 ounces country-style Italian bread, cut into 1-inch cubes (6 cups)
- 2 to 3 fresh jalapeño chile peppers, seeded and finely chopped (see note, page 182)
- 2 cups fat-free milk
- 1 cup refrigerated or frozen egg product, thawed, or 4 eggs, lightly beaten

**1** Lightly coat a 2-quart square baking dish with cooking spray; set aside. If using fresh corn, remove husks and silks from ears of corn. Using a sharp knife, cut corn kernels off cobs; set aside. In a large skillet cook onion in hot oil over medium heat for 3 to 4 minutes or until tender, stirring occasionally. Stir in fresh or thawed corn. Cook and stir for 2 minutes more. Cool slightly.

**2** In a large bowl combine corn mixture, bread cubes, and jalapeño peppers. In a medium bowl combine milk and egg product. Pour milk mixture over bread mixture; toss gently to coat. Transfer mixture to the prepared baking dish. Cover and chill for 2 to 24 hours.

**3** Preheat oven to 350°. Bake, uncovered, about 45 minutes or until center is set and top is light brown. Let stand for 10 minutes before serving.

**PER SERVING:** 136 cal., 2 g total fat (0 g sat. fat), 1 mg chol., 225 mg sodium, 22 g carbo., 2 g fiber, 7 g pro.

Corn on the Cob Pudding

Savory Peas and Apples

## Thyme-Roasted Asparagus

**MAKES:** 4 servings **PREP:** 25 minutes **BROIL:** 8 minutes
**STAND:** 15minutes **ROAST:** 10 minutes **OVEN:** Broil/400°

- **1 medium red sweet pepper**
- **1 pound fresh asparagus spears, trimmed**
- **2 tablespoons olive oil**
- **1 teaspoon snipped fresh thyme**
- **¼ teaspoon salt**
- **¼ teaspoon ground black pepper**
- **¼ cup shaved Parmesan cheese (1 ounce)**
- **2 tablespoons snipped fresh parsley**
- **Olive oil (optional)**
- **Cracked black pepper (optional)**

**1** To roast sweet pepper, preheat broiler. Line a baking sheet with foil; set aside. Halve pepper lengthwise; remove stem, seeds, and membranes. Place pepper halves, cut sides down, on the prepared baking sheet. Broil 4 to 5 inches from heat for 8 to 10 minutes or until skin is bubbly and brown. Bring foil up around pepper halves to enclose. Let stand about 15 minutes or until cool. Using a paring knife, gently pull off skin in strips and discard. Cut pepper into ½-inch strips; set aside.

**2** Meanwhile, adjust oven temperature to 400°. Place asparagus in a 15×10×1-inch baking pan. In a small bowl combine oil, thyme, salt, and the ground black pepper. Drizzle over asparagus; stir gently to coat. Roast for 10 to 12 minutes or until asparagus is tender and starting to brown, turning once.

**3** Arrange asparagus and sweet pepper on a warm serving platter. Top with cheese and parsley. If desired, drizzle with additional oil and sprinkle with cracked black pepper.

**PER SERVING:** 110 cal., 9 g total fat (2 g sat. fat), 5 mg chol., 269 mg sodium, 5 g carbo., 2 g fiber, 4 g pro.

## Savory Peas and Apples (30)

**MAKES:** 8 to 10 servings **START TO FINISH:** 20 minutes

- **3 slices turkey bacon, cut crosswise into thin strips**
- **2 teaspoons butter**
- **3 tart red cooking apples (such as Jonathan), cut into ½-inch slices**
- **⅔ cup chopped leeks (2 medium)**
- **4 cups fresh snow pea pods, trimmed and strings removed**
- **¼ teaspoon salt**
- **¼ teaspoon cracked black pepper**

**1** In a 12-inch skillet cook and stir bacon in hot butter over medium heat for 2 to 3 minutes or just until crisp. Add apples and leeks. Cook and stir for 3 to 4 minutes or just until apples are tender.

**2** Stir in pea pods. Cook, covered, for 1 to 2 minutes or until pea pods are crisp-tender. Sprinkle with salt and pepper.

**PER SERVING:** 68 cal., 2 g total fat (0 g sat. fat), 5 mg chol., 158 mg sodium, 11 g carbo., 2 g fiber, 2 g pro.

Roasting does magical things to vegetables. It caramelizes their sugars and gives them a tasty brown crust.

Thyme-Roasted Asparagus

Sweet Potatoes with Orange and Ginger

Sweet potatoes are the most nutrient-dense of all vegetables. They are high in dietary fiber and complex carbohydrates, and are loaded with cancer-fighting beta carotene and vitamins A, C, and E. Eat more of them!

Oven-Roasted Vegetables

## Oven-Roasted Vegetables

**MAKES:** 6 servings **PREP:** 15 minutes **ROAST:** 35 minutes
**OVEN:** 425°

- **1 pound medium sweet potatoes and/or white potatoes, peeled and cut into 1-inch pieces**
- **1 cup peeled baby carrots or 2 medium carrots, cut into 1-inch pieces**
- **1 medium parsnip, peeled and cut into 1-inch pieces**
- **1 medium red onion, cut into thin wedges (optional)**
- **1 tablespoon olive oil**
- **3 cloves garlic, minced**
- **1 teaspoon mixed dried herbs (such as marjoram, thyme, rosemary, and/or oregano), crushed**
- **¼ teaspoon salt**
- **⅛ teaspoon ground black pepper**

**1** Preheat oven to 425°. In a 13×9×2-inch baking pan arrange potatoes, carrots, parsnip, and, if desired, red onion. In a small bowl combine oil, garlic, mixed herbs, salt, and pepper. Drizzle oil mixture over vegetables; stir gently to coat.

**2** Cover with foil and roast for 30 minutes. Stir vegetables. Roast, uncovered, for 5 to 10 minutes more or until vegetables are tender and edges start to brown.

**PER SERVING:** 83 cal., 2 g total fat (0 g sat. fat), 0 mg chol., 110 mg sodium, 15 g carbo., 3 g fiber, 1 g pro.

## Apple-Rice Salad

**MAKES:** 6 servings **PREP:** 20 minutes **COOK:** 40 minutes
**CHILL:** 2 hours

- **1¾ cups water**
- **⅓ cup uncooked regular brown rice**
- **⅓ cup uncooked wild rice, rinsed and drained**
- **2 cups chopped apples (3 medium)**
- **1 cup thinly sliced celery (2 stalks)**
- **¼ cup sunflower kernels**
- **¼ cup dried currants or dried cranberries**
- **1 recipe Orange-Balsamic Vinaigrette**
- **Lettuce leaves (optional)**

**1** In a medium saucepan combine the water, brown rice, and wild rice. Bring to boiling; reduce heat. Simmer, covered, for 40 to 45 minutes or until rice is tender. Drain off any liquid. Transfer to a large bowl; cover and chill for at least 2 hours.

**2** Stir apples, celery, sunflower kernels, and currants into cooked rice. Drizzle with Orange-Balsamic Vinaigrette; toss gently to coat. If desired, serve on lettuce-lined salad plates.

**Orange-Balsamic Vinaigrette:** In a screw-top jar combine 2 tablespoons balsamic vinegar; 1 tablespoon olive oil; 2 teaspoons honey; 2 teaspoons brown mustard or Dijon-style mustard; 2 teaspoons finely shredded orange peel; 1 clove garlic, minced; and ¼ teaspoon salt. Cover and shake well.

**PER SERVING:** 191 cal., 6 g total fat (1 g sat. fat), 0 mg chol., 143 mg sodium, 32 g carbo., 4 g fiber, 4 g pro.

Orzo-Broccoli Pilaf

## Orzo-Broccoli Pilaf

**MAKES:** 6 servings **START TO FINISH:** 40 minutes

- 1 cup sliced fresh mushrooms
- ½ cup chopped onion (1 medium)
- 2 teaspoons olive oil
- ⅔ cup dried orzo pasta
- 1 14-ounce can reduced-sodium chicken broth
- 1 teaspoon dried marjoram, crushed
- ⅛ teaspoon ground black pepper
- 2 cups small broccoli florets
- ½ cup shredded carrot (1 medium)

**1** In a large saucepan cook mushrooms and onion in hot oil over medium-high heat for 5 to 7 minutes or until onion is tender, stirring occasionally. Stir in orzo. Cook and stir about 2 minutes or until orzo is light brown.
**2** Carefully stir in broth, marjoram, and pepper. Bring to boiling; reduce heat. Simmer, covered, for 12 minutes. Stir in broccoli and carrot. Return to boiling; reduce heat. Simmer, covered, about 3 minutes more or just until orzo is tender. Remove from heat. Let stand, covered, for 5 minutes before serving.

**PER SERVING:** 113 cal., 2 g total fat (0 g sat. fat), 0 mg chol., 209 mg sodium, 19 g carbo., 2 g fiber, 4 g pro.

## Barley Waldorf Salad

**MAKES:** 8 servings **PREP:** 20 minutes **COOK:** 45 minutes

- ¾ cup regular barley or quinoa
- 3¾ cups water
- ¼ teaspoon salt
- ¼ cup plain low-fat yogurt
- 3 tablespoons light mayonnaise or salad dressing
- ¼ teaspoon finely shredded lemon peel
- 1 tablespoon lemon juice
- ½ teaspoon salt
- ¼ teaspoon sugar
- 1½ cups seedless green and/or red grapes, halved
- ⅔ cup chopped apple (1 medium)
- ½ cup chopped celery (1 stalk)
- Romaine lettuce leaves
- ¼ cup coarsely chopped walnuts, toasted

**1** In a large saucepan cook barley over medium-low heat for 4 to 5 minutes or until golden, stirring occasionally. Add the water and the ¼ teaspoon salt. Bring to boiling; reduce heat. Simmer, covered, about 45 minutes for barley (about 15 minutes for quinoa) or until tender. Drain and cool.
**2** In a large bowl combine cooked barley, yogurt, mayonnaise, lemon peel, lemon juice, the ½ teaspoon salt, and sugar. Stir in grapes, apple, and celery.
**3** Spoon barley mixture onto 8 lettuce-lined salad plates. Sprinkle with walnuts.
**Note:** To make the salad ahead, prepare as directed through Step 2. Cover and chill for up to 24 hours. Before serving, stir in a little milk if necessary to moisten. Serve as directed in Step 3.

**PER SERVING:** 145 cal., 5 g total fat (1 g sat. fat), 2 mg chol., 281 mg sodium, 23 g carbo., 5 g fiber, 4 g pro.

Barley Waldorf Salad

Brown Rice Pilaf

In most cases, convenience foods come at a nutritional price. Instant brown rice is an exception. Regular brown rice takes 35 to 40 minutes to cook, while instant brown rice takes between 5 and 10 minutes—and there is no measurable nutritional difference between the two.

## Brown Rice Pilaf

**MAKES:** 4 servings **PREP:** 10 minutes **COOK:** 12 minutes **STAND:** 5 minutes

- 1 cup water
- 1 teaspoon instant chicken bouillon granules
- 1 cup sliced fresh mushrooms
- ¾ cup uncooked instant brown rice
- ½ cup shredded carrot (1 medium)
- ¾ teaspoon snipped fresh marjoram or ¼ teaspoon dried marjoram, crushed
- Dash ground black pepper
- ¼ cup thinly sliced green onions (2)
- 1 tablespoon snipped fresh parsley

**1** In a medium saucepan combine the water and bouillon granules. Bring to boiling. Stir in mushrooms, rice, carrot, marjoram, and pepper. Return to boiling; reduce heat. Simmer, covered, for 12 minutes. Remove from heat.
**2** Let stand, covered, for 5 minutes. Add green onions and parsley; fluff gently with a fork.

**PER SERVING:** 60 cal., 1 g total fat (0 g sat. fat), 0 mg chol., 230 mg sodium, 13 g carbo., 2 g fiber, 2 g pro.

## Mexicana Couscous 

**MAKES:** 6 servings **START TO FINISH:** 20 minutes

- ¾ cup chopped onion
- 2 cloves garlic, minced
- 1 tablespoon vegetable oil
- ½ teaspoon ground cumin
- 1 cup reduced-sodium chicken broth
- 1 cup coarsely chopped tomato
- ¾ cup frozen peas
- 2 tablespoons snipped fresh cilantro
- ¾ cup uncooked couscous
- Fresh cilantro sprigs (optional)

**1** In a medium saucepan cook onion and garlic in hot oil over medium heat until onion is tender, stirring occasionally. Stir in cumin; cook and stir for 30 seconds. Carefully add broth, tomato, frozen peas, and the 2 tablespoons cilantro.
**2** Bring to boiling; stir in couscous. Remove from heat. Cover and let stand about 5 minutes or until liquid is absorbed. Fluff with a fork. If desired, garnish with additional cilantro.

**PER SERVING:** 139 cal., 3 g total fat (0 g sat. fat), 0 mg chol., 121 mg sodium, 24 g carbo., 3 g fiber, 5 g pro.

Mexicana Couscous

Serve this 20-minute side with lime-marinated grilled chicken or steak.

# Menu

Roast chicken

Herbed Corn Bread Dressing [right]

Broccoli Rabe with Garlic [page 257]

Easy Apple Dumplings [page 290]

Herbed Corn Bread Dressing

## Herbed Corn Bread Dressing

**MAKES:** 8 servings **PREP:** 25 minutes **BAKE:** 20 minutes
**OVEN:** 375°

- Nonstick cooking spray
- 1 cup sliced celery (2 stalks)
- ¾ cup chopped onion
- 2 cloves garlic, minced
- 2 tablespoons olive oil or vegetable oil
- 4 cups crumbled corn bread
- 3 slices whole wheat bread, dried and crumbled
- ¼ cup snipped fresh parsley
- 1½ teaspoons dried sage, crushed, or 1 tablespoon finely snipped fresh sage
- 1 teaspoon dried thyme, crushed, or 2 teaspoons finely snipped fresh thyme
- ½ teaspoon dried marjoram, crushed, or 1 teaspoon finely snipped fresh marjoram
- ½ teaspoon ground black pepper
- ⅛ teaspoon salt
- ¾ cup refrigerated or frozen egg product, thawed, or 3 eggs, lightly beaten
- ½ to ¾ cup reduced-sodium chicken broth

**1** Preheat oven to 375°. Lightly coat a 2-quart rectangular baking dish with cooking spray; set aside. In a large skillet cook celery, onion, and garlic in hot oil over medium heat about 10 minutes or until tender.

**2** In an extra-large bowl combine corn bread and whole wheat bread. Stir in onion mixture, parsley, sage, thyme, marjoram, pepper, and salt. Add egg product; toss gently to coat. Drizzle with enough of the broth to moisten, tossing gently to combine.

**3** Spoon dressing into the prepared dish. Bake, uncovered, about 20 minutes or until heated through (165°).

**PER SERVING:** 226 cal., 8 g total fat (1 g sat. fat), 18 mg chol., 492 mg sodium, 32 g carbo., 3 g fiber, 7 g pro.

Buttermilk Corn Muffins

## Buttermilk Corn Muffins ✪

**MAKES:** 12 muffins **PREP:** 15 minutes **BAKE:** 15 minutes
**COOL:** 5 minutes **OVEN:** 400°

- Nonstick cooking spray
- 1 cup all-purpose flour
- ¾ cup cornmeal
- 1 tablespoon sugar
- 2 teaspoons baking powder
- ¼ teaspoon salt
- 1 cup buttermilk
- ¼ cup refrigerated or frozen egg product, thawed, or 1 egg, lightly beaten
- 1 tablespoon canola oil
- 1 tablespoon lower-fat margarine, melted
- 1 teaspoon vanilla
- ½ teaspoon butter flavoring

**1** Preheat oven to 400°. Lightly coat twelve 2½-inch muffin cups with cooking spray; set aside. In a medium bowl stir together flour, cornmeal, sugar, baking powder, and salt. Make a well in center of flour mixture; set aside.

**2** In a small bowl combine buttermilk, egg product, oil, melted margarine, vanilla, and butter flavoring. Add buttermilk mixture all at once to flour mixture. Stir just until moistened (batter should be lumpy).

**3** Spoon batter into prepared muffin cups, filling each two-thirds full. Bake for 15 minutes or until a toothpick inserted in centers comes out clean. Cool in muffin cups on a wire rack for 5 minutes. Remove from muffin cups; serve warm.

**PER MUFFIN:** 92 cal., 2 g total fat (0 g sat. fat), 1 mg chol., 15 g carbo., 129 mg sodium, 1 g fiber, 3 g pro.

No matter the shape it takes,

Orange Rye Spirals

## bread is a beautiful thing.

### Orange Rye Spirals

**MAKES:** 16 rolls **PREP:** 50 minutes **RISE:** 1½ hours
**BAKE:** 14 minutes **OVEN:** 375°

- **2¾ to 3¼ cups all-purpose flour**
- **1 package active dry yeast**
- **1 cup water**
- **¼ cup sugar**
- **¼ cup vegetable oil**
- **¾ teaspoon salt**
- **2 egg whites**
- **1¼ cups rye flour**
- **¼ cup finely chopped candied orange peel**
- **1 teaspoon caraway seeds, crushed**
- **¼ cup low-sugar orange marmalade or orange marmalade, melted**

**1** In a large bowl stir together 2 cups of the all-purpose flour and the yeast; set aside. In a medium saucepan heat and stir the water, sugar, oil, and salt just until warm (120° to 130°). Add to flour mixture; add egg whites. Beat with an electric mixer on low to medium speed for 30 seconds, scraping side of bowl constantly. Beat on high speed for 3 minutes. Using a wooden spoon, stir in rye flour, candied orange peel, caraway seeds, and as much of the remaining all-purpose flour as you can.
**2** Turn dough out onto a lightly floured surface. Knead in enough of the remaining all-purpose flour to make a moderately stiff dough that is smooth and elastic (6 to 8 minutes total). Shape dough into a ball. Place in a lightly greased bowl, turning once to grease surface. Cover and let rise in a warm place until double in size (1 to 1½ hours).
**3** Punch dough down. Turn out onto a lightly floured surface. Divide in half. Cover and let rest for 10 minutes. Meanwhile, grease 2 baking sheets; set aside.
**4** Divide each portion of dough into 8 pieces. Roll each piece into a 12-inch rope. Form each rope into an "S" shape, coiling each end snugly. Place rolls on the prepared baking sheets. Cover and let rise in a warm place until nearly double in size (about 30 minutes). Meanwhile, preheat oven to 375°.
**5** Bake about 14 minutes or until golden. Transfer to a wire rack; cool slightly. While warm, brush rolls with melted orange marmalade. Serve warm.

**PER ROLL:** 164 cal., 4 g total fat (0 g sat. fat), 0 mg chol., 390 mg sodium, 29 g carbo., 2 g fiber, 4 g pro.

### Pumpkin Seed Breadsticks

**MAKES:** about 24 breadsticks **PREP:** 15 minutes
**BAKE:** 8 minutes per batch **OVEN:** 425°

- **Nonstick cooking spray**
- **1 13.8-ounce package refrigerated pizza dough**
- **1 egg, lightly beaten**
- **1 to 3 tablespoons pumpkin seeds (pepitas), plain sesame seeds, and/or black sesame seeds**
- **Coarse salt or salt**

**1** Preheat oven to 425°. Lightly coat 2 large baking sheets with cooking spray. Unroll pizza dough onto a lightly floured surface. Using your hands, shape dough into a 12×9-inch rectangle. Brush dough with egg. Sprinkle with seeds; sprinkle lightly with salt. Using a floured long knife or pizza cutter, cut dough crosswise into ¼- to ½-inch strips.
**2** Place strips on the prepared baking sheets. Bake, 1 sheet at a time, for 8 to 10 minutes or until golden. Transfer breadsticks to wire racks; cool.

**PER BREADSTICK:** 39 cal., 1 g total fat (0 g sat. fat), 9 mg chol., 75 mg sodium, 6 g carbo., 0 g fiber, 1 g pro.

Pumpkin Seed Breadsticks

## Hearty Oat and Grain Bread

**MAKES:** 1 loaf (20 servings) **PREP:** 25 minutes **RISE:** 1½ hours
**BAKE:** 30 minutes **OVEN:** 375°

- 2 cups water
- ⅓ cup cracked wheat
- 2 tablespoons cooking oil
- 2 tablespoons molasses
- 1 package active dry yeast
- 1 cup rolled oats
- ¼ cup nonfat dry milk powder
- ¼ cup oat bran or toasted wheat germ
- 1 teaspoon salt
- 1½ cups whole wheat flour
- 1½ to 2 cups all-purpose flour
- Water
- 1 tablespoon rolled oats

**1** In a small saucepan bring the 2 cups water to boiling; add cracked wheat. Reduce heat. Cover and simmer for 5 minutes. Remove from heat; transfer mixture to a large bowl. Stir in oil and molasses. Cool to lukewarm (105° to 115°). Stir in yeast until dissolved. Add the 1 cup rolled oats, the dry milk powder, oat bran or wheat germ, and salt.
**2** Using a wooden spoon, stir in the whole wheat flour; stir in as much of the all-purpose flour as you can. Turn out onto a lightly floured surface. Knead in enough of the remaining all-purpose flour to make a moderately stiff dough that is smooth and elastic (6 to 8 minutes total). Shape into a ball. Place in a lightly greased bowl, turning once to grease surface. Cover and let rise in a warm place until double in size (about 1 hour).
**3** Punch dough down; cover and let rest for 10 minutes. Meanwhile, grease a baking sheet. Shape dough into an 8-inch round loaf; place on baking sheet. Cover and let rise in a warm place until nearly double in size (30 to 45 minutes).
**4** Preheat oven to 375°. Make 3 diagonal shallow slits across the top of the loaf. Brush lightly with water; sprinkle with the 1 tablespoon rolled oats.
**5** Bake for 30 to 35 minutes or until loaf sounds hollow when tapped.

**PER SERVING:** 115 cal., 2 g total fat (0 g sat. fat), 0 mg chol., 124 mg sodium, 21 g carbo., 3 g fiber, 4 g pro.

## Four-Grain Bread

**MAKES:** 1 loaf (16 servings) **PREP:** 45 minutes **RISE:** 1½ hours
**BAKE:** 40 minutes **OVEN:** 375°

- ⅓ cup quick-cooking rolled oats
- ⅓ cup quick-cooking barley
- 1¾ to 2¼ cups bread flour
- ½ cup whole wheat flour
- 1 tablespoon gluten flour*
- 1 package active dry yeast
- 1¼ cups warm water (120° to 130°)
- 2 tablespoons sugar
- 2 tablespoons vegetable oil
- 1¼ teaspoons salt
- ⅓ cup cornmeal

**1** Preheat oven to 375°. Spread oats and barley in a shallow baking pan. Bake about 10 minutes or until light brown, stirring occasionally. Cool. Transfer oats and barley to a blender or food processor. Cover and blend or process until mixture is the consistency of flour. Set aside.
**2** In a large bowl stir together 1 cup of the bread flour, the whole wheat flour, gluten flour, and yeast. Add the warm water, sugar, oil, and salt. Beat with an electric mixer on low to medium speed for 30 seconds, scraping side of bowl constantly. Beat on high speed for 3 minutes. Using a wooden spoon, stir in cornmeal, oat mixture, and as much of the remaining bread flour as you can.
**3** Turn out onto a lightly floured surface. Knead in enough of the remaining bread flour to make a moderately stiff dough that is smooth and elastic (6 to 8 minutes total). Shape dough into a ball. Place in a lightly greased bowl, turning once to grease surface. Cover and let rise in a warm place until double in size (1 to 1¼ hours).
**4** Punch dough down. Turn out onto a lightly floured surface. Cover and let rest for 10 minutes. Meanwhile, lightly grease an 8×4×2-inch loaf pan; set aside.
**5** Shape dough into a loaf by patting or rolling. To shape by patting, gently pat and pinch dough into a loaf shape, tucking edges underneath. To shape by rolling, on a lightly floured surface, roll dough into a 12×8-inch rectangle. Starting from a short side, tightly roll up, sealing seam with your fingertips. Place in the prepared pan. Cover and let rise in a warm place until nearly double in size (about 30 minutes). Meanwhile, preheat oven to 375°.
**6** Bake about 40 minutes or until top is golden and bread sounds hollow when lightly tapped. Immediately remove bread from pan. Cool on a wire rack.

**PER SERVING:** 118 cal., 2 g total fat (0 g sat. fat), 0 mg chol., 183 mg sodium, 21 g carbo., 2 g fiber, 4 g pro.

The aroma of homemade bread baking in the oven is the most welcoming smell there is.

Four-Grain Bread

page 286
page 294

# Sweet

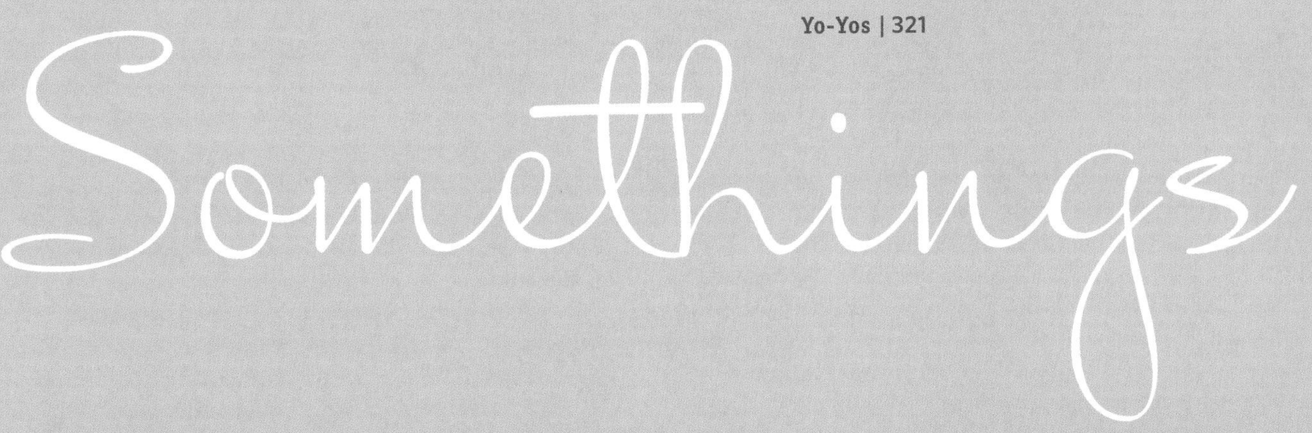
Somethings

Crisp Spice Cookies

## Crisp Spice Cookies

**MAKES:** about 66 cookies **PREP:** 45 minutes **CHILL:** 1 hour
**BAKE:** 5 minutes per batch **OVEN:** 375°

- **1⅓ cups all-purpose flour**
- **½ teaspoon ground ginger**
- **½ teaspoon apple pie spice**
- **¼ teaspoon ground cloves**
- **¼ teaspoon ground cardamom**
- **⅛ teaspoon cayenne pepper**
- **⅓ cup butter, softened**
- **⅓ cup mild-flavor molasses**
- **¼ cup packed dark brown sugar**

**1** In a medium bowl stir together flour, ginger, apple pie spice, cloves, cardamom, and cayenne pepper; set flour mixture aside.
**2** In a large mixing bowl beat butter with an electric mixer on medium speed for 30 seconds. Add molasses and brown sugar. Beat until combined, scraping side of bowl occasionally. Beat in flour mixture until just combined. Divide dough in half. Cover and chill dough about 1 hour or until easy to handle.
**3** Preheat oven to 350°. On a lightly floured surface, roll half of the dough at a time until 1/16 inch thick. Using a floured 2-inch round scalloped cookie cutter, cut out dough. Place cutouts 1 inch apart on an ungreased cookie sheet.
**4** Bake for 5 to 6 minutes or until edges are lightly browned. Transfer cookies to a wire rack; cool.

**PER 2 COOKIES:** 50 cal., 2 g total fat (1 g sat. fat), 5 mg chol., 22 mg sodium, 8 g carbo., 1 g pro.

## Simple Almond Cookies ✪

**MAKES:** 32 cookies **PREP:** 25 minutes
**BAKE:** 10 minutes per batch **OVEN:** 350°

- **Nonstick cooking spray (optional)**
- **2¼ cups whole almonds**
- **¾ cup sugar**
- **2 egg whites**
- **1 teaspoon almond extract or vanilla**
- **32 almond slices (2 tablespoons)**
- **2 ounces bittersweet chocolate, melted (optional)**

**1** Preheat oven to 350°. Line 2 large cookie sheets with parchment paper or coat with nonstick cooking spray; set aside. In a food processor combine whole almonds and sugar; cover and process until finely ground. Add egg whites and almond extract. Cover and process until well mixed.
**2** Using a well-rounded measuring teaspoonful of the almond mixture for each cookie, shape into a crescent shape or ball. Place 1 inch apart on prepared cookie sheets. Place an almond slice on top of each cookie.
**3** Bake for 10 to 12 minutes or just until cookies are starting to brown on the tops. Transfer to wire racks; let cool. If desired, transfer the warm melted chocolate to a resealable plastic bag. Seal bag; cut a small hole in one corner. Drizzle tops of cookies with melted chocolate.

**PER COOKIE:** 80 cal., 5 g total fat (0 g sat. fat), 0 mg chol., 4 mg sodium, 7 g carbo., 1 g fiber, 2 g pro.

These cookies are lovely to look at, delicious to eat, and can be indulged in with a clear conscience. Other than the healthful unsaturated fat contributed by the almonds, they contain no saturated fat from butter, shortening, or egg yolks.

## Chocolate-Cherry Biscotti

**MAKES:** about 24 cookies **PREP:** 25 minutes **BAKE:** 36 minutes
**COOL:** 1 hour **OVEN:** 375°/325°

- Nonstick cooking spray
- ¼ cup butter, softened
- ½ cup sugar
- ¼ cup unsweetened cocoa powder
- 1 teaspoon baking powder
- ¼ teaspoon baking soda
- 2 eggs
- ½ teaspoon vanilla
- 1⅔ cups all-purpose flour
- ⅓ cup finely chopped dried tart cherries

**1** Preheat oven to 375°. Lightly coat a large cookie sheet with cooking spray; set aside. In a large bowl beat butter with an electric mixer on medium to high speed for 30 seconds. Add sugar, cocoa powder, baking powder, and baking soda. Beat until combined, scraping side of bowl occasionally. Beat in eggs and vanilla until combined. Beat in as much of the flour as you can with the mixer. Using a wooden spoon, stir in any remaining flour and the dried cherries.
**2** Divide dough in half. Shape each portion into an 8-inch loaf. Place loaves about 3 inches apart on the prepared cookie sheet; flatten loaves slightly until about 2 inches wide. Bake for 18 to 20 minutes or until firm and a toothpick inserted near centers comes out clean. Cool on cookie sheet for 1 hour.
**3** Preheat oven to 325°. Using a serrated knife, cut each loaf diagonally into ½-inch slices. Place slices on an ungreased large cookie sheet. Bake for 10 minutes. Turn slices over; bake for 8 to 10 minutes more or until crisp and dry. Transfer to wire racks; cool.

**PER COOKIE:** 78 cal., 3 g total fat (1 g sat. fat), 23 mg chol., 56 mg sodium, 12 g carbo., 0 g fiber, 2 g pro.

Double-Pumpkin Bars

## Double Pumpkin Bars

**MAKES:** 8 bars **PREP:** 15 minutes **BAKE:** 20 minutes
**OVEN:** 350°

- Nonstick cooking spray
- 1 cup rolled oats
- ½ cup whole wheat pastry flour or white whole wheat flour
- ½ teaspoon baking soda
- ½ teaspoon ground cinnamon
- ½ teaspoon ground allspice
- ¼ teaspoon salt
- 1 egg, lightly beaten
- ½ cup canned pumpkin
- ¼ cup sugar
- ¼ cup canola oil
- 1 teaspoon vanilla
- ½ cup chopped pitted whole dates
- ¼ cup pumpkin seeds (pepitas) or chopped walnuts

**1** Preheat oven to 350°. Lightly coat an 8×8×2-inch baking pan with cooking spray; set aside.
**2** In a medium bowl stir together oats, flour, baking soda, cinnamon, allspice, and salt. In a small bowl combine egg, pumpkin, sugar, oil, and vanilla. Stir pumpkin mixture into flour mixture until combined. Stir in dates and pumpkin seeds. Spread batter evenly in the prepared pan.
**3** Bake about 20 minutes or until top is firm and a toothpick inserted near center comes out clean. Cool in pan on a wire rack. Cut into bars.

**PER BAR:** 264 cal., 12 g total fat (2 g sat. fat), 26 mg chol., 163 mg sodium, 34 g carbo., 4 g fiber, 8 g pro.

White whole wheat flour is a whole grain flour that is milled from white rather than red wheat. It contains the bran, germ, and endorsperm, but is light in color and has a mild flavor. It can be used in place of bleached flour—with more nutrition.

## Spiced Apricot Bars

**MAKES:** 24 bars **PREP:** 20 minutes **BAKE:** 15 minutes
**OVEN:** 350°

- Nonstick cooking spray
- ⅔ cup all-purpose flour
- ⅓ cup white whole wheat flour or whole wheat flour
- ½ teaspoon baking powder
- ¼ teaspoon baking soda
- ¼ teaspoon ground cardamom or ⅛ teaspoon ground nutmeg
- ½ cup packed brown sugar
- ½ cup apricot nectar or orange juice
- ¼ cup unsweetened applesauce
- ¼ cup refrigerated or frozen egg product, thawed, or 1 egg, lightly beaten
- 2 tablespoons canola oil
- ½ cup finely snipped dried apricots
- 1 recipe Apricot Icing

**1** Preheat oven to 350°. Coat an 11×7×1½-inch baking pan with cooking spray; set aside.
**2** In a medium bowl stir together all-purpose flour, whole wheat flour, baking powder, baking soda, and cardamom; set aside. In a small bowl combine brown sugar, apricot nectar, applesauce, egg product, and oil. Add brown sugar mixture to flour mixture, stirring just until combined. Stir in dried apricots. Spread batter evenly in the prepared pan.
**3** Bake for 15 to 20 minutes or until a toothpick inserted near center comes out clean. Cool in pan on a wire rack. Drizzle with Apricot Icing. Cut into bars.
**Apricot Icing:** In a small bowl stir together ½ cup powdered sugar and 2 to 3 teaspoons apricot nectar or orange juice to reach drizzling consistency.

**PER BAR:** 68 cal., 1 g total fat (0 g sat. fat), 0 mg chol., 27 mg sodium, 14 g carbo., 1 g fiber, 1 g pro.

## Easy Apple Dumplings ✪

**MAKES:** 8 servings **PREP:** 15 minutes **BAKE:** 25 minutes
**OVEN:** 375°

- ½ cup apple juice
- ⅓ cup packed brown sugar
- 2 tablespoons butter
- 2 tablespoons granulated sugar
- 1 teaspoon ground cinnamon
- 1 large cooking apple, peeled (if desired), cored, and cut into 8 wedges
- 1 8-ounce package (8) refrigerated crescent rolls
- 1 teaspoon coarse or granulated sugar
- Vanilla or cinnamon ice cream (optional)

**1** Preheat oven to 375°. Lightly grease a 2-quart square baking dish; set aside. In a small saucepan combine apple juice, brown sugar, and butter. Cook over medium-low heat until butter is melted, stirring to dissolve sugar. Set aside.
**2** In a medium bowl stir together the 2 tablespoons granulated sugar and cinnamon. Add apple; toss gently to coat.
**3** Unroll dough and separate at perforations. Place a coated apple wedge along the wide edge of each dough piece. Roll up dough around apple wedge. Arrange in the prepared baking dish. Gradually drizzle apple juice mixture over roll-ups. Sprinkle tops of roll-ups with coarse sugar.
**4** Bake for 25 to 30 minutes or until pastry is golden and apple is tender. Serve warm. If desired, serve with ice cream.

**PER SERVING:** 201 cal., 9 g total fat (4 g sat. fat), 8 mg chol., 245 mg sodium, 28 g carbo., 1 g fiber, 2 g pro.

These apple dumplings taste like they took all day to make but are ready for the oven in just 15 minutes.

Easy Apple Dumplings

Rasberry-Peach Crisp

## Raspberry-Peach Crisp

**MAKES:** 8 servings **PREP:** 30 minutes **BAKE:** 45 minutes
**OVEN:** 375°

- 4 cups sliced fresh peaches (4 medium) or frozen unsweetened peach slices
- 2 tablespoons granulated sugar
- 2 tablespoons sugar-free red raspberry preserves
- 1 tablespoon quick-cooking tapioca
- ⅔ cup quick-cooking rolled oats
- 2 tablespoons whole wheat flour
- 2 tablespoons packed brown sugar or brown sugar substitute* equal to 2 tablespoons brown sugar
- ½ teaspoon ground cinnamon
- 2 tablespoons butter
- Vanilla fat-free yogurt (optional)

**1** Preheat oven to 375°. For filling, thaw peach slices, if frozen; do not drain. In a large bowl combine fresh or thawed peach slices, granulated sugar, preserves, and tapioca. Transfer mixture to a 2-quart square baking dish.
**2** For topping, in a medium bowl combine oats, whole wheat flour, brown sugar, and cinnamon. Using a pastry blender, cut in butter until mixture resembles coarse crumbs. Sprinkle topping over peach mixture.
**3** Bake for 45 to 50 minutes or until topping is golden and filling is bubbly. Serve warm. If desired, serve with vanilla yogurt.

**PER SERVING:** 159 cal., 4 g total fat (2 g sat. fat), 8 mg chol., 22 mg sodium, 31 g carbo., 4 g fiber, 3 g pro.

## Caramelized Apple Tostadas 

**MAKES:** 4 servings **PREP:** 35 minutes **BAKE:** 10 minutes
**OVEN:** 400°

- 4 6- to 7-inch flour tortillas
- Butter-flavor nonstick cooking spray or nonstick cooking spray
- 2 teaspoons granulated sugar
- ¼ teaspoon pumpkin pie spice
- 4 cups peeled and sliced apples or pears (4 medium)
- 2 tablespoons packed brown sugar
- 1 teaspoon pumpkin pie spice
- 1 5.5-ounce can apple juice
- 2 tablespoons dried currants
- Powdered sugar (optional)

**1** Preheat oven to 400°. Place tortillas on a baking sheet. Lightly coat tortillas with cooking spray. In a small bowl stir together granulated sugar and the ¼ teaspoon pumpkin pie spice; sprinkle over tortillas. Bake about 10 minutes or until tortillas are crisp. Cool on a wire rack.
**2** Meanwhile, lightly coat a large nonstick skillet with cooking spray; heat skillet over medium heat. Add apples, brown sugar, and the 1 teaspoon pumpkin pie spice. Cook and stir about 10 minutes or until golden. Add apple juice and currants. Cook about 20 minutes more or until liquid is evaporated, stirring occasionally.
**3** To serve, spoon apple mixture over tortillas. If desired, sprinkle with powdered sugar.

**PER SERVING:** 199 cal., 2 g total fat (0 g sat. fat), 0 mg chol., 72 mg sodium, 29 g carbo., 5 g fiber, 2 g pro.

Caramelized Apple Tostadas

## Cherry Peach Cobbler

**MAKES:** 8 (about ¾-cup) servings **PREP:** 25 minutes **BAKE:** 30 minutes **OVEN:** 350°

- 1 pound peaches, halved, pitted, and sliced, or one 16-package frozen peaches, thawed*
- 1 pound dark sweet cherries, pitted, or one 16-ounce package frozen dark sweet cherries, thawed*
- ¼ cup cold water
- 4 teaspoons all-purpose flour
- ¾ cup all-purpose flour
- 2 tablespoons sugar
- 1½ teaspoons baking powder
- 2 tablespoons butter
- 1 egg, slightly beaten
- 3 tablespoons fat-free milk
- 1 teaspoon sugar
- ⅛ teaspoon ground cinnamon
- Frozen fat-free whipped dessert topping, thawed (optional)

**1** Preheat oven to 350°. Arrange sliced peaches and cherries in a 10-inch quiche dish. In a small bowl, combine the water and the 4 teaspoons flour; pour over fruit.
**2** For cobbler dough, in a medium bowl combine the ¾ cup flour, 2 tablespoons sugar, and the baking powder. Using a pastry blender, cut in butter until mixture resembles fine crumbs. Make a well in the center of the flour mixture; add egg and milk all at once. Stir just until moistened.
**3** Drop dough by spoonfuls into 8 to 10 mounds on top of the fruit. In a small bowl stir together 1 teaspoon sugar and the cinnamon; sprinkle over the dough.
**4** Bake for 30 to 40 minutes or until a toothpick inserted into the topping comes out clean and fruit mixture is bubbly on edges. Cool slightly on a wire rack. Serve warm. If desired, serve with dessert topping.
***Note:** If using frozen fruit, thaw it completely but do not drain the fruit before adding to the quiche dish.

**PER SERVING:** 142 cal., 4 g total fat (2 g sat. fat), 34 mg chol., 77 mg sodium, 25 g carbo., 2 g fiber, 3 g pro.

## Praline Baked Apples

**MAKES:** 4 servings **PREP:** 20 minutes **BAKE:** 30 minutes **OVEN:** 350°

- ½ cup apple juice
- ⅛ teaspoon ground cinnamon
- 4 small red baking apples
- ¼ cup pecans or walnuts, coarsely chopped
- ¼ cup packed brown sugar
- ⅛ teaspoon ground cinnamon

**1** Preheat oven to 350°. In a small bowl combine apple juice and ⅛ teaspoon cinnamon. Divide mixture among four 6-ounce custard cups. Using an apple corer or a sharp knife, remove cores from apples. Peel a strip from the top of each apple. Place apples in custard cups. Place custard cups in a shallow baking pan.
**2** In another small bowl combine nuts, brown sugar, and ⅛ teaspoon cinnamon. Sprinkle over apples. Bake, covered, for 30 to 40 minutes or until apples are tender.

**PER SERVING:** 195 cal., 5 g total fat (1 g sat. fat), 0 mg chol., 6 mg sodium, 39 g carbo., 4 g fiber, 1 g pro.

## Strawberry-Rhubarb Crisp

**MAKES:** 6 to 8 servings **PREP:** 20 minutes **BAKE:** 40 minutes **OVEN:** 375°

- ⅓ cup strawberry preserves
- ⅛ teaspoon ground cinnamon or nutmeg
- 2 cups sliced fresh strawberries
- 2 cups sliced fresh rhubarb
- 3 tablespoons all-purpose flour
- ½ cup quick-cooking rolled oats
- 2 tablespoons cornmeal
- 2 tablespoons honey
- 1 teaspoon vanilla

**1** Preheat oven to 375°. In a large bowl stir together preserves and cinnamon. Add strawberries and rhubarb; stir gently to coat. Sprinkle with flour; stir gently to combine. Spoon mixture into a 9-inch pie plate. Bake for 20 minutes.
**2** Meanwhile, for topping, in a small bowl stir together oats and cornmeal. Stir in honey and vanilla.
**3** Sprinkle topping over strawberry mixture. Bake about 20 minutes more or until topping is golden and fruit mixture is bubbly. Serve warm.

**PER SERVING:** 145 cal., 1 g total fat (0 g sat. fat), 0 mg chol., 9 mg sodium, 33 g carbo., 3 g fiber, 2 g pro.

Strawberry-Rhubarb Crisp

## Berry-Ginger Shortcakes

**MAKES:** 10 servings **PREP:** 25 minutes **BAKE:** 8 minutes
**OVEN:** 425°

- **3 cups fresh blueberries, raspberries, blackberries, and/or sliced strawberries**
- **2 tablespoons granulated sugar (optional)**
- **2 tablespoons finely chopped crystallized ginger**
- **1⅔ cups all-purpose flour**
- **1 tablespoon granulated sugar**
- **1½ teaspoons baking powder**
- **¼ teaspoon baking soda**
- **¼ cup butter**
- **½ cup buttermilk**
- **¼ cup refrigerated or frozen egg product, thawed, or 1 egg**
- **Nonstick cooking spray**
- **½ of an 8-ounce container frozen light whipped dessert topping, thawed**
- **¼ cup light sour cream**

**1** In a small bowl combine berries, the 2 tablespoons granulated sugar (if using), and the crystallized ginger. Set aside.

**2** Preheat oven to 425°. For shortcakes, in a medium bowl stir together flour, the 1 tablespoon granulated sugar, the baking powder, and baking soda. Using a pastry blender, cut in butter until mixture resembles coarse crumbs. Make a well in center of flour mixture. In a small bowl combine buttermilk and egg product. Add to flour mixture all at once, stirring just until moistened.

**3** Lightly coat a baking sheet with nonstick cooking spray; set aside. On a lightly floured surface, pat dough to ½-inch thickness. Using a floured 2½-inch round biscuit cutter, cut dough into rounds, rerolling scraps as necessary. Place on prepared baking sheet.

**4** Bake for 8 to 10 minutes or until golden. Cool slightly on a wire rack.

**5** Meanwhile, in a small bowl combine whipped topping and sour cream. Split shortcakes in half. Place bottoms on dessert plates. Spoon berry mixture and whipped topping mixture over bottoms. Replace shortcake tops.

**PER SERVING:** 183 cal., 5 g total fat (4 g sat. fat), 11 mg chol., 186 mg sodium, 30 g carbo., 2 g fiber, 4 g pro.

## Dream Cream Puffs ✪

**MAKES:** 8 servings **PREP:** 25 minutes **BAKE:** 30 minutes
**COOL:** 10 minutes **OVEN:** 400°

- Nonstick cooking spray
- ½ cup water
- 2 tablespoons butter
- ½ cup all-purpose flour
- 2 eggs
- 1 4-serving-size package sugar-free fat-free chocolate instant pudding and pie filling mix
- 2 cups fat-free milk
- ⅛ teaspoon peppermint extract
- Powdered sugar or unsweetened cocoa powder (optional)

**1** Preheat oven to 400°. Lightly coat a baking sheet with cooking spray; set aside.

**2** In a small saucepan combine the water and butter. Bring to boiling. Add flour all at once, stirring vigorously. Cook and stir until mixture forms a ball. Remove from heat. Cool for 10 minutes. Add eggs, one at a time, beating well with a wooden spoon after each addition.

**3** Drop dough in 8 mounds, 3 inches apart, onto the prepared baking sheet. Bake about 30 minutes or until golden and firm. Transfer to a wire rack; cool.

**4** Meanwhile, for filling, prepare pudding mix according to package directions using the fat-free milk. Stir in peppermint extract. Cover surface with plastic wrap and chill until ready to serve.

**5** To serve, cut tops from cream puffs; remove soft dough from insides. Spoon about 1/4 cup of the filling into the bottom half of each cream puff. Replace tops. If desired, sprinkle lightly with powdered sugar.

**Mocha Cream Puffs:** Prepare as directed, except omit peppermint extract. Add 2 teaspoons instant espresso coffee powder or instant coffee crystals with the milk when preparing the pudding.

**PER SERVING:** 112 cal., 4 g total fat (2 g sat. fat), 62 mg chol., 231 mg sodium, 13 g carbo., 0 g fiber, 5 g pro.

Dream Cream Puffs

Cream puffs are made with "choux" pastry—an unusual kind of dough made by stirring together boiling water and butter, flour, and eggs to make a thick paste that can be dropped or piped onto a baking sheet. The hot air from the oven causes the dough to puff up, creating crisp little pillows of pastry. Be sure to fill them just before serving or they will get soggy.

# Served chilled or warm, pudding

Citrus Trifle with Orange Custard

## Citrus Trifle with Orange Custard

**MAKES:** 10 (⅔-cup) servings **PREP:** 45 minutes **CHILL:** 2 hours

- **2 cups fat-free milk**
- **1 4-serving-size package fat-free sugar-free reduced-calorie vanilla instant pudding mix**
- **2 teaspoons finely shredded orange peel**
- **¼ cup orange juice**
- **½ of an 8-ounce package reduced-fat cream cheese (Neufchâtel), softened**
- **3 cups assorted citrus fruit sections (such as navel oranges, blood oranges, Cara Cara oranges, and/or grapefruit)**
- **½ of an 8-ounce angel food cake, cut into 1-inch cubes (about 4 cups)**

**1** In a medium bowl combine milk and pudding mix; beat with an electric mixer on low speed for 2 minutes. Beat in orange peel and 2 tablespoons of the orange juice. Set aside. In a large bowl beat cream cheese with an electric mixer on medium to high speed for 30 seconds. Gradually add pudding mixture, beating until well mixed.

**2** Divide half of the fruit among ten 6-ounce dessert glasses or dessert dishes. (Or arrange half of the fruit in a 1½-quart trifle bowl.) Arrange half the cake cubes over the fruit. Drizzle with 1 tablespoon of the remaining orange juice. Spoon half of the pudding mixture over cake. Repeat layers. Cover and chill for 2 hours before serving.

**PER SERVING:** 112 cal., 3 g total fat (2 g sat. fat), 10 mg chol., 283 mg sodium, 18 g carbo., 1 g fiber, 4 g pro.

## Cherry-Chocolate Bread Puddings

**MAKES:** 4 servings **PREP:** 20 minutes **BAKE:** 15 minutes
**OVEN:** 350°

- **Nonstick cooking spray**
- **2 cups firm-textured whole grain bread cubes**
- **3 tablespoons snipped dried tart cherries**
- **1 tablespoon toasted wheat germ**
- **⅔ cup fat-free milk**
- **¼ cup semisweet chocolate pieces**
- **⅓ cup refrigerated or frozen egg product, thawed, or 1 egg plus 1 egg white, lightly beaten**
- **1 teaspoon finely shredded orange peel**
- **½ teaspoon vanilla**
- **Frozen light whipped dessert topping, thawed (optional)**
- **Unsweetened cocoa powder (optional)**

**1** Preheat oven to 350°. Lightly coat four 6-ounce soufflé dishes or custard cups with cooking spray. Divide bread cubes, dried cherries, and wheat germ among the prepared dishes.

**2** In a small saucepan combine milk and chocolate. Cook and stir over low heat until chocolate is melted. Remove from heat. If necessary, beat with a wire whisk until smooth.

**3** Gradually stir chocolate mixture into egg product. Stir in orange peel and vanilla. Pour egg mixture over bread mixture in dishes; lightly press bread mixture with the back of a spoon to moisten.

**4** Bake for 15 to 20 minutes or until tops appear firm and a knife inserted near centers comes out clean. Serve warm. If desired, serve with whipped topping and sprinkle lightly with cocoa powder.

**Note:** To make ahead, prepare as directed through Step 3. Cover and chill for up to 2 hours. To serve, preheat oven to 350°. Bake and serve as directed.

**PER SERVING:** 155 cal., 4 g total fat (2 g sat. fat), 1 mg chol., 155 mg sodium, 27 g carbo., 3 g fiber, 7 g pro.

is always a crowd pleaser.

Cherry-Chocolate Bread Puddings

Chocolate-Filled Lemon Meringues

## Chocolate-Filled Lemon Meringues

**MAKES:** 6 servings **PREP:** 50 minutes **BAKE:** 25 minutes
**STAND:** 1 hour **OVEN:** 300°

- **2 egg whites**
- **⅔ cup sugar**
- **1 teaspoon finely shredded lemon peel**
- **¼ teaspoon cream of tartar**
- **4 teaspoons sugar**
- **1 tablespoon unsweetened cocoa powder**
- **⅓ cup mascarpone cheese or reduced-fat cream cheese (Neufchâtel) (about 3 ounces), softened**
- **½ teaspoon vanilla**
- **2 to 3 tablespoons fat-free milk**
- **1 cup fresh raspberries and/or blueberries**
- **Finely shredded lemon peel and/or unsweetened cocoa powder (optional)**

**1** Allow egg whites to stand at room temperature for 30 minutes. Meanwhile, preheat oven to 300°. Line a large baking sheet with parchment paper or foil. Draw twelve 2-inch circles 3 inches apart on the paper or foil; set aside.

**2** For meringue, in a small bowl stir together the ⅔ cup sugar and the 1 teaspoon lemon peel; set aside. In a large bowl combine egg whites and cream of tartar. Beat with an electric mixer on medium speed until soft peaks form (tips curl). Add sugar mixture, 1 tablespoon at a time, beating on high speed until stiff peaks form (tips stand straight). Spread meringue over circles on paper, building up sides to form shells.

**3** Bake for 25 minutes. Turn off oven; let meringues dry in oven with door closed for 1 hour. Lift meringues off paper. Transfer to a wire rack; cool.

**4** For filling, in a small bowl stir together the 4 teaspoons sugar and cocoa powder. In another small bowl combine mascarpone cheese and vanilla. Stir in cocoa mixture and enough of the milk to reach spreading consistency.

**5** Spread filling in meringue shells. Top with berries. If desired, garnish with additional lemon peel and/or cocoa powder.

**Note:** To make ahead, prepare as directed through Step 3. Transfer meringues to an airtight container; cover. Store at room temperature for up to 1 week. To serve, prepare filling and serve as directed.

**PER SERVING:** 181 cal., 7 g total fat (4 g sat. fat), 18 mg chol., 29 mg sodium, 29 g carbo., 2 g fiber, 5 g pro.

## Cinnamon-Chocolate Soufflés

**MAKES:** 2 servings **PREP:** 25 minutes **BAKE:** 23 minutes
**OVEN:** 350°

- **1 tablespoon sugar**
- **1 tablespoon unsweetened cocoa powder**
- **⅛ teaspoon ground cinnamon**
- **⅓ cup fat-free milk**
- **¼ teaspoon vanilla**
- **⅓ cup dried French bread cubes**
- **1 teaspoon vegetable oil**
- **1½ teaspoons all-purpose flour**
- **1 egg yolk**
- **1 egg white**
- **1 tablespoon sugar**
- **Unsweetened cocoa powder (optional)**

**1** Preheat oven to 350°. In a small bowl stir together 1 tablespoon sugar, the 1 tablespoon cocoa powder, and cinnamon. Stir in 2 tablespoons of the milk and the vanilla. Stir in bread cubes.

**2** In a small saucepan heat oil over medium heat. Stir in flour. Gradually stir in the remaining milk. Cook and stir just until mixture is thickened. Remove from heat.

**3** In a small bowl beat egg yolk with an electric mixer on high speed about 2½ minutes or until thick and lemon color. Gradually stir in thickened milk mixture. Stir in bread mixture.

**4** Wash beaters thoroughly. In a medium bowl beat egg white on medium speed until soft peaks form (tips curl). Gradually add 1 tablespoon sugar, beating on high speed until stiff peaks form (tips stand straight). Fold bread mixture into beaten egg white. Divide mixture between two 6-ounce soufflé dishes or custard cups.

**5** Bake for 23 to 25 minutes or until a knife inserted near centers comes out clean. If desired, sprinkle lightly with additional cocoa powder. Serve immediately.

**PER SERVING:** 159 cal., 5 g total fat (1 g sat. fat), 106 mg chol., 95 mg sodium, 22 g carbo., 0 g fiber, 6 g pro.

Cinnamon-Chocolate Soufflés

Soufflés depend on air whipped into egg whites to rise high and mighty. Be sure to thoroughly clean the beaters of your mixer after beating the egg yolk and before beating the egg white. Even a speck of fat in egg whites can keep them from getting as much volume as possible during the beating process.

Orange-Pumpkin Custards

## Orange-Pumpkin Custards

**MAKES:** 8 servings **PREP:** 15 minutes **BAKE:** 30 minutes **OVEN:** 375°

- 2 tablespoons orange juice
- 1 teaspoon vanilla
- ¼ cup golden raisins or dark raisins
- Nonstick cooking spray
- 1 15-ounce can pumpkin
- ⅔ cup evaporated fat-free milk
- ⅓ cup packed brown sugar
- ⅓ cup refrigerated or frozen egg product, thawed, or 1 egg plus 1 egg white, lightly beaten
- 1 teaspoon pumpkin pie spice
- ⅓ cup rolled oats
- 2 tablespoons packed brown sugar
- 2 teaspoons butter, melted

**1** In a small saucepan combine orange juice and vanilla. Heat over low heat just until hot but not boiling. Stir in raisins; cool.

**2** Meanwhile, preheat oven to 375°. Lightly coat eight 6-ounce soufflé dishes or custard cups or one 1-quart casserole with cooking spray. Place soufflé dishes or custard cups in a shallow baking pan; set aside.

**3** In a large bowl combine pumpkin, evaporated milk, the ⅓ cup brown sugar, egg product, and pumpkin pie spice. Stir in undrained raisin mixture. Spoon pumpkin mixture evenly into the prepared dishes.

**4** For topping, in a small bowl stir together oats and the 2 tablespoons brown sugar. Stir in melted butter. Sprinkle over pumpkin mixture.

**5** Bake about 30 minutes for individual custards (40 to 45 minutes for large custard) or until a knife inserted near centers comes out clean. Transfer to a wire rack; cool slightly.

**PER SERVING:** 128 cal., 1 g total fat (1 g sat. fat), 3 mg chol., 60 mg sodium, 26 g carbo., 2 g fiber, 5 g pro.

## Mini Cheesecakes ✪

**MAKES:** 10 servings **PREP:** 25 minutes **BAKE:** 18 minutes **COOL:** 5 minutes **CHILL:** 4 to 24 hours **OVEN:** 325°

- Nonstick cooking spray
- ⅓ cup crushed vanilla wafers (about 8 wafers)
- 1½ 8-ounce packages (12 ounces total) fat-free cream cheese, softened
- ½ cup sugar
- 1 tablespoon all-purpose flour
- ¼ cup refrigerated or frozen egg product, thawed, or 1 egg, lightly beaten
- 1 teaspoon vanilla
- ¾ cup assorted fresh fruit (such as raspberries or blueberries; halved grapes; cut-up pineapple, kiwifruit, or papaya; sliced strawberries or plums; and/or orange or grapefruit sections)

**1** Preheat oven to 325°. Lightly coat ten 2½-inch muffin cups with cooking spray. Sprinkle the bottom and side of each cup with 1 rounded teaspoon of the crushed vanilla wafers; set aside.

**2** For filling, in a medium bowl beat cream cheese with an electric mixer on medium speed until smooth. Add sugar and flour. Beat until combined, scraping side of bowl occasionally. Beat in egg product and vanilla on low speed just until combined. Divide filling evenly among muffin cups.

**3** Bake for 18 to 20 minutes or until filling is set. Cool in muffin cups on a wire rack for 5 minutes. Cover and chill for 4 to 24 hours.

**4** To serve, remove cheesecakes from muffin cups. Spoon fruit on top of cheesecakes.

**PER SERVING:** 107 cal., 1 g total fat (0 g sat. fat), 5 mg chol., 28 mg sodium, 18 g carbo., 0 g fiber, 6 g pro.

Mini Cheesecakes

Raspberry Custard Brûlée

## Raspberry Custard Brûlée

**MAKES:** 4 servings **PREP:** 30 minutes **CHILL:** 2 to 24 hours

- ¼ **cup sugar**
- 2 **teaspoons cornstarch**
- 1 **cup fat-free milk**
- 1 **egg, lightly beaten**
- 2 **tablespoons light sour cream**
- ½ **teaspoon vanilla**
- 3 **cups fresh red raspberries, blackberries, blueberries, and/or halved strawberries**

**1** For custard, in a small saucepan combine 2 tablespoons of the sugar and the cornstarch; stir in milk and egg. Cook and stir over medium heat just until mixture starts to bubble. Immediately pour into a small bowl; cool about 5 minutes. Stir in sour cream and vanilla. Cover and chill for 2 to 24 hours.

**2** To serve, divide berries evenly among 4 goblets or dessert dishes. Spoon custard over berries. (Thin custard if necessary with a little milk before spooning it over berries.) Set aside.

**3** For caramelized sugar, in a small heavy skillet or saucepan heat the remaining 2 tablespoons sugar over medium-high heat until sugar starts to melt, shaking skillet occasionally to heat evenly. Do not stir. Once the sugar starts to melt, reduce heat to low and cook until all of the sugar is syrupy and golden, stirring as necessary with a wooden spoon. Quickly drizzle caramelized sugar over custard. (If sugar hardens in the skillet, heat and stir until melted.) Serve immediately.

**PER SERVING:** 150 cal., 2 g total fat (1 g sat. fat), 55 mg chol., 56 mg sodium, 29 g carbo., 4 g fiber, 5 g pro.

## Cherry Dessert Crepes

**MAKES:** 8 servings **PREP:** 30 minutes **COOK:** 30 minutes

- 1¼ cups milk
- 1 cup all-purpose flour
- 1 egg
- 1 teaspoon sugar
- 1 teaspoon vanilla
- 1 teaspoon canola oil
- ¼ teaspoon baking powder
- 1 teaspoon finely shredded orange peel
- ½ cup orange juice
- ½ cup white Zinfandel
- ⅛ teaspoon ground nutmeg
- 1½ to 2 pounds dark sweet cherries, pitted
- 1½ teaspoons cornstarch
- 1½ teaspoons cold water

**1** For crepes, in a blender combine milk, flour, egg, sugar, vanilla, oil, and baking powder. Cover and blend until smooth.

**2** Heat a nonstick or lightly greased 6-inch skillet over medium-high heat; remove from heat. Spoon in 2 tablespoons of the batter; lift and tilt skillet to spread batter over bottom of pan. Return to heat. Cook about 1 minute or until light brown. Turn with a spatula; cook for 30 seconds. Invert crepe onto a clean work surface; cover loosely to keep warm. Repeat with the remaining batter to make 16 crepes total, lightly greasing skillet if necessary.

**3** For sauce, in a large skillet combine orange peel, orange juice, wine, and nutmeg. Stir in cherries. Bring to boiling; reduce heat. Simmer, uncovered, for 4 to 5 minutes or until cherries are tender. Using a slotted spoon, transfer cherries to a bowl. Return wine mixture to boiling; reduce heat. Boil gently, uncovered, for 2 to 3 minutes or until reduced to ½ cup.

**4** In a small bowl stir together cornstarch and the water; stir into wine mixture. Cook and stir until thickened and bubbly. Cook and stir for 2 minutes more. Pour sauce over cherries; stir gently to combine.

**5** Spoon about 2 tablespoons of the sauce onto each crepe; carefully roll up crepes. Serve warm.

**PER SERVING:** 148 cal., 3 g total fat (1 g sat. fat), 30 mg chol., 41 mg sodium, 25 g carbo., 2 g fiber, 4 g pro.

Chocolate-Cream Cheese Cupcakes

## Chocolate-Cream Cheese Cupcakes 

**MAKES:** 18 cupcakes **PREP:** 30 minutes **BAKE:** 25 minutes **COOL:** 10 minutes **OVEN:** 350°

- ½ of an 8-ounce package fat-free cream cheese, softened
- ⅓ cup sugar
- ¼ cup fresh or frozen egg product, thawed, or 1 egg, lightly beaten
- ⅓ cup miniature semisweet chocolate pieces
- 1½ cups all-purpose flour
- 1 cup sugar
- ¼ cup unsweetened cocoa powder
- 1 teaspoon baking powder
- ¼ teaspoon baking soda
- ⅛ teaspoon salt
- 1 cup water
- ⅓ cup vegetable oil
- 1 tablespoon vinegar
- 1 teaspoon vanilla
- ½ cup plain low-fat granola

**1** Preheat oven to 350°. Line eighteen 2½-inch muffin cups with paper bake cups; set aside.

**2** In a small bowl beat cream cheese with an electric mixer on medium speed until smooth. Add the ⅓ cup sugar and egg product; beat until combined. Stir in chocolate pieces.

**3** In a bowl stir together flour, 1 cup sugar, cocoa powder, baking powder, baking soda, and salt. Add water, oil, vinegar, and vanilla. Beat on medium speed for 2 minutes. Spoon batter into the prepared muffin cups, filling each about half full. Spoon about 1 tablespoon cream cheese mixture into each cup. Sprinkle with granola.

**4** Bake for 25 to 30 minutes or until tops spring back when lightly touched. Cool in muffin cups on wire racks for 10 minutes. Remove from muffin cups; cool completely.

**PER CUPCAKE:** 166 cal., 5 g total fat (1 g sat. fat), 1 mg chol., 62 mg sodium, 27 g carbo., 0 g fiber, 3 g pro.

Citrus Angel Cake

## Citrus Angel Cake

**MAKES:** 12 servings **PREP:** 50 minutes **BAKE:** 40 minutes
**OVEN:** 350°

- **1½ cups egg whites (10 to 12 large)**
- **1½ cups powdered sugar**
- **1 cup cake flour or all-purpose flour**
- **1 teaspoon cream of tartar**
- **3 tablespoons frozen juice concentrate (limeade, lemonade, or orange juice), thawed**
- **¾ cup granulated sugar**

**1** Allow egg whites to stand at room temperature for 30 minutes. Meanwhile, preheat oven to 350°. Sift powdered sugar and flour together three times; set aside.

**2** In an extra-large bowl combine egg whites and cream of tartar. Beat with an electric mixer on medium speed until soft peaks form (tips curl). Add juice concentrate. Gradually add granulated sugar, about 2 tablespoons at a time, beating on high speed until stiff peaks form (tips stand straight).

**3** Sift about one-fourth of the flour mixture over beaten egg whites; fold in gently. Repeat, folding in the remaining flour mixture by fourths.

**4** Pour batter into an ungreased 10-inch tube pan. Gently cut through batter with a narrow metal spatula to remove air pockets. Bake on the lowest oven rack for 40 to 45 minutes or until top springs back when lightly touched. Immediately invert cake; cool completely in the inverted pan.*

**5** Loosen side and center of cake from pan; remove cake. Using a serrated knife, cut into wedges.

***Note:** If the cake has risen higher than the pan, invert it over a jar or bottle so the top of the cake does not touch the countertop.

**PER SERVING:** 152 cal., 0 g total fat, 0 mg chol., 51 mg sodium, 34 g carbo., 0 g fiber, 4 g pro.

## Mocha Cake with Berries

**MAKES:** 12 servings **PREP:** 25 minutes **BAKE:** 30 minutes
**COOL:** 10 minutes **OVEN:** 350°

- **Nonstick cooking spray**
- **¾ cup sugar**
- **½ cup water**
- **1 tablespoon instant espresso coffee powder or 2 tablespoons instant coffee crystals**
- **3 ounces bittersweet or semisweet chocolate, chopped**
- **2 egg yolks**
- **1 teaspoon vanilla**
- **½ cup unsweetened cocoa powder**
- **⅓ cup all-purpose flour**
- **¼ teaspoon baking powder**
- **5 egg whites**
- **Unsweetened cocoa powder (optional)**
- **½ of an 8-ounce container frozen light whipped dessert topping, thawed**
- **1½ cups fresh red raspberries, blackberries, and/or blueberries**

**1** Preheat oven to 350°. Lightly coat a 9-inch springform pan with cooking spray; set aside. In a medium saucepan stir together sugar, the water, and coffee powder. Cook and stir over medium-low heat until sugar is dissolved and mixture nearly boils. Stir in chocolate until melted. Remove from heat. In a small bowl lightly beat egg yolks with a fork. Gradually stir hot chocolate mixture into egg yolks; stir in vanilla (mixture may appear slightly grainy). Set aside.

**2** In a medium bowl stir together the ½ cup cocoa powder, flour, and baking powder. Stir in chocolate mixture until smooth. In a large bowl beat egg whites with an electric mixer on medium to high speed until stiff peaks form (tips stand straight). Stir a small amount of the beaten egg whites into chocolate mixture to lighten. Fold chocolate mixture into the remaining beaten egg whites. Pour batter into the prepared pan, spreading evenly.

**3** Bake about 30 minutes or until top springs back when lightly touched. Cool in pan on a wire rack for 10 minutes. Loosen cake from side of pan; remove side of pan. Cool completely on rack (cake may fall slightly but evenly during cooling).

**4** To serve, cut cake into wedges. If desired, sprinkle 12 dessert plates with additional cocoa powder. Place cake wedges on plates. Top with whipped topping and berries.

**PER SERVING:** 152 cal., 5 g total fat (3 g sat. fat), 34 mg chol., 31 mg sodium, 24 g carbo., 2 g fiber, 4 g pro.

Mocha Cake with Berries

# A wedge of warm gingerbread

## Gingerbread ✪

**MAKES:** 9 servings **PREP:** 15 minutes **BAKE:** 20 minutes **COOL:** 10 minutes **OVEN:** 350°

- Nonstick cooking spray
- 1½ cups all-purpose flour
- ¼ cup sugar
- 1 teaspoon ground ginger
- 1 teaspoon ground cinnamon
- ½ teaspoon baking powder
- ½ teaspoon baking soda
- ¼ teaspoon salt
- ½ cup water
- ⅓ cup full-flavor molasses
- 3 tablespoons butter or margarine, melted
- 2 egg whites
- Frozen light whipped dessert topping, thawed (optional)

**1** Lightly coat an 8×8×2-inch baking pan with nonstick cooking spray; dust lightly with flour. Set aside.
**2** In a large mixing bowl combine the 1½ cups flour, the sugar, ginger, cinnamon, baking powder, baking soda, and salt. Add the water, molasses, butter, and egg whites. Beat with an electric mixer on low to medium speed until combined. Beat on high speed for 2 minutes. Spread into prepared pan.
**3** Bake in a 350° oven about 20 minutes or until a wooden toothpick inserted near the center comes out clean. Cool in the pan on a wire rack for 10 minutes. Remove cake from pan. Serve warm and, if desired, with dessert topping.

**PER SERVING:** 163 cal., 4 g total fat (3 g sat. fat), 11 mg chol., 216 mg sodium, 28 g carbo., 1 g fiber, 3 g pro.

Gingerbread

## Persimmon Streusel Cake

**MAKES:** 20 servings **PREP:** 20 minutes **BAKE:** 35 minutes **OVEN:** 350°

- Nonstick cooking spray
- 1¼ cups all-purpose flour
- ¾ cup whole wheat pastry flour
- 2 tablespoons toasted wheat germ
- 2 teaspoons baking powder
- 1 teaspoon pumpkin pie spice or apple pie spice
- ¼ teaspoon salt
- ¾ cup sugar
- ⅓ cup cooking oil
- ¼ cup refrigerated egg product, thawed, or 1 egg
- 1 teaspoon vanilla
- 1 cup fat-free milk
- 3 medium fresh persimmons or 6 plums, pitted and chopped (2½ to 3 cups)
- Streusel Topping
- Frozen light whipped dessert topping, thawed (optional)

**1** Preheat oven to 350°. Lightly coat a 13×9×2-inch baking pan with cooking spray; set pan aside. In a medium bowl combine all-purpose flour, whole wheat pastry flour, wheat germ, baking powder, pumpkin pie spice or apple pie spice, and salt; set aside.
**2** In a large bowl combine sugar and oil; beat with an electric mixer on medium speed until combined. Add egg and vanilla to sugar mixture; beat on medium speed about 1 minute or until creamy, scraping side of bowl occasionally. Stir in milk. Using a wooden spoon, stir flour mixture into egg mixture. Pour batter into the prepared pan. Arrange chopped persimmons or plums over batter. Sprinkle Streusel Topping over fruit.
**3** Bake for 35 to 45 minutes or until a toothpick inserted near the center comes out clean. Serve warm or cool. Cut into squares and, if desired, top with dessert topping.
**Streusel Topping:** In a small bowl combine 3 tablespoons sugar, 2 tablespoons all-purpose flour, 2 tablespoons whole wheat pastry flour, 2 tablespoons toasted wheat germ, and ½ teaspoon pumpkin pie spice or apple pie spice. Stir in 1 tablespoon melted butter until well combined.

**PER SERVING:** 130 cal., 5 g total fat (1 g sat. fat), 2 mg chol., 68 mg sodium, 21 g carbo., 1 g fiber, 3 g pro.

will put a smile on your face.

## Date-Ginger Cake

**MAKES:** 9 servings **PREP:** 25 minutes **BAKE:** 30 minutes
**OVEN:** 350°

- 1 cup all-purpose flour
- 1 teaspoon baking powder
- ¼ teaspoon baking soda
- ½ cup sugar
- ¼ cup vegetable oil
- 1 teaspoon grated fresh ginger or ½ teaspoon ground ginger
- ½ cup orange or lemon low-fat yogurt
- ¼ cup refrigerated or frozen egg product, thawed, or 1 egg, lightly beaten
- 2 tablespoons fat-free milk
- ¾ cup pitted whole dates, snipped
- 2 tablespoons all-purpose flour
- 1 recipe Orange Sauce

**1** Preheat oven to 350°. Grease and lightly flour an 8×8×2-inch baking pan; set aside. In a small bowl stir together the 1 cup flour, baking powder, and baking soda; set aside.
**2** In a medium bowl combine sugar, oil, and ginger. Stir in yogurt, egg product, and milk. Add flour mixture to yogurt mixture, stirring just until combined.
**3** In a small bowl combine dates and the 2 tablespoons flour; toss gently to coat. Fold into batter. Pour batter into the prepared pan, spreading evenly.
**4** Bake for 30 to 35 minutes or until a toothpick inserted in center comes out clean. Serve warm with Orange Sauce.

**Orange Sauce:** In a small saucepan combine ¼ cup sugar, 2 teaspoons cornstarch, 1 teaspoon grated fresh ginger or ½ teaspoon ground ginger, and ¼ teaspoon finely shredded orange peel. Stir in ¾ cup orange juice. Cook and stir over medium heat until thickened and bubbly. Cook and stir for 2 minutes more. Serve warm. Makes about ¾ cup.

**PER SERVING:** 247 cal., 6 g total fat (1 g sat. fat), 1 mg chol., 85 mg sodium, 46 g carbo., 2 g fiber, 4 g pro.

Sunshine Cake

## Sunshine Cake

**MAKES:** 16 servings **PREP:** 50 minutes **BAKE:** 35 minutes
**OVEN:** 375°

- 1½ cups egg whites (10 to 12 large)
- 1½ cups sugar
- 1 cup cake flour or all-purpose flour
- 2 teaspoons vanilla
- 1½ teaspoons cream of tartar
- 4 egg yolks
- 1 recipe Lemon Fluff
- Fresh raspberries (optional)
- Orange and/or lemon peel strips (optional)

**1** Allow egg whites to stand at room temperature for 30 minutes. Meanwhile, preheat oven to 375°. Sift ¾ cup of the sugar and the flour together three times; set aside.
**2** In an extra-large bowl combine egg whites, vanilla, and cream of tartar. Beat with an electric mixer on medium speed until soft peaks form (tips curl). Gradually add the remaining ¾ cup sugar, about 2 tablespoons at a time, beating on high speed until stiff peaks form (tips stand straight).
**3** Sift about one-fourth of the flour mixture over beaten egg whites; fold in gently. Repeat, folding in the remaining flour mixture by fourths. Transfer half of the egg white mixture to another bowl; set both bowls aside.
**4** In a medium bowl beat egg yolks on high speed about 5 minutes or until thick and lemon color. Fold beaten egg yolks into one portion of the egg white mixture. Alternately add spoonfuls of yellow and white batters to an ungreased 10-inch tube pan. Gently cut through batters with a narrow metal spatula to remove any large air pockets.
**5** Bake on the lowest oven rack for 35 to 40 minutes or until top springs back when lightly touched. Immediately invert cake; cool completely in the inverted pan. Loosen side and center of cake from pan; remove cake.
**6** Frost cake with Lemon Fluff. If desired, garnish with raspberries and orange and/or lemon peel strips. Store, covered, in the refrigerator.

**Lemon Fluff:** Thaw one 12-ounce container frozen light whipped dessert topping. Fold in 1 teaspoon finely shredded lemon peel and 2 tablespoons lemon juice. (Add more peel and/or juice for a more intense flavor.)

**PER SERVING:** 169 cal., 4 g total fat (3 g sat. fat), 51 mg chol., 37 mg sodium, 29 g carbo., 0 g fiber, 3 g pro.

Oatmeal-Applesauce Cake

## Oatmeal-Applesauce Cake

**MAKES:** 20 servings **PREP:** 25 minutes **BAKE:** 25 minutes
**OVEN:** 350°

- Nonstick cooking spray
- 1 cup all-purpose flour
- 1 cup whole wheat pastry flour
- ⅔ cup quick-cooking rolled oats
- 2 teaspoons baking powder
- 1½ teaspoons ground cinnamon
- ½ teaspoon baking soda
- ¼ teaspoon salt
- ¼ teaspoon ground nutmeg
- ⅔ cup packed brown sugar
- ⅓ cup butter, softened
- ¼ cup refrigerated or frozen egg product, thawed, or 1 egg, lightly beaten
- 2 teaspoons vanilla
- 1¾ cups unsweetened applesauce
- ¾ cup mixed dried fruit bits or raisins
- ½ cup quick-cooking rolled oats
- 3 tablespoons toasted wheat germ
- 2 tablespoons packed brown sugar
- Fresh raspberries (optional)

**1** Preheat oven to 350°. Lightly coat a 13×9×2-inch baking pan with cooking spray; set aside. In a bowl stir together all-purpose flour, whole wheat pastry flour, the ⅔ cup oats, baking powder, cinnamon, baking soda, salt, and nutmeg.
**2** In a large bowl combine the ⅔ cup brown sugar and butter. Beat with an electric mixer on medium speed until smooth. Add egg product and vanilla; beat until combined. Alternately add flour mixture and applesauce to butter mixture, beating on low speed after each addition. Stir in dried fruit bits. Pour batter into the prepared pan.
**3** In a bowl combine ½ cup oats, wheat germ, and the 2 tablespoons brown sugar. Sprinkle oat mixture over batter. Bake for 25 to 30 minutes or until a toothpick inserted near center comes out clean. Cool on a wire rack. If desired, top with raspberries.

**PER SERVING:** 150 cal., 4 g total fat (2 g sat. fat), 9 mg chol., 121 mg sodium, 27 g carbo., 2 g fiber, 3 g pro.

Strawberry Cream Pie

## Strawberry Cream Pie

**MAKES:** 8 servings **PREP:** 30 minutes **CHILL:** 4 hours

- 2½ cups fresh strawberries
- ¼ cup sugar
- 1 envelope unflavored gelatin
- 2 tablespoons frozen limeade or lemonade concentrate, thawed
- 3 egg whites, lightly beaten
- 1 tablespoon tequila or orange juice
- 1 3-ounce package ladyfingers, split
- 2 tablespoons orange juice
- ½ of an 8-ounce container frozen light whipped dessert topping, thawed
- Sliced fresh strawberries (optional)
- Fresh mint sprigs (optional)

**1** Place 2½ cups strawberries in a blender or food processor. Cover and blend or process until nearly smooth. Measure pureed strawberries (you should have about 1½ cups).
**2** In a medium saucepan stir together sugar and gelatin. Stir in pureed strawberries and limeade concentrate. Cook and stir over medium heat until mixture is bubbly and gelatin is dissolved. Gradually stir about half of the hot gelatin mixture into egg whites. Return egg white mixture to saucepan. Cook and stir over low heat about 3 minutes or until mixture is slightly thickened (do not boil). Pour into a bowl; stir in tequila. Cover and chill about 2 hours or until mixture mounds when spooned, stirring occasionally.
**3** Meanwhile, cut half of the split ladyfingers in half crosswise; stand on end around the outside edge of a 9-inch tart pan or springform pan that has a removable bottom. Arrange the remaining split ladyfingers in the bottom of the pan. Drizzle the 2 tablespoons orange juice over ladyfingers.
**4** Fold whipped topping into strawberry mixture. Pour mixture into the prepared pan, spreading evenly. Cover and chill about 2 hours or until set. If desired, garnish with additional strawberries and mint.

**PER SERVING:** 130 cal., 3 g total fat (2 g sat. fat), 39 mg chol., 48 mg sodium, 22 g carbo., 1 g fiber, 4 g pro.

## Lattice-Topped Apple Pie ✪

**MAKES:** 8 servings **PREP:** 30 minutes **BAKE:** 40 minutes
**OVEN:** 375°

- 6 cups sliced unpeeled cooking apples (such as Jonathan or Rome Beauty) (6 medium)
- 3 tablespoons sugar
- 1 teaspoon ground cinnamon
- 1 tablespoon cornstarch
- 1 recipe Pastry for Lattice-Top Pie
- Fat-free milk

**1** Place apples in a 2-quart rectangular baking dish; set aside. In a small bowl combine sugar and cinnamon; set aside 1 teaspoon of the mixture. Stir cornstarch into the remaining sugar mixture. Sprinkle cornstarch mixture over apples; toss gently to combine.
**2** Preheat oven to 375°. Prepare Pastry for Lattice-Top Pie. On a lightly floured surface, slightly flatten dough. Roll dough from center to edge into a 10×5-inch rectangle. Cut pastry lengthwise into nine ½-inch strips. Place 4 strips lengthwise and 5 strips crosswise on top of apple mixture, spacing strips evenly to form a lattice-style crust. Trim pastry strips; tuck ends into dish. Brush pastry with milk; sprinkle with the reserved 1 teaspoon sugar mixture.
**3** Bake for 40 to 45 minutes or until pastry is golden and apples are tender. Serve warm or cool completely.
**Pastry for Lattice-Top Pie:** In a medium bowl stir together ½ cup all-purpose flour, ¼ cup whole wheat pastry flour or whole wheat flour, 2 tablespoons toasted wheat germ, and ⅛ teaspoon ground nutmeg. Using a pastry blender, cut in 3 tablespoons butter until mixture resembles coarse crumbs. Sprinkle 1 tablespoon cold water over part of the flour mixture; toss gently with a fork. Push moistened dough to side of bowl. Repeat with additional cold water, 1 tablespoon at a time (2 to 3 tablespoons total), until all of the flour mixture is moistened. Shape into a ball.

**PER SERVING:** 152 cal., 5 g total fat (2 g sat. fat), 12 mg chol., 48 mg sodium, 26 g carbo., 3 g fiber, 2 g pro.

## Honey-Apricot Frozen Yogurt

**MAKES:** 12 servings **PREP:** 35 minutes **STAND:** 20 minutes
**FREEZE:** 10 hours

- 1 **32-ounce carton or five 6-ounce cartons vanilla low-fat yogurt**
- 3 **cups finely chopped fresh apricots* or nectarines**
- 2 **tablespoons honey**
- **Fresh apricot or nectarine slices (optional)**

**1** In a large food processor combine yogurt, half of the chopped apricots, and the honey. Cover and process until smooth. (If using a blender or small food processor, do this step in two batches.)
**2** Transfer mixture to a 2-quart freezer container. Stir in the remaining chopped apricots. Cover and freeze about 4 hours or until firm.
**3** Chill the large mixer bowl for a heavy stand electric mixer. Spoon the frozen mixture into the chilled bowl. Beat with mixer on medium speed until slightly fluffy, starting slowly and gradually increasing the speed. Return mixture to the freezer container. Cover and freeze about 6 hours or until firm.
**4** Let frozen yogurt stand at room temperature for 20 minutes before serving. If desired, garnish each serving with apricot slices.
***Note:** If fresh apricots aren't available, use three 15-ounce cans unpeeled apricot halves in light syrup, drained.

**PER SERVING:** 93 cal., 1 g total fat (1 g sat. fat), 4 mg chol., 50 mg sodium, 18 g carbo., 1 g fiber, 4 g pro.

## Tropical Fruit Pops

**MAKES:** 12 to 14 frozen pops **PREP:** 20 minutes **FREEZE:** 3 hours

- 2 **cups peeled and chopped mango**
- 1 **8-ounce can crushed pineapple (juice pack), undrained**
- 1 **medium banana, sliced**
- 1/4 **cup frozen orange juice concentrate, thawed**
- 1/4 **teaspoon ground ginger**

**1** In a blender or food processor combine mango, undrained pineapple, banana, orange juice concentrate, and ginger. Cover and blend or process until smooth.
**2** Divide fruit mixture among twelve to fourteen 3-ounce paper cups. Cover each cup with foil. Cut a small slit in center of each foil cover; insert a wooden craft stick or plastic spoon into each pop. (Or divide mixture among 12 to 14 compartments of a plastic frozen pop mold. Insert a pop mold stick into each compartment.) Freeze about 3 hours or until firm.
**3** To serve, remove foil and tear paper cups from pops or remove pops from compartments in mold.

**PER POP:** 47 cal., 0 g total fat, 0 mg chol., 1 mg sodium, 12 g carbo., 1 g fiber, 0 g pro.

## Frozen Chocolate-Banana Bites 

**MAKES:** 4 servings **PREP:** 15 minutes **FREEZE:** 1 to 2 hours

- 2 **medium bananas**
- 1/3 **cup dark chocolate pieces**

**1** Line a baking sheet with waxed paper. Cut bananas into 1/2-inch pieces. Arrange banana pieces close together in a single layer on the prepared baking sheet.
**2** In a saucepan cook and stir chocolate over low heat until melted. Cool slightly. Drizzle melted chocolate over banana pieces. Cover and freeze for 1 to 2 hours or until firm.

**PER SERVING:** 109 cal., 4 g total fat (0 g sat. fat), 1 mg chol., 1 mg sodium, 20 g carbo., 2 g fiber, 1 g pro.

Frozen Chocolate-Banana Bites

These bite-size ice cream sandwiches are perfectly fun fare for a child's tea party or girls' night out.

Yo-Yos

## Yo-Yos ✪

**MAKES:** 12 servings **PREP:** 30 minutes **FREEZE:** 1 to 4 hours

- **¼ cup semisweet chocolate pieces**
- **¼ teaspoon shortening**
- **24 amaretti or vanilla wafers**
- **⅓ cup vanilla or fruit-flavor low-fat or light ice cream**

**1** In a small saucepan combine chocolate and shortening. Cook and stir over low heat just until melted. Cool slightly. Spread about 1 teaspoon of the melted chocolate on bottom of each cookie. Let stand until chocolate is set.

**2** Using a melon baller*, place a small scoop of ice cream (about 1 rounded teaspoon) on chocolate side of half of the cookies. Top with the remaining cookies, chocolate sides down. Cover and freeze for 1 to 4 hours.

***Note:** Dip the melon baller into water between scoops so the ice cream comes out of the scoop neatly.

**PER SERVING:** 73 cal., 3 g total fat (1 g sat. fat), 1 mg chol., 8 mg sodium, 12 g carbo., 0 g fiber, 1 g pro.

## Sunrise Ice Pops ✪

**MAKES:** 8 frozen pops **PREP:** 20 minutes
**FREEZE:** 1 hour + overnight

- **½ cup low-calorie cranberry juice**
- **2 tablespoons lime juice**
- **2 teaspoons honey**
- **1 drop red food coloring (optional)**
- **1½ cups orange juice**
- **¼ cup diet lemon-lime carbonated beverage**

**1** In a liquid measuring cup combine cranberry juice, lime juice, honey, and, if desired, food coloring. Using eight 3-ounce paper cups or compartments of a plastic frozen pop mold, pour 4 teaspoons of the juice mixture into each cup or compartment. Freeze about 1 hour or just until firm.

**2** In another liquid measuring cup combine orange juice and carbonated beverage. Pour orange juice mixture over cranberry mixture. Cover each paper cup with foil. Cut a small slit in center of each foil cover; insert a wooden craft stick into each pop. Freeze overnight.

**3** To serve, remove foil and tear paper cups from pops or remove pops from compartments in mold.

**PER POP:** 30 cal., 0 g total fat, 0 mg chol., 2 mg sodium, 7 g carbo., 0 g fiber, 0 g pro.

Strawberry Sherbet

## Strawberry Sherbet

**MAKES:** 12 servings **PREP:** 15 minutes **CHILL:** 1 hour
**FREEZE:** per manufacturer's directions + 3 hours

- **¼ cup sugar**
- **4 teaspoons cornstarch**
- **1 teaspoon finely shredded lemon peel**
- **1 12-ounce can evaporated fat-free milk**
- **1½ teaspoons vanilla**
- **2 10-ounce packages frozen strawberries in light syrup, thawed**
- **1 tablespoon lemon juice**
- **Fresh strawberries, halved (optional)**

**1** In a small saucepan stir together sugar, cornstarch, and lemon peel. Stir in evaporated milk. Cook and stir over medium heat until thickened and bubbly. Cook and stir for 2 minutes more. Stir in vanilla. Cover and chill about 1 hour or until completely chilled.

**2** In a blender or food processor combine strawberries in light syrup and lemon juice. Cover and blend or process until smooth. Stir strawberry mixture into chilled milk mixture.

**3** Freeze mixture in a 2-quart ice cream freezer according to the manufacturer's directions. Transfer to a freezer container. Cover and freeze about 3 hours or until firm. If desired, garnish each serving with fresh strawberries.

**PER SERVING:** 68 cal., 0 g total fat, 1 mg chol., 33 mg sodium, 14 g carbo., 0 g fiber, 2 g pro.

Note: **Boldfaced** page numbers indicate photographs.

## N



## O

P

## U



## W



## Y



## Z

## In-a-Pinch Substitutions

It can happen to the best of us: Halfway through a recipe, you find you're completely out of a key ingredient. Here's what to do:

| Recipe Calls For: | You May Substitute: |
|---|---|
| 1 square unsweetened chocolate | 3 Tbsp unsweetened cocoa powder + 1 Tbsp butter/margarine |
| 1 cup cake flour | 1 cup less 2 Tbsp all-purpose flour |
| 2 Tbsp flour (for thickening) | 1 Tbsp cornstarch |
| 1 tsp baking powder | ¼ tsp baking soda + ½ tsp cream of tartar + ¼ tsp cornstarch |
| 1 cup corn syrup | 1 cup sugar + ¼ cup additional liquid used in recipe |
| 1 cup milk | ½ cup evaporated milk + ½ cup water |
| 1 cup buttermilk or sour milk | 1 Tbsp vinegar or lemon juice + enough milk to make 1 cup |
| 1 cup sour cream (for baking) | 1 cup plain yogurt |
| 1 cup firmly packed brown sugar | 1 cup sugar + 2 Tbsp molasses |
| 1 tsp lemon juice | ¼ tsp vinegar (not balsamic) |
| ¼ cup chopped onion | 1 Tbsp instant minced |
| 1 clove garlic | ¼ tsp garlic powder |
| 2 cups tomato sauce | ¾ cup tomato paste + 1 cup water |
| 1 Tbsp prepared mustard | 1 tsp dry mustard + 1 Tbsp water |

## How to Know What You Need

Making a shopping list based on a recipe can be tricky if you don't know how many tomatoes yields 3 cups chopped. Our handy translations:

| When the Recipe Calls For: | You Need: |
|---|---|
| 4 cups shredded cabbage | 1 small cabbage |
| 1 cup grated raw carrot | 1 large carrot |
| 2½ cups sliced carrots | 1 pound raw carrots |
| 4 cups cooked cut fresh green beans | 1 pound beans |
| 1 cup chopped onion | 1 large onion |
| 4 cups sliced raw potatoes | 4 medium-size potatoes |
| 1 cup chopped sweet pepper | 1 large pepper |
| 1 cup chopped tomato | 1 large tomato |
| 2 cups canned tomatoes | 16 oz can |
| 4 cups sliced apples | 4 medium-size apples |
| 1 cup mashed banana | 3 medium-size bananas |
| 1 tsp grated lemon rind | 1 medium-size lemon |
| 2 Tbsp lemon juice | 1 medium-size lemon |
| 4 tsp grated orange rind | 1 medium-size orange |
| 1 cup orange juice | 3 medium-size oranges |
| 4 cups sliced peaches | 8 medium-size peaches |
| 2 cups sliced strawberries | 1 pint |
| 1 cup soft bread crumbs | 2 slices fresh bread |
| 1 cup bread cubes | 2 slices fresh bread |
| 2 cups shredded Swiss or Cheddar cheese | 8 oz cheese |
| 1 cup egg whites | 6 or 7 large eggs |
| 1 egg white | 2 tsp egg white powder + 2 Tbsp water |
| 4 cups chopped walnuts or pecans | 1 pound shelled |